Women
and Health
Psychology
MENTAL HEALTH ISSUES

ENVIRONMENT AND HEALTH
Andrew Baum and Jerome E. Singer, Series Editors

Women and Health Psychology

MENTAL HEALTH ISSUES

Cheryl Brown Travis

University of Tennessee

LAWRENCE ERLBAUM ASSOCIATES, PUBLISHERS

1988   *Hillsdale, New Jersey*   *Hove and London*

Lawrence Erlbaum Associates, Inc., Publishers
365 Broadway
Hillsdale, New Jersey 07642

Library of Congress Cataloging-in-Publication Data

Travis, Cheryl Brown, 1944–
  Women & health psychology.

  Includes bibliographies and index.
  1. Women—Mental health. 2. Clinical health
psychology. I. Title. II. Title: Women and health
psychology. [DNLM: 1. Mental Health. 2. Women—
psychology. WA 305 T782w]
RC451.4.W6T73 1988   155.6'33   88-3878
ISBN 0-8058-0253-3

Printed in the United States of America
10 9 8 7 6 5 4 3 2 1

To
Joy and J. C. Brown,
parents of the first order

Contents

Preface

There are two basic themes of the following chapters. First, social frameworks are eventually experienced and expressed as personal frameworks, that is, as part of the self and all the beliefs and feelings and actions that contribute to the self. Second, specific diagnostic conditions, such as depression, alcoholism, or eating disorders, emerge from dynamics that are experienced by most women. Therefore, the following chapters are pertinent to women in general and not only to women who are eligible for a formal diagnosis. Conditions, events, and experiences that contribute to serious problems for a percentage of women, will at some point be experienced by all. Both the experience and management of those conditions are shaped by gender.

Acknowledgments

The interest and enthusiasm of students in the Women and Health Psychology classes was a source of continuing motivation for this book, as were the persistent inquiries of good friends about the progress of the book. Pam Moore and Bonnie Bowers made the chapters on psychotropic drugs and eating disorders truly enjoyable endeavors. Marlyne Kilbey and Joanne Popour Sobeck composed their chapters on alcoholism with a confidence born of many years of experience in the field, and in so doing they made a significant contribution to the book. Bette Lesh, who helped me discover feminism before we had a name for it, edited several early chapters and forever improved my writing style. Linda Samataro contributed considerable expertise as a reference librarian with specialization in health and psychology. Connie Ogle managed many details of manuscript preparation and periodic sessions of attitude adjustment. Nancy Vineyard shared her expertise in medical terminology and gave invaluable assistance in constructing the index. Sharon Anthony gave continuing support and reassurance. Curtis Travis listened to much of the general analysis on numerous long distance training runs and has been a source of inspiration and insight. I express my thanks and appreciation to all.

The Psychology of Gender: Mental Health Implications

1

FEMINIST ANALYSES

Liberal
Radical
Socialist/Marxist

VISIONS OF WOMEN

Psychoanalytic Frameworks
Feminist Object Relations
Relational Androgyny
Social Constructionism

ANDROGYNY

Definition and Measurement
Correlates of Androgyny
Mental Health Implications
Criticisms of Androgyny

SUMMARY AND CONCLUSIONS

The social psychological construction of gender plays a major role in the definition and diagnosis of illness, timing and expression of symptoms, treatment strategies, and theoretical explanations. Thus, mental illness is as much a social as a personal event. Understanding, treating, and preventing psychological dysfunction is conceptualized here to fall within both self and social frameworks. The major feminist perspectives allocate different levels of significance to self and social frameworks but collectively offer a method for integrating many related issues.

In this chapter, basic feminist perspectives are reviewed, views of women and the nature of male-female relationships are summarized and contrasted with a model of androgyny. The following chapters on depression, use of psychotropic drugs, alcoholism, and eating disorders each illustrate the complexity of integrating self and social events.

FEMINIST ANALYSES

Divisions between various feminist perspectives are always arbitrary to some degree, and other reviews have offered different classifications (Firestone, 1970; Fee, 1975; Jagger & Struhl, 1978; Sayers, 1982). Individual advocates typically incorporate perspectives, methods, and objectives of more than one approach. Although there is considerable overlap and blurring of boundaries, each perspective does have a general core that distinguishes it from others. A more extensive version of this review is also presented in volume I of this series but is reiterated here because feminist analyses provide a valuable context in which to view the more specialized theories of gender and mental health discussed in the following chapters.

Liberal

Liberal and radical positions can be partly distinguished by their focus on the nature and source of differences between the sexes. The liberal position holds that the biological basis for sex differences is minimal. Those differences that do appear may be understood best in terms of the social construction of gender and more generally in terms of sexism. Sexism is defined as "the entire range of attitudes, beliefs, practices, policies, laws, and behaviors discriminating against women (or against men) on the basis of their gender" (Safilios-Rothschild, 1974, p. 1). The main problem is that society has segregated women and men in virtually all life experiences: personal sense of self, friendships, sexuality, work, play, and religion. This segregation has invariably led to conditions whereby men have more power, access to financial resources, status, autonomy, and choice than women. It is enforced by official policies and de facto social conditions. The implications and consequences of this sexism (segregation and discrimination) have been explored by several feminists, Friedan (1963) and Bird (1968).

The problem is defined as both situational and personal, involving self and social frameworks. It is situational because women and men have been assigned discrete, nonoverlapping roles. Men work outside the home and publicly demonstrate their ability to achieve; women work privately inside the home and often achieve by nurturing others. It is personal because characteristics thought appropriate for the performance of these discrete roles have been idealized as masculinity and femininity. Men are strong, aggressive, instrumental, confident, and active. Women are submissive, communal, expressive, careful, and quiescent. Thus, the very experience of self is involved; however to some extent, it is an arbitrary experience based on a social construction of work roles and relationships.

Three concerns have characterized liberal analyses: (a) the sexist division of labor justified on the basis of supposed biological differences between the sexes, (b) barriers to equal opportunity as they have emerged in educational and occupational settings, and (c) limited choices in the expression of self imposed by categorical definitions of masculinity and femininity. These concerns incorporate issues addressed on molar levels in terms of social-situational frameworks and in terms of personal-self frameworks.

The liberal position tends to minimize the role of biology and evolution in sex differences. In contrast, popular accounts of evolution and sociobiology have relied heavily on biological arguments for current divisions of status and power (Ardrey, 1966; Morris, 1967; Tiger & Fox, 1971). These renditions of human evolution suggest that the current sexual division of labor is firmly based in biology, reflecting an appropriate natural order. The chauvinism of popular sociobiology has been amply demonstrated (Morgan, 1972; Fisher, 1979; Hubbard, Henifin & Fried, 1979; Hubbard & Lowe, 1979; Tobach & Rosoff, 1978). Feminists, many of whom are fine biologists, do not discount biology as a legitimate science; rather, they argue for careful formulation of hypotheses, methodology, and analyses of data. The tendency to overgeneralize and extrapolate from a two or three animal species to human behavior is severely criticized. It has been argued that "Not the biological facts but man's social attitudes toward women—attitudes that are based on prejudiced interpretation of the facts—require revisions" (Montague, 1952, p. 55).

Liberal feminists argue that biology is very much a social phenomena (Sayers, 1982). This perspective is supported by research on sex differences (O'Leary, Wallston, & Unger, 1985; Hyde, 1985; Hyde & Linn, 1986).

Psychological research on the nature and extent of sex differences, for example, in spatial perception, verbal memory, and mathematical reasoning, has been critiqued by feminist scientists as biased and sexist from initial inception to final interpretation (Unger, 1979; Block, 1984; Wallston, 1985). Empirical support for supposed sex differences has been extensively reviewed elsewhere (Maccoby & Jacklin, 1974). Sex differences appear to be influenced by the nature of the task and several other variables, including the sex of authors of articles (Eagly, 1983). These findings have led feminists to focus on situational and personal factors rather than biological ones.

Because sex differences are judged to be minimal from a liberal perspective, problems of equal opportunity, prejudice, and discrimination become political-economic and personal events. Equal opportunity issues have been addressed in the areas of equal protection in law (Schulder, 1970; DeCrow, 1974), education (Serbin, 1973; Frey, 1979), language (Lakoff, 1973; Schulz, 1975), and numerous other areas, including the practice of medicine. The liberal position is generally based on an assimilation model of social change (Rossi, 1976) where integration is the key element. The focus here is to facilitate the entry of women into full citizenship and the transactions of commerce, law, politics, education, and so on.

Personal redress has been proposed in new conceptions of gender. Masculinity and femininity are no longer conceived as mutually exclusive characteristics. Tests and measures that construct gender as a single bipolar phenomenon are criticized (Constantinople, 1973). A variety of instruments and scales have been developed in psychological research based on this new conception of integrated gender, androgyny (Bem, 1974; Spence & Helmreich, 1978). The concept of androgyny has strongly influenced feminist models of mental health and will be presented in more detail in Chapter 6. Although there are problems with the popularization of androgyny (Wallston, 1985), it has been an unspoken assumption that if women and men could be more personally and psychologically integrated, social-situational integration would be facilitated.

The impact of liberal analysis on women's health has been evidenced in several areas. By law, admissions to all health training and education programs must be nondiscriminatory. Increased access to training and certification for women professionals in the health area has been a major goal. A liberal analysis advocates an informed consumer role for women seeking counseling or therapy (Strickland, 1984). Providing information about therapists and counselors in consumer manuals is one type of activity related to this goal. Making health care available to more women, for example through community funded centers and haven houses for victims of abuse, is another goal consistent with the liberal focus.

Additionally, liberal feminists maintain a critical appraisal and monitoring of federal funding for health care programs and health-related research. For example, much of the theory development, research, and federally funded treatment programs on alcoholism have been designed around men, with only limited attention to women. Efforts to insure better educated and better trained clinical therapists are also reflected in a liberal focus, which encourages the inclusion of courses on the psychology of gender in the graduate curriculum of accredited programs, in particular advocating training in crisis intervention for problems typically experienced by women and in areas of reproductive decision making.

Radical

Radical perspectives give greater emphasis to essential differences between the sexes and thus maximize the unique features of maleness and femaleness. According to radical perspectives, there is less overlap between the sexes, and core differences tend to precipitate conflict, especially conflict over power and status. Women are seen as representing a perspective and style that is uniquely feminine. This style is characterized by trust, cooperation, and creativity. Men are seen as more likely to adopt destructive competitive styles, to exploit others in a zero-sum strategy, and to have difficulty in trusting others. Representative works include Firestone's *Dialectics of Sex* (1970), Millet's *Sexual Politics* (1970), and Frankfort's *Vaginal Politics* (1972). A broad sampling of radical feminism is available in an edited volume by the same title (Koedt, Levine, and Rapone, 1973).

The radical perspective recognizes at the outset that biology itself is the key factor in sexual dualism. Radical feminists argue that in order to eliminate the sexual class system, women must seize control of reproduction and reassert ownership of their own bodies (Firestone, 1970). The objective is not to simply provide adequate services for women but to restore to women the power to look after themselves.

At least one school of thought locates the conflict within the psyche of men, who universally are awed by women, envious of women, and simultaneously fear women (Lederer, 1968; Dinnerstein, 1976; Daly, 1978). Women are held in awe as being intimate with the most powerful forces of nature and creation, for example, Earthmother and Mother Nature. The images of women as potential destroyers, for example, Medussa, amazons, sirens, and harpies, are seen as a partial reflection of the fear of women and the power of that which is female.

Partly because of the psychological flaws of men (their fear, envy, and contempt of women), radical feminists have encouraged women to look to other women for emotional sustenance and as collaborators in social change. Consciousness raising through personal sharing has legitimated the experiences of women, and women's feelings have become a valid basis for political analysis.

Causes of conflict and frustration are no longer located totally within the personalities of women but are seen as products of a male-dominated system. Additionally, leadership, authority, and influence have been reconsidered. The nature of power relations has been interpreted as corrupting to all parties; therefore, it is not adequate simply to replace men with women in positions of power. The *process* of reaching and implementing decisions and allocating resources must be reconstructed.

Consistent with the focus on female biology, much of the radical impact of women's health care has been in the areas of gynecology and reproductive health. Male domination in the area of childbirth has especially been criticized (Ostrum, 1975; Rich, 1977). Access to safe contraception has also been a major concern (Dowie & Johnston, 1977; Seaman, 1977). Freedom of choice regarding abortion has been consistently supported on the basis that forced gestation violates the integrity of women. Control of one's body is seen as a primary requirement for other freedoms. To the extent that women's choices are restricted by laws made by men, men are in a position to dominate women.

Radical innovations in women's health care have included the development of cooperative health care centers for women. In these centers women discuss their personal health concerns and learn elements of self-help in group settings. Individual therapy is often supplemented by support groups, and problem analysis incorporates issues of social political origin rather than simply focusing on intraindividual explanations. Further, the focus tends to be on promoting broad-based change in social institutions rather than adaptation on the part of the individual.

Criticisms of the radical perspective include the fact that not all women experiencing mental health problems are prepared to explore them from such a broad perspective. Often, the implications of therapy produce threats to longstanding marital and family relationships, which for some women may create more traumatic conflict than the presenting symptoms.

The potential of radical strategies to instigate effectively broad-based social change is another problem of radical analyses. One of the more common attacks made by critics of women's liberation is to accuse public advocates of being man-haters and lesbians. Disregarding the accuracy of such attacks, the fact remains that in the public eye these claims have been, to some degree, accepted. One result is that radical feminists have lost credibility and effectiveness as advocates of social change. Additionally, grassroots support has been undermined. Women who could enthusiastically support equal pay for comparable work may be subdued by the implication that to do so they must renounce emotional ties with traditionally significant others. Thus, the integration of self and social frameworks has been a significant problem among feminist analyses in general and is addressed in repeatedly in the following chapters.

Socialist/Marxist

Socialist and Marxist perspectives are not completely overlapping but have a common orientation and are discussed jointly here for purposes of convenience. Both emphasize a structural, rather than personal, basis for sexism and discrimination (Robinson, 1978). Marxist analyses propose that all societies are identified by the mode of production characteristic of that society; all manifestations of power, status, or conflict can be traced to the mode of production. The essential divisions in society are divisions of class. The key historical period in this analysis is the shift from a feudal system to capitalism (Hamilton, 1978). Marxist analyses point out that women do not represent a single class. Working and middle class women are divided on a number of issues based on economic rather than sexist factors (Sayers, 1982). The family is a unit within the capitalist system, which helps maintain order, replenish the supply of workers, and serves as a unit for consumption of goods. Significant change in society, therefore, must also include significant changes regarding the family.

Socialist analyses argue that sex-gender systems constitute a level of reality more basic than economic class and thus share an orientation similar to radical analyses. Gender is seen as the master class, extending across all other divisions (Laws, 1979), structuring personal, social, and political realities. Sex-gender systems have permeated societies throughout history, from the concepts of yin and yang to more recent divisions elaborated by Western society. The discovery of paternity and the associated transition from group to pair marriage is seen as the origin of sex-gender systems practiced today. Forces that require women to devote their energies to child rearing and caring for husbands result in reduced choices for women and eventually a diminished sense of self-esteem and competence (Rossi, 1964; Jones, 1970). Socialists point out that these patriarchal family systems continue to exist even in working class (proletariat) families and in socialist societies.

Socialist and Marxist analyses agree that modes of production and reproduction are often parallel in their consequences and, therefore, may be inextricably entertwined (Chodorow, 1979). Current constructions of production and sex-gender systems result in divisions whereby men are associated with the work of production and women with that of consumption. Men accomplish their tasks in public settings and women perform household chores in isolation. Underlying explanations rely on structural, not personal, factors. Thus, from both perspectives, patriarchy and the nuclear family are major factors in the oppression of women. The compatibility of the two analyses is suggested by the title of a volume edited by Eisenstein (1979), *Capitalist Patriarchy and the Case of Socialist Feminism*. Since the source of oppression is institutionalized, collective action is a prerequisite for effective social change (Dunbar, 1971).

A major theme of the socialist/Marxist analysis is that the medical system has become a means of social control utilized by the capitalist state (Ehrenreich & Ehrenreich, 1974). The state and the medical system operate in an interlocking system of support. The state uses health care as an instrument of social control by increasing funding and offering programs during periods of protest and unrest, but these are quickly withdrawn as the impetus for social change is dissipated (Navarro, 1975). The medical system is also used to control social change by defining what is healthy, what is reasonable care, and what is hazardous to health. The direction of benefit is mutual, and the state approves or blocks legislation according to principles that insure a profit base for the medical system (Felkner, 1982).

Socialist/Marxist analyses regarding the status of women and women's health are only tangentially concerned with women's biology. Socialist analyses see the discovery of paternity as the origin of patriarchy; and, therefore, the biological role of women as reproducers of male property is an important factor in the subsequent low status of women. Marxist analyses have encouraged women to view themselves as part of a larger conflict and to share the goals of other exploited groups. The exploitation of women derives from the same source found in the exploitation of men: class distinction in power and differential access to the means of production (Eisenstein, 1979). Women are encouraged to take a broader view of social change.

Other analyses within the socialist/Marxist orientation have focused on the job of housewife and homemaker. Much of the problem stems from the peculiar sexual division of labor in society. Men work outside the home for wages while women work inside the home for no wages. The housewife role is a form of exploitation because the housewife is prevented access to the means of production and wages. Because women do not receive wages for their role as housewife, the job is seen as valueless and the women who perform it are, therefore, without value (Benston, 1969; Chodorow, 1979). As will be seen in later chapters, some theorists view the housewife role as a major risk to women's mental health.

Feminists have discussed the issue of pay for housework from several viewpoints. Estimates of the dollar value of domestic work have been based on court litigation for wrongful death (where a husband is reimbursed for the loss of his wife), divorce settlements, and in attempts to improve the accuracy of measures of the gross national product (Baker, et al., 1980). These analyses demonstrate that, when practical need arises, a dollar value can be attached to housewife functions. However, attaching a dollar value to work does not change the nature of the work, and the goals of social change should include more than simply shifting paychecks around.

Criticisms of women's health care have addressed a number of issues: domestic violence against women, funding of child care, reproductive and safety hazards in the work place, and national health insurance (Marieskind, 1980). Health care practitioners have been criticized regarding a number of aspects of domestic violence. First, practitioners and the health care system in general have defined wife abuse as a private event and not properly subject to intervention. The health care system has ignored the needs of battered women and their children for even minimal relief or shelter. Resource centers and shelters have been provided by volunteer and charitable groups, with little or no assistance from the medical establishment. Additionally, physicians have treated only the symptoms of abuse and have contributed to the problem by tranquilizing "depressed" women so they may tolerate their circumstances.

Criticisms of the socialist/Marxist approach can be formulated from a number of perspectives. Liberal analysts accept the position that women should have greater access to employment opportunities but place more emphasis on equitable pay and salary issues. Getting women out of the home and into a wage earner position will not, in and of itself, alleviate sexism or harrassment in the workplace. The fact that men's work is often evaluated more highly than that of women, simply because it is men's work, is a phenomenon that extends beyond getting a job in the first place.

Radical analyses argue that moving women into the work force does little to change the sexism and exploitation of women as homemakers. When women are employed outside the home, they continue to have primary responsibility for child care and household tasks. Estimates are that full-time housewives spend about 63 hours each week on household tasks, and women employed outside the home spend about 42 hours each week on these tasks (Baker et al., 1980).

Thus, both liberal and radical perspectives accept the value of an economic base for women's liberation. However, liberal analyses insist that the nature of the workplace and work relationships must change, whereas radical perspectives argue that the nature of domestic and family relationships must change. Even feminists of the socialist/Marxist persuasion have had some doubts as to the implementation of feminist goals within the socialist movement (Stacey, 1979). In a review of the status of women in socialist countries, Scott (1974) details continuing sexism and discrimination.

In spite of the several differences outlined in preceding paragraphs, feminist perspectives share some important similarities. Most feminists agree on three points: (a) women are oppressed, (b) the personal is political, and (c) process shares equal importance with outcome. In describing and explaining oppression, liberals tend to focus on sexism and discrimination, radicals focus on biological and psychological bases of power conflicts between males and females, and socialist/Marxists emphasize capitalistic patriarchy. All feminists agree that the personal experiences of women can be understood in a broader social/political context, evidenced by discriminatory laws, male fear and anger, or profit motives. Egalitarian participation in the process of problem solving is a third common value. It may involve participation in educational and professional settings, communal cooperation in life-styles, or collaboration in managing the means of production.

Subsequent chapters are designed to provide the best sources of factual information currently available on women's health. No attempt is made to favor one feminist perspective over another; readers are invited to apply theoretical formulations according to the heuristic criterion of whether or not the formulations enhance overall comprehension.

VISIONS OF WOMEN

The classic questions regarding women are phrased in choices between passivity and activity, dependence and individuation, nurturance and achievement. These choices are universally presented as personal events, quite independent of social frameworks. Women, to the extent they are given the opportunity, must choose between diverging paths. The assumption that masculinity and femininity are opposites of a single dimension underlies much of this philosophy. The implication has been that healthy men follow one pattern of development and healthy women another. The motivating forces of one sex are antithetical to the other. Within this perspective, women must not only be defined in terms of activity and passivity, but also by the manner in which they relate to men. This imagery permeates both occidental and oriental philosophy and is reflected in much contemporary theory.

The myth of Demeter, goddess of life, and her four daughters, Persephone, Psyche, Athena, and Artemis dramatically illustrates this point (see a more complete recounting by Chesler, *Women and Madness*, 1972). The myth depicts each daughter as following stereotyped developmental paths with respect to activity-passivity and men in general. Those who choose attachment and mothering must forego adventure and companionship. Those who pursue adventure and companionship must forego a marital bond. There is no vision that integrates instrumental activity and affective bonds with men. Persephone is captured by Hades and becomes a queen slave. Psyche chooses wedded bliss and is married to Eros, whom she encounters only at night and is forbidden to gaze upon. Athena is reborn as a man to assist men in their adventures, and Artemis dedicates herself to active womenhood and the Amazon societies.

Psychoanalytic Frameworks

Individual development, within the psychoanalytic tradition, can be best understood as a product of the Oedipal complex and its resolution. Anatomical distinctions between the sexes are key to the origins and resolution of the Oedipal complex and to subsequent psychological development. Indeed, the investment of libido in appropriate anatomical structures is essential to healthy development. Freud discussed and clarified his views on these points over a period of several decades (Freud, 1905, 1925, 1931).

The male sequence begins with an investment of libido in the mother. The intense wish for total possession of the mother is recognized as unacceptable, especially to the father, a competitor and potential aggressor. Compelled by castration anxiety, the boy subsequently renounces the mother, allowing identification with the father. It is the complete and forceful resolution of the Oedipal complex that accounts for much of male character. Males are capable of greater control of emotions and a generally higher degree of moral comprehension based on objective principle.

The female sequence begins with confirmation of the existence of the penis, recognized for its imposing size and inherent value, leading to penis envy. Through a gradual process, the girl eventually accepts that she is permanently female and will not acquire a penis. Lacking a forceful resolution to the Oedipal complex, the girl accepts femininity as the only role reasonably attainable.

Normal development for women, according to Freud, necessitates a shift of erotogenic zones. This change involves (a) suppression or abandonment of the clitoris as an essential erotogenic zone, (b) reorientation from masculine to feminine psyche, (c) transition from active to passive, (d) abandonment in the belief in a universal penis, and (e) adoption of a suitable feminine identification. A sense that the worst has already happened, that is, castration, leaves women with a lingering, if vague, yearning, tendencies toward neuroticism, and equivocal moral comprehension.

Other theorists contemporary with Freud adapted his initial insights in further analyses of female development and sexuality. Wilhelm Reich (1942) placed orgasmic competence at the core of psychological health for both sexes, holding that the fear of pleasure was basically the fear of an independent or free life-style. Hysterical and neurotic patients, often women, were designated as ill because of a lack of genital gratification. He based these conclusions on the insights of Freud and his own clinical experience.

An incident Reich found particularly instructive was the case of a woman referred to Freud by a Viennese physician. Her symptoms included acute anxiety attacks and virginity after 18 years of marriage. (The fact that her husband was impotent is mentioned only in passing, since the problem is clearly located in the woman.) The private opinion of the physician was that the appropriate prescription was, "Penis normalis, dosim. Repetatur" (Reich, 1942, p. 95).

One expects that a serious scientist adopting the position that orgasmic capacity is fundamental to mental health would provide appropriate instruction regarding this essential experience. Reich suggests that in women, mature orgasms are achieved by stimulation of the posterior wall of the vagina, hardly consistent with accepted facts about female arousal.

The clitoris and clitoral excitation have continued to be identified with narcissistic and infantile development. The erotic qualities of the clitoris are partially blamed for the immature development of women, because the clitoris gives one solitary pleasure, in contrast with the vagina which is identified as an organ of social pleasure. "In this sense the clitoris is the sexual organ most typical of women, . . . because it is invested with the same narcissistic enhancement with which the woman invests her body" (Grunberger, 1964, p. 79).

This analysis has led some feminists to charge that psychoanalysis is an attempt to psychically castrate women and, therefore, simply represents another instance of men trying to control women. Women are designated as having partial frigidity if they are clitorally responsive but cannot achieve orgasm vaginally. This position has been espoused by psychoanalysis well after the time when Masters and Johnson (1966) published their initial work on sexuality. Nagera, writing in 1975, acknowledged that few women actually have vaginal orgasm. However, he supports the traditional theoretical analysis that "To complete the move into the passive-feminine position, a wave of repression must usually dispose of or at least suspend the masculine-clitoral strivings" (Nagera, 1975, p. 47).

In addition to poor moral comprehension and unresolved clitoral strivings, psychoanalytic frameworks also support the proposition that narcissism is endemic to women. Because women are deprived of adequate narcissistic confirmation from the beginning of their lives, they project their unfulfilled needs onto relations with their later partners. Girls are described by modern psychoanalytic theorists as attempting to gain confirmation (previously withheld by the mother) through later love objects. In contrast, males are assured of their worth and are less dependent on confirmation by others. This fact obviously has implications for locus of control, agency and communion, activity and passivity, and attachment and autonomy.

Narcissism has been used to explain why girls are more interested in their relationships (girlfriends, boyfriends, etc.) and are, therefore, more dependent on their love objects than are boys (Grunberger, 1964). It does seem to be the case that in any elementary school playground, most boys are engaged in active, rough and tumble play. Girls disperse themselves around the edges of playing fields and talk, typically about their families, friends, and relationships. In their comprehensive review of sex differences literature, Maccoby and Jacklin (1974) found results suggesting that this is a stable and real difference. But whether this difference in behavior is based on boys' tendencies to be competitive or girls' greater verbal abilities is not clear.

Additionally, it is argued that girls can sometimes achieve a state of narcissistic autonomy in that they may take themselves as their love object, focusing their energies on becoming beautiful, charming, and desirable. In this case, the girl always has herself as the core of her object world. That these behaviors may represent acquiescence to social norms and sanctions is seldom acknowledged.

Subsequent elaborations of the psychoanalytic perspective introduced object relations (Freud, 1933; Fairbairn, 1952). In object relations, the focus is on pre-Oedipal events, and critical aspects of development are rephrased in terms of individuation and differentiation. The human experience is conceptualized as a universal dilemma involving the polarity of individuality and connectedness. Although somewhat different terms are applied, the central question of development remains the resolution of the conflict between attachment and autonomy.

The primary cathexis is to someone the infant does not initially differentiate from self; instead there is a fusion of self, other, and world. Objects are people, aspects of people, or symbols of people incorporated into psychic representations. It is these earliest social relations and object representations that determine subsequent psychological growth. Because nurturance is imperfect, a sense of self gradually emerges as separate from other objects. These dynamics are most salient in the primary relationship of mother-child.

Object relations theory retains the psychoanalytic perspective that males and females follow different patterns of development but differs somewhat in that diverging patterns of development are conceptualized in terms of the resolution of attachment and autonomy. However, the resultant differences in basic male and female personality are retained very much as described in psychoanalytic foundations.

Feminist Object Relations

Feminist object relations accept the basic tenant of traditional object relations, namely that male development proceeds along a pattern of separation, autonomy, and individuation, whereas female development is characterized by attachment and greater dependency. Feminist theorists point out that this pattern is particularly costly for women and that women often lack the sense of entitlement that allows them to fully individuate. Two features of this approach make it particularly feminist, the view that these issues must be resolved to bring about social change and that the experience of the self is founded in the social context of parenting patterns.

These theorists hold that understanding the tension between attachment and autonomy and the different experiences of women and men with respect to that tension is a necessary precondition for social change. The basis for men's prejudice and fear of women is buried in the most intimate aspects of self events. Dinnerstein (*The Mermaid and the Minotaur*, 1976) argues that the most potent forces of sexual conservatism are buried in the psychological substrate of connectedness and separation. To change male-female relations, the basic psychological conditions that promote prejudice, discrimination, and violence against women must be addressed. That is, simply changing laws and social customs will not change the essential relationships of men and women. Laws, educational practice, economic restrictions, and social customs that constitute the instruments of oppression are simply reflections of much deeper phenomena.

Dinnerstein (1976) views the intensive and exclusive mothering of children by women as a critical element in shaping male-female relations. She argues that current relations will remain unchanged until the monopoly of females on mothering has been broken. The earliest sense of existence is in relation to a woman, and it is at a woman's breast that the infant experiences its first major social encounter. Therefore, the dynamics of separation, individuation, and ego development are played out vis-a-vis females.

That girls are mothered by a person of the same sex has several consequences for object relations and resolution of the Oedipal complex. Oedipal dynamics initiate a turning away from the mother, the first love object (Chodorow, 1978). In addition to the chagrin of a lost love, girls experience a feeling that their mother has somehow betrayed them. Girls discover that they must compete with other females for the erotic resources of males and so may never recapture the mother closeness men may seek in an adult pairing with a woman (Dinnerstein, 1976).

The father becomes someone important who can help the girl get away from the mother. In the stereotypes promoted in U.S. society, only men (fathers) embody active selfhood. Women (mothers) do not exhibit this autonomy. A consequence is that development proceeds on the assumption that there is an absolute split between nurturance and freedom (Benjamin, 1984). The girl's inability to see her mother as an active subject (rather than a passive object) makes her doubt her own ability to engage in agentic activity.

Because her mother is of the same sex, the girl comes to experience herself as only partly separate from the mother. Further, to the extent that she anticipates eventually performing the roles of mother, she cannot reject the mother without rejecting her own future. Complete separation from the mother is not psychologically necessary for the girl because she can hope to have one day that same influence, that is, to be the mother of children.

The girl's emotional identification with her mother is strengthened as she becomes aware of gender, but she also learns that it is her father who demonstrates freedom. Thus, emotional attachment is to the mother, but admiration is reserved for the father. The fact that autonomy and individuation are modeled by men and not by women implies that to achieve freedom she must, in a sense, become like a man. "The disparity between the ideal of autonomy and the ideal of femininity is a concrete dilemma for early girlhood, one which persists consciously and unconsciously into adult life" (Benjamin, 1984, p. 43).

Implications for mother-daughter relationships are extensively discussed by object relations theorists. Although conceptually rich, these analyses often locate many of the mechanisms of adult neuroses within the mother and her inadequacies, perpetuated by her own poor resolution of the attachment-autonomy polarity. Therefore, this perspective on object relations analyses may be employed by some theorists in the service of blaming women for their own oppression.

Because mothers are incompletely nurturant and incompletely reliable, their daughters' needs are only partially and unpredictably fulfilled. Ambivalence in responding to the daughter's needs in early infancy communicates a message that the daughter cannot fully rely on the mother. The mother unconsciously restrains and limits her daughter's expectations because the mother is aware of the limits of a woman's lot. This produces anxiety and confusion for the daughter. In an attempt to come to an understanding, the daughter infers that something is wrong with her needs or that she herself is unworthy. The daughter takes in the notion that she shouldn't expect too much, that life is inconsistent, and that something is wrong with who she is (Eichenbaum & Orbach, 1984). A sense of unentitlement follows and is embodied in feelings of unworthiness and self-hate. This analysis ignores the fact that fathers may also shape girls expectations or reward dependency (Osofsky & O'Connell, 1972).

Paradoxically, when the daughter seeks to fulfill her needs elsewhere, the mother cannot give her permission. Failure to psychologically release her daughter is based on the mother's own dependence and investment in her daughter as an emotional confidant. The mother, deeply flawed herself, cannot support the daughter in her separation and individuation. Instead, she evokes emotions of guilt and shame, interrupting the daughter's adventures and exploration of her separateness. The daughter's move toward separation is experienced as a psychological loss and abandonment. Instead of finding the self-completion in her daughter she had hoped for, the mother faces rejection. As the cycle advances, the daughter, never completely separated and still dependent on the mother, in her turn becomes the unreliable nurturer and needy mother (Eichenbaum & Orbach, 1984).

Object relations to some extent forecasts the nature of the resolution of the Oedipal complex among boys (Chodorow, 1978). Boys come to define themselves as more separate and distinct, with a greater sense of rigid ego boundaries and differentiation. Boys renounce their emotional dependence on the mother more completely than do girls. The compulsory resolution of the Oedipal complex among boys (because of castration anxiety) prepares them psychologically for an orientation to that which lies in the public sphere of activity, that is, roles in society and the work world. Men must seek their masculinity outside the home. Therefore, it is important for men to see the public realm as distinct from that which is feminine and additionally to see women as incompetent in this realm. To the extent that autonomy and attachment are perceived as incompatible, personal and social events are also judged as separate and conflicting. The resolution of the Oedipal complex for boys also prepares them to be obedient to authority and to recognize the values of status and dominance.

A further dynamic is that because of the exclusive nurturance of infants by women, men are embued with a deeply ingrained sense of the psychological power of women. This emerges from infantile experiences of helplessness and dependence on the mother. The mother is seen as omnipotent, because she has been the source of every pleasure and discomfort in the infant's life. As adults, men exhibit a desire for unilateral possessiveness of women. This does not simply represent the desire of the infant to possess the mother but is also a response to the deeper fear that the power of women must be controlled.

Recognition of female sexuality is frightening because it reminds men of the uncontrollable mother. As a consequence, female sexuality becomes constrained and sequestered, producing even more latent fears. Women acquiesce to this control because in a sense they acquire a measure of power. They are slaves, but they are magical slaves.

Other theorists within feminist object relations have focused on exactly how it is that only women have been assigned the role of nurturing children and how this role is maintained through generations of tradition. Chodorow describes this phenomenon as the *Reproduction of Mothering* (Chodorow, 1978). Chodorow sees the mother role as integrated within a social system of production. As such, it is socially defined, organized, and reproduced. Chodorow's work represents one of the first feminist efforts to integrate the issues of the dynamic intrapsychic events with social norms and traditions. The self events that emerge in the context of infancy and mothering are seen to occur in a social framework.

Relational Androgyny

The second feminist approach to attachment and autonomy accepts the initial tenants outlined by object relations, that is, women and men have substantially different orientations that are often in apparent conflict. However, relational androgyny attempts to eliminate the perjorative analysis of female development and is aimed at healing the split between individuation and attachment (Miller, 1976; Surrey, 1983; Stiver, 1984). This perspective builds on the earlier theoretical work on androgyny in gender identification (Constantinople, 1973; Bem, 1974, 1975a). Relational androgyny challenges the conceptualization of dependency and autonomy as polar opposites and argues that incorporation of both behavior patterns in the same individual is a step toward healthy psychological development. The implications of androgyny for mental health will be reviewed in the next section.

Relational androgyny additionally offers a different view of attachment and dependency as aspects of strength, necessary for psychological growth. Miller (1976), for example, argues that the ability to grow psychologically is an ongoing process that inevitably involves repeated feelings of vulnerability.

In no society does the person—male or female—emerge full-grown. A necessary part of all experience is a recognition of one's weaknesses and limitations. That most valuable of human qualities—the ability to grow psychologically—is necessarily an ongoing process, involving repeated feelings of vulnerability all through life. (Miller, 1976, p. 31)

According to Miller, people need to learn that feelings of weakness, dependency, and vulnerability are not shameful or abhorrent. Compared to men, women are better able to be consciously aware of their own neediness; therefore, women have ready access to psychological strengths essential to growth. In this sense, the ability to admit weakness is an important resource. These feelings can form the platform from which an individual can move on to find paths to new strengths. In contrast to women, men seem to flee from these feelings *before* they experience them.

Relational androgyny is critical of traditional theory for providing a limited view of development. In traditional theory, healthy development and the acquisition of a sense of self proceed through the experience of separation. For example, Erikson suggested a staged process of development, with each stage involving greater separation and sense of self (Erikson, 1950). Feminist analysts argue that development of a sense of self is much more complicated than the process suggested by traditional object relations, that is, escape from fusion (Miller, 1984).

Relational androgyny supports the contention that a sense of self can be acquired through interaction and relation to others. In this framework, being related to others, understanding the feelings of others, and being attuned to the condition of relationship with others, can enhance a sense of self, empowerment, and motivation (Miller, 1984). Furthermore, ties to other people need not be an exercise in dependency (Miller, 1976).

A recurrent theme in this analysis is that both women and men deny their dependency needs, with men seeing dependency as a threat to autonomy and women seeing it as selfishness. Adoption of a male model has led to a perception of adulthood based on autonomy. Adoption of a male model has influenced psychological theories of mental health such that autonomy is considered more mature and normative. Indeed, Stiver (1984) points out that much psychological theory discusses dependency in a biased and perjorative fashion, associating any and all dependency needs as childish and regressive. Surrey (1983) questions the implications of traditional theory where healthy development is based on a foundation of disconnection (with the mother) and elaboration of the separateness of women and men.

Relational androgyny accepts the basic analysis of object relations that girls are less separated from their mothers than are boys. However, rather than viewing this as a negative or weak condition, it is suggested that women acquire special, uniquely feminine patterns of relating to others. *The female self is a self in relationship.*

A consequence is that women find it easier to move back and forth between the roles of givers and receivers of support and generally to have a greater capacity for empathy (Chodorow, 1978; Jordan, 1983; Stiver, 1984). Because girls are less differentiated and are more continuous with the object world, girls have an ongoing preoccupation with both internalized object relationships and external relationships. Feminine personality comes to be based on a retention and continuity of relationships. This approach is consistent with a radical feminist perspective, which holds that there is a uniquely female way of being in the world that is particularly valuable and should be fostered.

Relational androgyny attempts to alleviate the rigid dichotomizing of male and female spheres of activity by attacking the conceptualization of dependency and autonomy as opposites. If women and men could both acknowledge and work within their needs for connectedness and communal attachment, there would be less need for insisting that male and female must be opposites.

Social Constructionism

A third feminist perspective, the social constructionist approach, argues that current classifications are based on a socially constructed understanding of dependency and autonomy (Lerner, 1983). This perspective is most compatible with a liberal feminist analysis. A review suggests that much of what has been labeled as passive and dependent (because women do it) is, in fact, functionally instrumental and goal directed. These behaviors may be best understood in terms a social framework, especially status and power.

Unger (1979) has reviewed a number of social behaviors, such as conformity, influence strategies, and nonverbal acts, which illustrate this point. The main thrust is that anyone, female or male, in low status, low prestige positions, and having limited resources, is likely to adopt certain coping styles to avoid negative sanctions and gain access to rewards. The "cheerful" obsequious manners of slaves may be understood in this same light.

Social constructionism suggests that dependency behavior on the part of women does not reflect a lack of differentiation of the internal self but instead represents a functional strategy by which women maintain important relationships (Lerner, 1983). Women's displays of dependent behavior may be viewed as serving a protective function for a family or marital system.

Girls are taught that attracting men and securing relationships with them is primarily determined by women's actions and characteristics. Women have an obligation to protect, soothe, and build the ego of their male partner. There is an implicit warning that men are weak and need to be protected. To fulfill this function, women may forego their own development. To the extent that women "de-self," their male partners gain in "pseudo-self" (Bowen, 1978). There is then a hidden assumption that relationships are built and maintained by the woman's subordination of her interests, needs, and so on. In this sense, dependency behavior may be highly instrumental. Admonitions for women to become more independent and autonomous, if adopted, may be costly in terms of breakups of relationships or followed by the emergence of symptoms in other family members in an effort to maintain the family system (Lerner, 1983).

Social constructionism argues that the analysis of male autonomy in contrast to female dependency works well as long as dependency is defined as emotional attachment to others. However, if dependency is assigned a broader operational definition, the validity of the analysis becomes questionable. For example, men frequently rely on a wife to manage their home, care for their children, express their emotional concern through birthday and sympathy cards purchased by the wife (or secretary), and maintain sociable relations with friends and acquaintances.

Suppose dependency were defined as letting someone else choose one's underwear, clean one's clothes, cook one's meals, arrange details of one's vacation? That men do not become competent in these spheres or exert energy in fulfilling these tasks is not perceived as dependency or failure to separate. Men are not thought to suffer emotionally or psychologically from this condition, nor are they perceived to be less developed as individuals. Rather men are thought to be exhibiting their independence of women and home by pursuing public activities.

The social constructionist analysis offers a broad perspective on the general social classification of that which is female or male. The interpretation of women's behavior as dependency derives in part from a dichotomous assignment of females to "nature" (biological, personal, private variables, and experiences) and males to "culture" (rational, social, public facts). Social definitions of that which is cultural and that which is personal, or that which is valued and that which is disregarded, have largely shaped our understanding of development and the nature of women. A significant consequence of this is a division of labor that assigns domestic events to women and public acts to men. Thus, women are seen to engage in activities that require little or no skill, since they come "naturally." Such natural activities do not deserve high regard or recognition.

Public actions, those performed by men, are established according to normative and social criteria, often codefied in extensive and formally developed rules. This is variously termed society, culture, or the real world; and the people who do these acts are considered fully adult, mature, and agentic. Domestic labor, performed privately and in isolation, is incompletely subject to observation and determined by informal expectations. Thus, domestic activities are perceived to be influenced by personal characteristics and traits. These conditions lend themselves to an interpretation of motherhood as natural and biologically determined. This reinforces the sense that women are closer to their biology than men and that women are somehow less developed as complete human beings.

Feminist perspectives suggest that in any analysis where culture (that which is performed publicly according to acknowledged skills) is pitted against natural acts (those performed privately without the necessity of training), it is always culture that is valued and esteemed. The public sphere dominates the private sphere. To the extent that the public dominates the domestic, men dominate women.

The systematic control of women's individual and private life experiences by collective social arrangements is partly reflected in the feminist insight that "the personal is political." This perspective suggests not only that self and social frameworks are interwoven but that self events are constructed by prepotent social structures. Furthermore, these social structures reflect vested interests, not simply accidental social traditions.

Summary

Visions of women have traditionally been based on dichotomous categories of masculinity and femininity, variously presented as active-passive, public-private, autonomy-attachment, and so on. This dichotomy appears to be based at least partly on a division of the experience of self and social events, and theorists have only recently begun to examine how to integrate self and social frameworks involving gender.

As is obvious, feminist criticisms and analyses represent a rather complex and diverse grouping. Each offers a somewhat different perspective on self and social frameworks. Feminist object relations proposes that social events can best be understood in terms of self events. The elimination of conflict and discrimination must begin with an understanding of the essential psychic conflict between attachment and autonomy. Feminist object relations accepts the basic psychoanalytic tenet that male and female needs are categorically different and individuation proceeds along different paths. Attachment needs of the female are seen to be particularly costly in terms of individuation.

Relational androgyny accepts the tenet that the focus of women and men is qualitatively different but attempts to resolve the dichotomous classification of gender and promotes a more favorable view of attachment and the traditional feminine styles of behavior. Relational androgyny suggests that the principles of attachment and care that focus women's energies are essentially creative and tend to enhance actualization.

The social constructionist view of these issues is most compatible with a relativistic approach to knowledge and tends to place more emphasis on social frameworks. That is, the observer always influences to some degree the recorded measurements of a phenomenon, whether it be a photon of light or human experience. According to social constructionism, the basic starting point of feminist object relations and relational androgyny is false. Social constructionism offers an entirely different perspective, that both women and men exhibit both types of behavior and are driven to meet both types of needs. The identification of women with attachment and dependency and of men with independence and autonomy is artifactual. That is, male behavior is labeled as reflecting autonomy simply because a male exhibits it, and behaviors typical of women are automatically labeled dependent simply because a woman exhibits them.

ANDROGYNY

Data on the incidence, symptomatology, and timing of mental disorders reveal consistent sex differences that will be elaborated more fully later. These data suggest that gender is a master variable in the realm of mental health. If this is so, then analysis, treatment, and prevention must include some understanding of the nature of gender. The concept of androgyny represents a contemporary revolution in thinking about gender and has been proposed as a potential model of mental health. This section reviews the concept and measurement of androgyny; examines correlates of androgyny; and presents some of the major theoretical, methodological, and empirical limitations of androgyny.

Definition and Measurement

The construction of masculinity and femininity as mutually exclusive has long been reflected in operational definitions and psychometric methods of assessment. Traditional measures of masculinity and femininity are based on an assumed dichotomy, illustrated in psychoanalytic and object relations analyses. Since males and females were considered opposites, high masculinity precluded high femininity and vice versa.

An additional underlying assumption of traditional measures is that masculinity and femininity represent a single dimension of human function and, therefore, can be described by the development of a single score (Constantinople, 1973). One might contrast this approach with measures of intelligence, which typically incorporate a variety of subcomponents and compound scores.

Alternative approaches to the measurement of gender identification have advocated the value of integrating diverse functions and orientations within each individual. These functions and orientations have been variously referred to as agentic and communal (Bakan, 1966), instrumental and expressive (Parsons & Bales, 1955), and anima and animus (Jung, 1953).

Two standardized measures were developed in response to this philosophy and have served as major instruments for research on a variety of issues and problems related to gender: the Bem Sex Role Inventory (Bem, 1974, 1975a) and the Personal Attributes Questionnaire (Spence, Helmreich, & Stapp, 1974). Both measures are based on the premise that gender identification does not have to be categorical. Integration of both dimensions in the same individual is termed androgynous.

Items contained on the Bem Sex Role Inventory (BSRI) identified as masculine valued include self-reliant, independent, assertive, forceful, and competitive; whereas those identified as feminine valued include yielding, cheerful, shy, affectionate, and gentle. Individuals provide a rating on each trait reflecting the extent to which they are characterized by that trait. A high score on both masculine and feminine traits is classified as androgynous.

A major hypothesis developed by Bem is that androgynous individuals are behaviorally flexible. That is, as situational demands change, these individuals also vary their behavior to adopt the most appropriate response, regardless of the sex-typed nature of the response. In a series of laboratory studies, Bem and her colleagues demonstrated that androgynous individuals do exhibit effective task oriented behavior, as well as nurturance, depending on situational demands (Bem, 1975b; Bem & Lenney, 1976).

Spence, Helmreich, and Stapp (1974) developed the Personal Attributes Questionnaire (PAQ) from an earlier research instrument on sex role stereotypes (Rosenkrantz, et al., 1968). Feminine valued items include emotional, considerate, tactful, gentle, and kind, while masculine valued items include independent, competitive, adventurous, outgoing, and leader. Psychometric foundations of this measure are excellent, with high internal consistency and test retest reliability. Cross validation has been conducted as well. Scores on the PAQ are only modestly related to measures of social desirability.

Although these measures represent a significant advance in conceptualization and measurement of gender, they continue to lend themselves to a dualistic perspective. Hyde (1985) has suggested that future development in the conceptualization and measurement of gender will include truly multidimensional scaling. Gender identification can be manifested in work-achievement domains, interpersonal style, cognitive-emotional frameworks, world schema, and so on. These dimensions may be only tangentially related, and could therefore be measured independently to provide a more comprehensive view of an individual. In fact, gender may become a somewhat less prominent characteristic, when more complexity is incorporated into conceptions of individuals.

Is androgyny becoming the norm? Are people less likely to rely on stereotypes for gender? Although the data is somewhat mixed, the answer appears to be no. Positive data include the fact that readers of *Psychology Today* tended to describe androgynous individuals when asked to identify their ideal woman or man (Tavris, 1977). Androgynous individuals are perceived to be higher on instrumentality and expressiveness and to be better adjusted and more likeable (Jackson, 1983). Also, in a somewhat positive vein, historical trends in androgyny between 1958 and 1978 indicate that males are perhaps more likely to be androgynous than females (Heilbrun & Schwartz, 1982).

Other research suggests that sex stereotypes remain firmly in place. Stereotypic views of gender, life goals, and a reluctance to be identified as a feminist have been observed in high school and college students, as well as employed women (Travis, 1976; Der-Karabetian & Smith, 1977). Other studies indicate that men continue to rely on stereotypes regarding ideals for women and men, and that this is true even among androgynous men (McPherson & Spetrino, 1983). It has also been demonstrated that much of general information processing is influenced by a gender schema. That is, concepts, perceptions, and memory for events continue to be organized in terms of gender (Bem, 1981).

Implicitly stereotyped visions of gender have been revealed by college students in a unique research design (Foushee, Helmreich, & Spence, 1979). College students were presented descriptions of males or females using items from the PAQ that were male valued or female valued, depending on the sex of the stimulus person. They were then presented with a list of characteristics valued for the other sex and asked to estimate the probability that the stimulus person would also possess that trait. Results indicated that college students tended to see the two sets of traits as opposite and dualistic, rather than independent. For example, if a man were described as possessing male-valued traits, students estimated the probability that he would also have feminine traits as very small. Likewise, the possession of masculine traits was estimated as highly improbable for feminine women.

Correlates of Androgyny

The hypothesis that androgynous people are behaviorally flexible suggests that these individuals have a complex view of the world and their own environment. Generally speaking, such individuals should consider situations and problems as containing many viable options for action. This implies a tolerance for ambiguity and a certain degree of cognitive complexity. The direction of causal influence is, of course, unclear at this point. Androgyny may be a product of cognitive complexity or it may promote cognitive complexity.

The relationship of androgyny to cognitive complexity and tolerance for ambiguity was investigated by Rotter and O'Connell (1982). College students were administered the BSRI, a measure of cognitive complexity, and a measure of tolerance for ambiguity. Results indicated that cross-sex identification in men and androgynous identification in women were correlated positively with cognitive complexity and tolerance for ambiguity. These authors suggest that androgynous women tend to see new situations as interesting and nonthreatening and that their perceptions reflect more complexity and less stereotyping than others.

Other research correlating psychological traits and characteristics with androgyny indicates that androgynous individuals score higher on self-actualizing values, self-regard, synergy, flexibility, and social presence (Allgeier, 1979). Other studies, relying on paper and pencil measures, have reported high flexibility and self-esteem among androgynous subjects and low self-esteem and low flexibility among undifferentiated subjects (Orlofsky & Windle, 1978).

Problems with research investigating flexibility and androgyny have been outlined by several researchers. Paper and pencil measures do not represent a direct measure of behavioral patterns, and individuals may not exhibit a one-to-one correspondence between traits and behaviors (Helmreich, et al., 1979). Furthermore, generalizations from a few situations to sex related behaviors in everyday settings may not be warranted (Kaplan & Sedney, 1980).

A review of the relationship between trait femininity and masculinity and other categories of sex role variables reveals generally weak relationships (Cook, 1985). The relationship may be even weaker than available data suggest, because nonsignificant findings tend not to be submitted or published. Thus, for every published article reporting nonsignificant associations between gender and other variables, there may be several more unpublished studies with similar nonsignificant findings.

In addition to weak relationships and potential artifacts of editorial policy, Cook (1985) suggests that emphasizing individual traits may obscure the impact of more potent situational demands. A major feminist criticism of psychological theories and visions of women is that these theories tend to locate all major motivational and causal variables in the individual or as a product of personal relationships. Cook's analysis represents a liberal feminist perspective and offers encouragement for a social action or civil rights focus on development and mental health.

Mental Health Implications

Traditional theory has suggested that stereotypic gender identification is a precondition for mental health (Rychlak & Legerski, 1967). Parsons and Bales (1955) proposed that a sex role division of labor along the dimension of instrumentality and expressiveness was not only healthy for individuals but also beneficial to society. Mental health implications have been assessed for four categories of gender identification: traditional masculine, traditional feminine, androgynous, and undifferentiated. Recent research has indicated that individuals with low or minimal sex typing (as revealed on a sex role stereotype questionnaire) were also likely to score high on scales of depression (Chevron, Quinlan, & Blatt, 1978).

Evidence contradicting conventional wisdom indicates that women with traditionally feminine gender identification are likely to have low self-esteem and high anxiety (Consentino & Heilbrun, 1964; Gall, 1969). Additionally, certain features of traditional femininity seem to be related to mental illness, especially nonexpression of negative feelings, passivity, learned helplessness, and other-directedness (Brodsky & Hare-Mustin, 1980; Gilbert, 1981). These characteristics are associated with vicarious actualization and manipulative influence strategies because traditional female roles are lacking in control and power (Unger, 1979). As Cook (1985) points out, traditional masculinity also has associated weaknesses, for example, compulsive risk taking, emotional rigidity, and reflexive aggressive acts.

Some theorists have argued for androgyny as a model of mental health among women (A. G. Kaplan, 1976). In particular, androgynous women were thought to benefit from the flexibility to be assertive when challenged and, for example, to be tender with children. As social and cultural conditions change, androgyny may become more adaptive than traditional sex roles (Marecek, 1979). These conditions include decreased family size, increased life expectancy, and changing work roles. Those who are flexible in their behavior patterns may experience the least amount of stress. This may be even more apparent when multiple indicators are incorporated into models of mental health, for example, attitude toward self, self-actualization, and environmental mastery (Maffeo, 1982).

Empirical data from a variety of subject groups have provided support for the contention that androgyny may be a component of good mental health. An early study of high school girls found that retiring, passive, feminine typed girls had the lowest profiles on self-acceptance and well-being; but girls classed as ascendant had generally positive profiles (Williams, 1973). Data on a college student population revealed that androgyny is positively correlated with self-esteem for both sexes (Spence,

Helmreich, & Stapp, 1975). Data on hospitalized women patients indicated that androgynous women have significantly less depression and social introversion than traditionally feminine women (Burchardt & Serbin, 1982).

Criticisms of Androgyny

Criticisms of androgyny as a model of mental health cover three general areas. The first set of problems concerns basic issues of test construction and interpretation. The second set involves a growing database that indicates masculinity and androgyny may have essentially the same implications for mental health. A third set addresses philosophical issues regarding feminist values.

Recent data suggest that correlations between androgyny scores and social desirability are higher than initially supposed (Lee, 1982). This implies that androgyny may simply be an artifact of wanting to appear acceptable in modern culture. Other studies have failed to verify the two-factor interpretation of the BSRI, indicating that while a masculinity factor is psychometrically well formed, femininity appears to encompass two factors (Pedhazur & Tetenbaum, 1979). This would indicate that androgyny is more than simply high scores on both masculinity and femininity. Furthermore, it appears that some of the positive associations between androgyny, as measured by the BSRI, and self-esteem may be determined to a large extent by the nature of the self-esteem test employed (Dorgan, Goebel, & House, 1983). That is, with one measure of self-esteem correlations may be positive, but no significant relationships emerge when a different self-esteem measure is used.

Another problem is that research designs have been correlational in nature. Thus, in many cases it is difficult to infer a clear causal relationship. For example, whether androgyny shapes self-esteem or self-esteem shapes gender identification is difficult to determine. Nor is it possible to eliminate the possibility that a third master variable has influenced both.

The second set of criticisms deals with the nature of substantive findings. For example, it has been suggested that self-esteem is not theoretically related to gender. It has been argued that gender behavior is probably situation specific and may fluctuate dramatically (Locksley & Colten, 1979). This suggests that situational variables may be more important than personality traits.

Additionally, androgyny has not always been associated with the highest scores on measures of mental health (Kelly, & Worell, 1977; Jones,

Chernovetz, & Hanson, 1978). The model suggests that androgynous individuals should score highest on self-monitoring, internal locus of control, and expectations for success. However, in many instances it is the masculinity score alone, not androgyny, that accounts for the greater amount of variance (Lee & Scheurer, 1983).

Advice to counselors has begun to incorporate this new set of information and supports the contention that although androgyny may not always be better than masculinity on traditional measures of mental health, it is consistently better than traditional femininity (Gilbert, 1981).

Implications of androgyny for mental health may be equivocal in other respects as well. For example, androgyny implies an ideal behavior set. An individual should not only incorporate feminine and masculine traits, but acquire behavioral skills commensurate with these traits (Lott, 1981). Thus, an individual is expected to be supportive, tolerant, and nurturant while making homemade bread and is also expected to be assertive, dominant, and dextrous while changing spark plugs on the car. Thus, the ideal is presented as a superhuman, competent in all spheres. The children's Halloween costumes must be creatively designed and handcrafted, while also preparing an acceptance speech for the National Academy of Sciences award for scientific contributions to polymer chemistry. Other problems arise from the fact that although individuals may be androgynous, they must still recognize situational cues as to whether masculine or feminine behavior is appropriate. Failure to properly identify the situation may lead to inappropriate behavior (A. G. Kaplan, 1979). It may also be the case that androgyny on the part of women may be perceived as inappropriate role violation. Where men are perceived as assertive and energetic, women may be perceived as pushy and obsessive.

Philosophical criticisms reflect a number of feminist issues. To a certain extent, the ideal of androgyny may be interpreted as devaluing that which is feminine in orientation. The criticism here is that androgyny represents a sellout to men, with the ideal to become more like a man (Orloff, 1978). Devaluation of a feminine style may create a certain amount of risk for some clients who are strongly sex typed as feminine (Kenworthy, 1979).

In practical application, the ideal of androgyny does fall short in changing male-female relationships. Women are encouraged to "be more like a man," for their own mental health and ultimate success in the work world. However, men are not encouraged to the same degree to acquire feminine characteristics, for example, to become yielding, shy, or gullible. In the day-to-day division of labor and responsibilities, women are the ones who really occupy the multiple roles of companionate spouse, nurturant mother, domestic administrator, and business person. The primary role of men continues to be that of "good provider."

Comment

A final comment must be that theorists and researchers have continued to identify behaviors that are learned according to socially specified values as reflecting a gender-based substrate (Lott, 1981). The initial dichotomy reflected by the Demeter myth continues to influence much of our thinking. Behavior is not identified primarily in terms of effectiveness or social expectations but rather in terms of masculinity or femininity. Data presented in the following chapters suggest that this categorical classification of individuals and their behavior accounts for a significant degree of the variation in mental health exhibited by women and men.

SUMMARY AND CONCLUSIONS

The major thesis of this and succeeding chapters can be summarized in a few points. First, mental health is a social, as well as a personal, phenomenon. Further, women are not more susceptible to mental health symptoms than are men, and much of what has been assumed to be inherent sex differences is shaped instead by culture. Second, measures of health status, risk, treatments, and outcomes for all areas of medical and psychological health reflect various confounds, errors, and artifacts. That is, most descriptions and analyses of cause and effect are only relatively accurate and must in nearly all cases be qualified by special assumptions or conditions. In subsequent chapters, problems of research design and limitations of existing data are outlined for separate topics. The following chapters deal with events commonly treated under mental health plans: depression, psychotropic drug dependence, alcoholism, eating disorders, and psychotherapy. Each chapter presents these problems as relevant to the individual's experience of self and as an expression of the social construction of gender. The complexity of these events supports the thesis that health, especially women's health, occurs within a personal and a social framework.

Gender and Mental Health Status | 2

Here, as elsewhere, conceptualizations of mental health and research methodology have shaped conclusions. That is to say, mental health is a socially constructed phenomenon. By some definitions of mental health, women have a poor prognosis; however, other approaches suggest equivalence in the mental health status of women and men. One strategy in assessing sex differences in mental health has been to look at rates of utilization of services. Typically, this involves examination of admission records. However, admission records may not reflect the true incidence of disorder in the general population.

INDICATORS OF MENTAL HEALTH

Community Surveys

Community surveys, usually involving personal interviews, are a second approach to assessing mental health. A recent community survey of mental health status, the Epidemiological Catchment Area (ECA) study, attempted to determine rates of psychological dysfunction in the population at large. This study involved household interviews using the Diagnostic Interview Schedule (DIS) with nearly 9,000 respondents. The Diagnostic Interview schedule allows classification into 15 diagnostic categories corresponding to those described in the Diagnostic and Statistical Manual of Mental Disorders (DSM III) constructed by the American Psychiatric Association. Interviews were conducted in three locations: New Haven, Baltimore, and St. Louis. Details of the study methods are presented elsewhere (Eaton et al., 1984; Regier et al., 1984; Robins et al., 1984).

General findings of the ECA study provide a background or baseline against which to evaluate sex differences in incidence of psychological disorder and diagnostic classifications (Shapiro et al., 1984). Approximately 59% of all respondents had had a general health or mental health visit to a physician or therapist in the 6 months before the interview. Only 6% to 15% of all health visits involved psychological or mental health problems. However, 68% of individuals receiving a diagnosis on the Diagnostic Interview Survey (DIS) had made a health visit; 18% of these visits were specified as mental health related. Thus, individuals with a mental health classification were more likely than the average person to visit a physician for general health purposes and also were more likely to have mental health visits. These data lend support to the validity of the diagnostic instrument.

The lifetime probability of having one of the 15 mental disorders diagnosed in the survey was estimated to be approximately 30%. Thus, approximately one third of the general population will experience psychological dysfunction at some time in their lives. The six most frequent DIS classifications are listed below in descending order.

1. Anxiety (phobic, panic, obsessive-compulsive)
2. Affective (dysthymia, depression)
3. Substance Abuse/Dependence (alcohol, illicit drugs)
4. Severe Cognitive Impairment
5. Schizophrenia
6. Antisocial Personality

Percent of respondents having a general or mental health visit in the past 6 months is illustrated in Figure 2.1. Women tend to have slightly more health visits for all indicators (general and mental health) than men and a relatively higher percentage of these visits are mental health related (Shapiro et al., 1984). This latter finding however, was quite variable from city to city, with sex differences ranging between 1% and 18%.

An additional finding of some interest was that women reporting mental health visits frequently received care from a general practitioner, while men were much more likely to receive care from a mental health specialist. This finding is illustrated in Figure 2.2. Thus, the ECA data indicate that women are more likely than men to have a mental health visit, but this frequently occurs in the context of general medical care. Men, who are relatively less likely to have a mental health visit, are most likely to receive that care from a mental health specialist.

FIGURE 2.1 Sex comparisons in percent of all health visits designated as mental health related for three communities. Source: S. Shapiro et al. (1984). Utilization of health and mental health services. *Archives of General Psychiatry, 41,* 971–978.

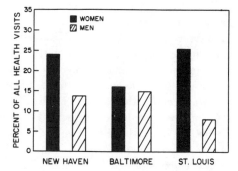

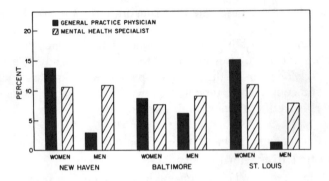

FIGURE 2.2   Sources of mental health care for women and men in three communities. Source: S. Shapiro et al. (1984). Utilization of health and mental health services. *Archives of General Psychiatry, 41,* 971–978.

Differential Diagnoses and Gender

Sex differences in diagnoses were significant for several classifications but were most pronounced for alcohol dependence and depression (Myers et al., 1984; Robins, et al., 1984). Males were most likely to receive diagnoses for antisocial personality and alcohol abuse, with four to five times as many males with these classifications as women. Women were approximately twice as likely as men to receive a diagnosis of depression or phobia. Other community-based surveys and related studies have reported similar findings with respect to diagnoses that have been found to be consistent across a variety of service facilities (Belle & Goldman, 1980). This basic pattern is illustrated in Figure 2.3. Numerous measures indicate women have higher rates of depression than men. This is true for admissions to psychiatric facilities, private outpatient care, and community surveys. The lifetime risk of depression is 20%–26% among women and 8%–12% among men (Wetzel, 1984).

The ages at which various dysfunctions are likely to become problematic are interesting and indirectly may reveal information on causation. Men have high rates of alcohol and drug dependence during their teens and middle adulthood (18–44), with rates sharply declining among men in older age brackets. Rates for alcohol and drug dependence among women are always much lower than those for men and show a peak in the late teens and early adulthood, 18–25. This pattern is illustrated in Figure 2.4. Incidence of depression reveals similar age trends, but the sexes are reversed. Women have high rates of depression in their late teens, a peak in middle adulthood (25–44), and sharp decreases in older age brackets. Men have consistently lower rates of depression, but male rates also peak in younger age brackets. This pattern is illustrated in Figure 2.5. The fact

Diagnostic Categories
Inpatient Care

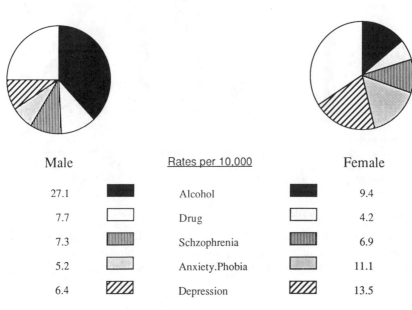

Male	Rates per 10,000	Female
27.1	Alcohol	9.4
7.7	Drug	4.2
7.3	Schzophrenia	6.9
5.2	Anxiety.Phobia	11.1
6.4	Depression	13.5

FIGURE 2.3   1984 Vital & Health Stat. series 13 # 46

FIGURE 2.4   Rates of drug and alcohol abuse among women and men by age. Source: J. K. Myers, et al. (1984). Six-month prevalence of psychiatric disorders in three communities. *Archives of General Psychiatry, 41,* 959–976.

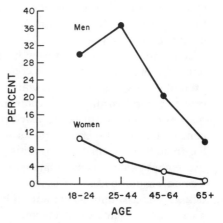

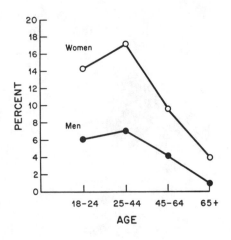

FIGURE 2.5 Rates of depression among women and men by age. Source: J. K. Myers, et al. (1984). Six-month prevalence of psychiatric disorders in three communities. *Archives of General Psychiatry, 41*, 959–976.

that the patterns illustrated in Figures 2.4 and 2.5 are so similar suggests that early and middle adulthood present stressful life tasks for both women and men. The impact of the stress is simply evidenced in different symptoms.

Sources of Artifact

The variety of facilities offering mental health services is a major source of artifact in admissions data. For example, state and county mental hospitals and community mental health centers offer 24-hour emergency care, as well as diagnostic and rehabilitation services. Additionally, general care hospitals often have inpatient psychiatric units. The number of private mental hospitals has also increased in the last decade. Special treatment for children and adolescents represent another area of growth in mental health service facilities.

The importance of this variety is that women and men may be admitted or receive services on a differential basis at different facilities. For example, compared to men, women are more likely to be admitted to private mental hospitals and to receive treatment at outpatient and community mental health centers. Men are more likely to be admitted to general hospital psychiatric units and state and county mental health hospitals (Belle, 1980).

Another problem with admission records is that utilization of services may be shaped by factors other than symptoms experienced by an individual. For example, women often have flexible roles that allow them to seek care without loss of income, whereas men are less likely to have similar opportunities for care. Thus, it is simply less costly (in terms of lost income) for women to seek care.

Admission to mental health services is also subject to clinical bias and artificial labeling. It has been suggested that some diagnostic categories of the DSM III are sex biased (M. Kaplan, 1983a, 1983b). Conditions reflecting extreme exaggerations of the traditional feminine personality—dependence and passivity—are subject to classification as mental disorder. However, conditions reflecting exaggerations of the traditional masculine personality, for example, obstreperous or independent personality, are not assigned diagnostic classifications. Thus, by being too extreme in her femininity a woman might well be classified as mentally ill.

Perceptions of dysfunction may be shaped by sex role expectations in other ways as well. In a study of self-referred intake interviews and subsequent recommendation for hospitalization, results indicated that women who presented with typically male syndromes, such as personality disorders or substance abuse, were more than twice as likely to be hospitalized than men reporting the same symptoms. Alternatively, men presenting symptoms of neuroses or depression were more likely to be hospitalized than women (Rosenfield, 1982). Thus, it would appear that when symptomatology violates sex role expectations of psychological dysfunction, individuals are more likely to be perceived as severely impaired. Women and men presenting symptoms of schizophrenia (a gender neutral diagnosis) were equally likely to be hospitalized. This pattern is illustrated in Figure 2.6.

Community surveys also have methodological problems that require caution in generalization to all women and men (Goldman & Ravid, 1980). Different community surveys may use different methods for determining mental illness. For example, some studies may rely on clinical judgment while others employ a checklist score. Even when the same checklist is used, different teams may adopt different criterion scores.

Additionally, the type of mental illness under study may be quite selective. Many studies have focused on anxiety and depression as opposed to drug dependence or personality disorder. Considerable argument has been devoted to the work of Gove and Tudor (1973) because they specifically excluded drug dependence and sociopathy (conditions frequently diagnosed among men). Their justification was that individuals with these diagnoses did not suffer mental anguish from their conditions.

Sex differences in reporting styles have also been suggested as explanations for results of community surveys (Phillips & Segal, 1969). Several factors may, in fact, be operating to produce an artificially high level of symptoms among women. A tendency to "yeasay" or agree with interviewers may be more prevalent among women, possibly due to women's

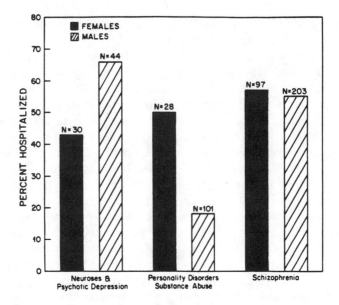

FIGURE 2.6   Hospital admission rates as a function of sex and symp-
tomology. Source: S. Rosenfield (1982). Sex roles and societal reaction to
mental illness: The labeling of deviant behavior. *Journal of Health and Social
Behavior, 23,* 18–24.

desire to be helpful. Women may also hope to please or gain the approval
of the interviewer. Gender roles for women make it acceptable to discuss
emotional responses and to bring these to the attention of interviewers
and physicians (Cooperstock, 1971). Further, men may engage in denial
of symptoms. This suggestion is consistent with the fact that nearly 67%
of men seeking general health care in "not sick" visits actually receive a
sick diagnosis from the physician (Verbrugge, 1983).

The potential artifact of reporting style has been questioned in several
studies. Gove and his co-workers (Clancy & Gove, 1974; Gove & Geerken, 1976) conducted surveys through extensive telephone interviews
ultimately involving nearly 3,000 respondents. These studies evaluated
the role of social desirability and approval needs in reporting of psychological symptoms. Results indicated that reporting bias could not explain
observed sex differences in number of reported symptoms.

A further examination of reporting bias involved household interviews
with over 700 respondents (Byrne, 1981). Only depressive symptomatology was examined in this study, but the symptoms were divided into
somatic and affective classes on the supposition that sex differences are
simply a matter of affective sensitivity on the part of women. It was
expected that sex differences would be observed on affective but not

somatic symptoms. However, results indicated significant sex differences on both classes of symptoms. Byrne (1981) concluded that sex differences in reported depression reflect a legitimate phenomenon.

Summary

Mental health indicators are subject to a number of confounding influences in reporting, recording, and diagnosis. Whether women or men have better mental health profiles is not entirely clear. It is clear that women and men consistently receive care from diverse providers and service facilities. Differential diagnoses also appear to be quite consistent, regardless of provider or service variables. Age patterns for the onset of symptoms suggest that young and middle adulthood are particularly trying times for both women and men but that coping strategies lead to different sets of symptoms.

THE NATURE OF DEPRESSION

Analyses of depression continue to reflect the issues of self and social variables and their relative importance. Four theoretical orientations on depression have been developed and are reviewed here: psychoanalytic, cognitive/behavioral, role and life events stress, and neurobiological models of depression. The first three represent a graded emphasis from self to social variables. In each case, gender constitutes an important factor in risk, etiology, and resolution of depression. Neurobiological models offer a focus on physiological mechanisms and pathways by which the various symptoms of depression are evidenced. Neurobiological models are most pertinent to treatment of depression and are thus also related to issues raised in chapters three and four concerning psychotropic drug use among women.

Probably no single model is adequate to the complete description of depression. Depression is not a unitary event and various models highlight different features. Symptoms of depression include affective feeling states, cognitive thought process, behavior, and physical functioning. Typical symptoms are listed in Table 2.1.

Psychoanalytic Constructs

Considerable space has already been devoted to psychoanalytic constructs and will only be reviewed briefly here. Early psychoanalytic formulations conceptualized depression as a reaction to the loss of a love object. The

Table 2.1 Symptoms of Depression

Affective
Depressed mood, feeling sad, despondent, gloomy
Anxiety
Decreased capacity to experience pleasure
Feelings of worthlessness, self-reproach, or shame

Cognitive
Retardation of speech and thought
Loss of interest in work and usual activities
Diminished ability to think or concentrate
Fall in self-esteem
Pessimism and helplessness
Thoughts of death

Behavior
Changes in posture
Indifferent grooming
Agitation, restlessness
Decreased sexual activity

Physical Functioning
Change in appetite, usually leading to weight loss
Sleep disturbance, hyposomnia or hypersomnia
Loss of energy, fatigue, lethargy
Bodily complaints

hostility associated with this loss was repressed and eventually turned inward against the self. Depression-prone people, therefore, are especially dependent on support, nurturance, and acceptance from others, characteristics endemic to female psychology, according to psychoanalytic formulations.

Psychoanalytic theory offers an explanation for higher rates of depression among women based on Oedipal dynamics. Freud suggested that the unique resolution of the Oedipal complex among girls laid the foundation for an adult personality characterized by narcissism, masochism, and dependency. This was due largely to the fact that girls never experience a castration anxiety and thus are never forced to absolutely separate themselves from their preferred love object. Additionally, since females experience penis envy, they necessarily feel inadequate and never are able to accept entirely the inadequacies perpetuated on them by their mothers. Therefore, females are incomplete, unfinished, and psychologically vulnerable.

In Freud's 1917 monograph, *Mourning and Melancholia*, he established loss as the central component of depression. The energy cathected to the love object is subsequently transferred to a symbolic representation of the love object internal to the individual. The individual identifies so completely with the lost love object that anger meant for the abandoning love object is instead vented within the self. Emotional states vary between rage, fear, longing, and, guilt. Symptoms of depression are produced by rage at not receiving a fair deal and fear of expressing that rage. These feelings fluctuate with a longing to regain the love object and simultaneously feeling guilty about anger the individual wishes to express. Anger and hostility that cannot be expressed may be interpreted unconsciously as a cause, and not as a result, of the loss. Therefore, the anger is turned inward as a form of reparation.

In the object relations framework, vulnerability to depression is closely related to attachment, bonding, and separation. Internal representations of the "caretaker" reassure the individual that the bond with the caretaker continues to exist. While individuals have a developmental task to separate from the caretaker, they also experience fear of abandonment, anger, and denial of anger, followed by a general denial of the frustrating aspects of the loved object. Clinical case studies indicate that depressed patients do indeed report that when they were children their parents were perceived to be insensitive, unavailable, or overly intrusive. These data support the contention that psychological representations of the parent are central aspects of depression (Blatt, Wein, Chevron, & Quinlan, 1979).

In more recent analyses, Kohut & Wolf (1978) suggest that parent-child relations are central to predispositions toward depression. A central feature of this system is the establishment of a correspondence between ideal and real images of self and others. Two systems or tasks must be successfully accomplished in early development. One is the child's move from grandiosity to mature self-esteem. Second, the idealized conceptualizations of parents must be gradually internalized. Should either task be interrupted or uncompleted, the individual will be psychologically vulnerable.

Repair of the splitting and denial is a major goal of therapy. The focus is on cognitive function and structure, not actual behaviors. Ventilation of anger is delayed until good self and object representations have been developed. Although anger may be explored in controlled fashion, the release of pent-up emotion is not the goal of therapy. Therapeutic focus is on ideational and emotional processing (Horowitz, 1980).

Cognitive Behavioral Hypotheses

The fact that depression regularly includes cognitive and behavioral symptoms has stimulated another set of hypotheses that focus on learned behavior and information processing. These theories tend to focus on proximal rather than distal causes, including both environmental and internal cognitive events.

Support for cognitive behavioral approaches was initially inferred from immediate and long-term reactions to catastrophic events. Initial work along these lines was conducted in an extensive study of soldiers during World War II (Fox, 1945). War neuroses, stress reactions, and depressive episodes were linked to soldiers' sense of being out of control. Other studies monitored the effects of catastrophic events. Leopold and Dillon (1963) conducted a 4-year study of survivors of a collision at sea between a gasoline tanker and a freighter. All survivors had symptoms of stress, anxiety, and depression at the initial interview. Over the 4-year period, the number of symptoms actually increased, including sleep disturbance, feelings of depression, and general upset. Although all survivors had spent many years in maritime service, none had been able to return to sea duty. Additional research has been reviewed elsewhere (Bootzin & Max, 1980).

Issues of predictability, control, and dependence are critical to this set of hypotheses. When individuals lose predictability and sense of control of their environment, feelings of dependence and resentment often follow. However, prolonged experience of loss of control may produce a sense of helplessness and depression.

The concept of *efficacy* is central to these analyses and has been introduced by Bandura (1977). One component of efficacy is to identify the appropriate, effective behavior that will lead to a successful conclusion. A second component is the belief that one can, in fact, perform this behavior. Efficacy, therefore, is based on being certain that effective behavior can be specified and that one is capable of executing those actions.

The concept of *learned helplessness* is one that has received much attention within this framework. Learned helplessness, attributed to the work of Seligman (Seligman, 1975; Maier & Seligman, 1976; Miller, Rosellini, & Seligman, 1977; Abramson, Seligman, & Teasdale, 1978; Hannum, Rosellini, & Seligman, 1978; Seligman & Weiss, 1980), was initially observed in laboratory research with dogs. The basic paradigm involved escape or avoidance conditioning with electric shock or other noxious stimuli. Typically two animals are yoked or paired in the administration of trials and outcomes. However, one animal is allowed to engage in escape behavior that, if performed correctly and within a specified time, will lead to avoidance of the noxious stimulus. The yoked animal has no options of escape and simply receives the same success or punishment incurred by the test animal. Once an escape response is established, the rules are changed so that no response is effective in avoiding punishment. Typically, after a period of ferocious activity the test animal becomes quiescent, failing even to attempt escape under conditions where it subsequently becomes possible. This phenomenon is termed learned helplessness. Yoked animals that have not been extinguished on escape behavior do not exhibit this pattern.

Learned helplessness as a factor in the etiology of depression among women probably has a more indirect effect than that observed in animal models. A more complex model would necessarily incorporate the fact that women have a generally lower power base or status than men. Being of lower status has several implications for the probability of initiating effective action in the world. First, it is hard to get attention or to gain the responsiveness of those one wishes to influence. Second, undertaking any behavior directed at changing the status quo incurs more energetic costs for women than men. Third, influence attempts must often be disguised.

Girls (and women) must learn how to gain attention and influence opportunities without invoking negative sanctions for violating their low status role. Other minority groups experience similar difficulties, for example, the "pushy jew" and the "uppity nigger." A reasonable response to this delicate balance is to adopt indirect strategies. The first goal then is to ingratiate one's self with dominant individuals, thus acquiring a certain degree of protection and idiosyncrasy credit. This goal may be accomplished by being helpful, nurturant, and supportive of dominants; it may also be accomplished by being generally pleasing and entertaining or by being attractive and appealing.

This same pattern may be observed in much of the daily life experiences of women, a pattern which I term the *invisible woman phenomenon*. The simple fact is that women tend to be ignored much of the time. Thus, their sense of efficacy is undermined in many subtle ways. A few examples will make the experience more obvious.

1. Carlene goes to the grocery store with her husband and pays for their purchases in cash, whereupon the checker returns the change to Carlene's husband.

2. A telephone salesperson announces that the woman of the household has won a promotional prize, but it can only be acquired if her husband accompanies her to accept it.

3. Kathy participates in a meeting on how to improve safety at work. Kathy makes a suggestion; however, the discussion continues along other lines until Dave makes the same suggestion, which is greeted with enthusiasm and eventually adopted as Dave's idea.

4. A husband and wife approach an airline check-in counter where the attendant asks if they prefer seating in smoking or nonsmoking. The woman hands both tickets to the attendant and responds, "No smoking please." The attendant fills out the appropriate cards and says, "Thank you sir."

These experiences tend to make women feel that what they do is not significant and that they have little impact or control of what happens. These experiences also communicate to women that they may have to exert intense energy in order to gain ascendence in a particular situation. The attention and social deference accorded to men as part of normal social exchange must be repeatedly won by women. Questions about the ultimate cost-benefit ratio or potential gains, therefore, are more salient to women than men. Estimates of energy costs may lead to lethargy, indifference, and depression.

These experiences also tend to teach girls that acquiring attention and gaining the responsiveness of others must be sought through extra normal or indirect channels. The birthright of the male must be purchased by the female. Girls enter a system of social exchange early in their development where attention and approval are objects of barter. Girls learn to adhere to the expectations and value systems of adults in order to successfully execute social exchange. One consequence is that girls learn to care for the needs of others and are also taught to be other directed and controlled by the expectations of others.

Women, socialized to please others, learn to be attuned to those things that interest mates and children. Since they too have needs, their dependence on others for happiness may result in manipulative behavior in order to get those needs met (Wetzel, 1984). The lack of environmental control combined with the fundamental attribution error that one is basically responsible for events may be a fatal combination for depression.

Chesler (1972) has suggested that much depressive behavior, lethargy, fatigue, illness, etc., may be interpreted as manifestations of what is basically a slave culture. The requirement that women cater to the needs of others and feel guilt over pursuit of their own preferences sets up a psychological substrate for depression. However, it is the lack of environmental control, diminished reinforcement, and punishment for violations that ultimately produces symptoms of depression. The fact that we term it depression rather than oppression reveals a bias to locate causes for events within individuals.

The potential for effective contingent behavior and opportunities for reinforcement are critical issues in understanding these phenomena. However, even behavior theorists tend to focus on individuals rather than larger systems. For example, Lewinsohn (1975) lists three risk factors for depression, none of which reflect Chesler's (1972) analysis. According to Lewinsohn, an individual is particularly at risk for depression when there are few potentially reinforcing events related to personal characteristics, little reinforcement in the environment, and few effective behaviors or coping skills available to the individual (Lewinsohn, 1975). Other researchers have additionally located some of the cause of depression within the individual. In this perspective, the depressed person may act in such a way as to cause others to withdraw, thus reducing opportunities for reinforcement (Lazarus, 1968).

Cognitive variables may act in synergistic fashion to exacerbate the problem. Among cognitive patterns lending themselves to depression are tendencies to abstract selectively on the basis of a single negative episode, to overgeneralize from limited encounters, and to magnify negative implications and minimize positive ones (Beck, 1967; Beck & Greenberg, 1974; Beck, Rush, Shaw, & Emery, 1979). Individuals may set unrealistic goals of perfection for themselves; thus, anything short of perfection is failure. The belief that one must always be in agreement with others also establishes a predisposition to anxiety and depression.

The analysis presented here suggests that women have access to a weak power base and occupy generally low status. Other hypotheses suggest that it is specific life roles, events, and associated stress that precipitate depression.

Role Stress

Role theories of stress and depression focus on the fact that married women and men have different rates of mental illness, suggesting that the housewife role may be a factor in depression. Analysis of the traditional housewife role reveals patterns identified by cognitive and behavioral theories as high risk factors for depression, namely, limited reinforcement and minimal control. The role stress hypothesis has been proposed by Gove as an explanation for the higher incidence of depression among women (Gove, 1972; Gove & Tudor, 1973).

This hypothesis is supported by the fact that psychosomatic complaints are found to be highest among married women in traditional housewife roles, especially when children are present (Gove & Geerken, 1976; Gove, 1978). Additional support is indicated by the fact that when environmental and role obligations are controlled, sex differences in general health disappear or are substantially reduced (Gove & Hughes, 1979). Recent studies suggest that multiple roles, particularly employment outside the home may have a protective benefit for general and mental health of women (Haw, 1982; Verbrugge, 1983).

In a traditional scenario, the housewife role is the only major social role of the woman, constituting limited opportunity for alternative sources of esteem or accomplishment. The role itself has little prestige and is often performed in unstructured settings where there is little to distinguish success from failure. Major functions of the housewife role are performed in isolation; thus, loneliness may become a major factor in symptomatology. Further, the structure of the household routine is often determined by other individuals in the family or agencies outside the home, contributing to a sense of lack of control. Critical to this scenario is the general low power of the housewife role (Horwitz, 1982).

The subpanel on the mental health of women for the President's Commission on Mental Health (1978a) made a noteworthy observation about family life in this respect:

> Society clings to the myth of the family as a haven of safety and a source of mental health for women. Yet, the family is the most frequent single locus of all kinds of violence, including wife abuse, child battering, incest, and homicide. (President's Commission on Mental Health, 1978)

Subcomponents of the housewife role may be particularly risky. In particular, childrearing responsibilities may contribute to rates of depression among women. The mere presence of children in the home has been found to significantly increase the probability of depression (Brown & Harris, 1978; Wetzel, 1984). Feelings that one is continually confronted by demands from others, desires to be alone, and feelings of loneliness are correlated with the number of children in the home and with the age of the youngest child (Gove & Geerken, 1977). This may be true because women assume more childrearing responsibilities. It may also be that conflicted feelings of lack of control and anger toward children and oblivious spouses may precipitate depressive affect.

Life span development issues may also operate in some cases. The work of Pauline Bart (1971) is most relevant to this perspective. In an intensive study of depression among middle-aged women, she observed a general pattern. Depressed women tended to make perfectionist demands on themselves, feel generally inadequate, and often puritanical and embarrassed about sex. Additionally, many of these women relied on their daughters as confidants when the daughters were in their teens. One consequence of emotional reliance on children was that as children left home, the women were more likely to experience a sense of isolation.

The full-time housewife role, for better or worse, is not a career that can easily be extended beyond the high school education of children. Thus, women are forced to make significant adjustments in their career behavior at a time when their spouses may be just beginning to reap the rewards of long service and achievement in their careers. Overt and latent conflict with adult children in fact, may be a significant component of depressive syndromes among women (Deykin, Jacobson, Klerman, & Solomon, 1966).

Additionally, issues of emotional support may operate. For example, women are encouraged to provide emotional sustenance for loved ones, but men seldom have similar training or encouragement. When women need reciprocal support, they may find a distant, nonresponsive husband. Thus, women often must face stressful life events without emotional support. After repetitions of such one-sided interactions, women may experience anger, anxiety over expression of anger, and eventually depression.

The issue of anger in depression has been empirically studied in a long-term project involving extended interviews and self-report questionnaires of 40 depressed and 40 control women (Weissman & Paykel, 1974). Assessment was conducted before, during, and in follow-up after psychotherapy. Ages of subjects and controls ranged from 25 to 58, with an average age of 42. The majority were Italian Catholic, and most were from middle to lower socioeconomic classes. Most subjects and controls were housewives.

Results suggested that depressed women had more hostility and friction than controls. As therapy and recovery progressed, levels of hostility and domineering behavior declined toward that of "normal" women. Interestingly, greatest friction was recorded when children were in the home. This pattern of increased hostility and friction lends support to the role stress hypothesis of depression. Women who worked outside the home showed less impairment in work than housewives at initial intake. Weissman and Paykel (1974) concluded that an outside occupation has a protective effect.

The extensive evidence pertinent to role theories of depression among women is mitigated somewhat by other studies. The entire hypothesis is based on the assumption that women, in fact, do experience more mental illness than men. As reviewed earlier, a number of artifacts may contribute to this assumed sex difference. A major criticism has been the definition of psychological disorder adopted by Gove and his coworkers. The definition accepted by Gove excludes drug dependence or substance abuse as diagnostic categories. Other theorists have argued for a broader definition and inclusiveness among diagnostic categories (Dohrenwend & Dohrenwend, 1976).

Other mitigating factors are that empirical findings do not consistently condemn marriage roles as risk factors in mental health. In a recent review of marriage and psychological well-being, Gove and his co-workers conclude that marriage can have a beneficial effect when the marriage relationship and attendant roles are personally satisfying (Gove, Hughes, & Style, 1983). Other researchers have reported that educational level interacts significantly with marital status. Differential rates of mental disorder among married and never married women are most dramatic at lower educational levels and tend to become statistically nonsignificant among women with high school or higher educational levels (Meile, Johnson, & Peter, 1976).

Additionally, studies of sex differences in depression that have recruited both housewives and employed women have reported higher rates
of depression among women, regardless of roles, than those observed for
men (Radloff, 1975). It has been suggested that marital roles per se are
not at issue; rather, status differences are key to understanding psychological dysfunction (Martin, 1976).

Life Events Stress

A second stress hypothesis focuses on life events rather than specific
roles. A number of early researchers provided observational and epidemiological support for this hypothesis. The connection between psychological well-being and environmental events was initially suggested by
Braatoy (1937) and based on data indicating that rates of schizophrenia
covaried with social class. Subsequent research supported these initial
findings (Tietze, Lemkau, & Cooper, 1941; Pasamanick, Knobloch and
Lilienfeld, 1956). The importance of life events stress was also discussed
by Janis (1951) in relation to World War II.

Contemporary research has been shaped by conceptualizations and
empirical data provided by the Dohrenwends and colleagues (Dohrenwend, 1961; Crandell & Dohrenwend, 1967; Dohrenwend & Dohrenwend, 1967, 1969) and by others (Langer & Michael, 1963; Forrest,
Fraser, & Priest, 1965; Hudgens, Morrison, & Barchha, 1967; Holmes &
Rahe, 1967; Cadoret, Winokur, Dorzab, & Baker, 1972). The general
thrust is that life events, such as changing jobs, getting married, moving,
and so on, are likely to precipitate stress reactions, including depression.

The life events hypothesis suggests that the reason for covariation of
mental disorder and social class is that members of lower classes experience relatively more stressful life events. In this framework, personality
type and unresolved psychodynamic tasks are irrelevant. It has been further suggested that the role of life events stress may impact more on the
timing of psychological symptoms than their actual nature or diagnostic
classification (Beck & Worthen, 1972; Benjaminsen, 1981).

Dohrenwend and Dohrenwend (1969) presented the issues of life
events stress around dichotomies of nature versus nurture in the etiology
of mental disorder. They reported that stressful life events produce reversible symptoms, particularly well illustrated by war neuroses and survivors of disasters. A high incidence of depression among people who had
experienced relocation for purposes of urban renewal also tended to support the life events hypothesis (Fried, 1963). Similar depressive patterns
were observed after President Kennedy's assassination (Sheatsley & Feldman, 1964).

In a major study of the life events hypothesis, Dohrenwend and Dohrenwend (1969) recruited a subject pool of over 1,000 people living in Manhattan (including Jews, Irish, Puerto Rican, and blacks). Subjects were surveyed for psychological disorder using a 22-item questionnaire assessing worry, sleep disturbance, incapacitating lethargy, restlessness, etc. Stressful events were classed into those involving security and those involving achievement, for example, changing jobs, birth of a child, divorce, leaving parental home, move to a new neighborhood, and job training for new skills. Results indicated a correlation between life events and social class, with lower social classes experiencing more life events.

Applications of life events hypotheses to depression among women is particularly fruitful. In one survey of over 900 women, symptoms of psychological dysfunction were strongly related to the occurrence of stressful life events, especially marital discord and job-related conflicts (Marecek, Kravetz, & Finn, 1979). Housewives were more vulnerable to such stressful life events than employed women.

An additional factor that may increase the risk of exposure to stressful life events is the strategies by which women, especially young women, plan their lives. *Contingency planning* among women is an important factor in shaping women's locus of control, influencing anxiety levels, and ultimately their sense of self-worth. Women generally must plan their lives around contingencies determined by other people. Primary contingencies often involve adjustments for career requirements of a male companion. In particular, young women are likely to be uncertain about their own career plans because the male in their romantic life is starting his own career, and her plans must be made compatible with his. Additionally, women frequently choose a career that will enable them to accommodate to the traditional demands of children and motherhood at some time in the ill-defined future. In the same context, women may be asked to manage more life events stress of the day-to-day variety than men.

Moving to a new city has been found to be more risky for women than men (Wetzel, 1984). This is likely to be explained by the fact that moves are often initiated to facilitate the career advancement of a spouse. Thus, the woman's sense of potential rewards are limited to vicarious gains. Additionally, social supports are eroded and social-self roles may be seriously restricted, for example, positions of responsibility in volunteer and community organizations.

Although life events models have received much interest and empirical support, methodological flaws continue to limit conclusions (Paykel, 1980). Many studies rely on retrospective reporting. Research on memory for life events indicates that people may fail to recall up to 5% of events with each intervening month (Brown, Harris, & Peto, 1973; Brown & Harris, 1982; Paykel, 1980). Further, in studies comparing hospitalized patients with community controls, the difference in actual number of events is often not particularly striking for controls and target groups.

Although few researchers or clinicians question the negative impact of major life events, especially loss of a spouse or family member, the actual size of the impact has been questioned. The amount of variance in psychological functioning explained by life events has not been determined, nor have the relative odds of psychological disorder been estimated. A major problem in estimating the amount of variance explained or in establishing relative risk is the fact that much of the research is correlational and retrospective in nature. Therefore, inferences regarding causal direction must remain speculative.

An additional problem is that modifying factors have not been investigated. The same event may have a different impact on different people. Current views are that some individuals are vulnerable to life events stress and that this vulnerability is determined by modifying or intervening variables. For example, some individuals may be vulnerable because they have limited social support networks. Thus, stressful events have differential impact. However, factors that create vulnerability may themselves produce symptoms of depression or stress (Jenkins, 1979; Paykel, 1980; Solomon & Bromet, 1982).

The impact of social networks in role and life events stress is also seen in other problem areas, such as addictive behavior discussed in the next chapters. Recognition of the importance of social situational factors in general for the mental health of women is an important tenant of feminist therapy.

Neurobiological Theory

Several lines of evidence link depression to neurological or physiological states, including sleep disturbance, endocrine changes, and alteration in neurotransmitters. The fact that sleep disturbance is a universal symptom associated with depression further suggests neurobiological mechanisms. Evidence from sleep research has been studied and promises some advances in assessment of depression and the effectiveness of pharmacologic treatments (Kupfer & Reynolds, 1983).

1. Sleep disturbance: Depressed patients frequently exhibit hyposomnia and early morning awakening, although sometimes there may be hypersomnia.

2. Alteration in EEG patterns: There is a reduction in slow-wave or delta sleep and, in some cases, a total absence of stage 3 and 4 sleep, known as deep sleep. There is correspondingly more stage 1 sleep.

3. Shortened onset of REM: Rapid Eye Movement typically indicates dream states and is associated with stage 1 sleep. There is a general increase in the amount of light sleep and this is paired with more dream activity.

Depression is also associated with comprehensive changes in the endocrine system. Depression is found to correlate with increased levels of cortisol, reduced growth hormone, reduced gonadotropins, gonadal steroids, and several other endocrine functions. The extremely complex interaction of the endocrine system makes it difficult to determine whether each measurement represents a unique effect or may perhaps be the result of changes in some master component, such as cortisol (Rubin & Poland, 1983).

Some research has attempted to determine if these physiological functions associated with depression are genetically transmitted. To this end, a few kinship studies have been conducted. Results indicate a higher incidence of depression among individuals with a stricken relative than among individuals with no family history of depression. Twin separation studies have been extremely limited and have not provided sufficient information to draw firm conclusions (Wetzel, 1984). Kinship studies typically share a major confound; subjects not only share varying degrees of genetic relatedness, but they also share a similar family ecology as well.

A considerable amount of neurobiological research on depression has centered around the *norepinephrine hypothesis* (Jacobsen, 1964; Bunney & Davis, 1965; Schildkraut, 1965). Norepinephrine is a neurotransmitter in the catecholamine family, generally associated with sympathetic nervous system arousal. The early justification for making an association between catecholamines and depression stems from the theory of *fight or flight* developed by Cannon (1929). Catecholamines (epinephrine and norepinephrine) are secreted in larger quantities during states of arousal. By inference, low levels of these compounds could lead to depressed activity. This perspective suggests that depression is more correctly viewed as a state of lowered physiological responsiveness. Initial data in support of this hypothesis were first discovered in the treatment of hypertension. Drug treatments for hypertension were also reported to produce depressive mood as a side effect. These compounds were known to have the effect of lowering levels of several neurotransmitters, reserpine, dopamine, serotonin, and norepinephrine. Alternatively, drugs that elevated amounts of these neurotransmitters, such as monoamine oxidase inhibitors (MAOI), were found to elevate mood.

The hypothesis suggests that lowered levels of norepinephrine function in a causal fashion to produce many of the symptoms of depression. Studies typically measure a by-product of norepinephrine. When norepinephrine is metabolized in the central nervous system, by-products known as MHPG (3-methoxy-4-hydroxyphenethylene) and DHPG (dihydroxyphenethylene) are formed. These by-products can be found in urine and blood plasma and are accepted as indicators of the actual levels of norepinephrine in the brain.

Depressed patients often have lower levels of MHPG than healthy controls (Maas, Fawcett, & Dekirmenjian, 1972). MHPG has been found to fluctuate with mood in depressed patients who also have manic phases to their illness. Additionally, higher levels of MHPG have been associated with reported states of anxiety (Sweeney, Gold, Pottash, & Davies, 1980). These human studies are correlational in nature; however, true experiments have been conducted with animals and tend to support causal interpretations (Porsolt, 1983).

Research has recently been developed in the study of naturally occurring opiate-like substances, especially endorphins (Herz & Emrich, 1983). Opiates are known to have tranquilizing, sedative, hypnotic, and possibly antidepressant effects. Exercise physiology has discovered that exercise can increase the levels of certain opiate-like substances produced naturally by the body, endorphins, and may account for the commonly reported sense of well-being or "runners' high" following exercise. Studies measuring endorphin levels in cerebrospinal fluid have had mixed results, with some results indicating that increased levels are found during manic states and lowered levels during depressed states. Because opiates are highly addicting, their clinical application is limited. Additionally, the impact of endorphins may only be effective under conditions where metabolism is altered by the illness state itself. Further, it may be the case that the functional problem is not one of absolute levels of endorphins produced but rather in an impaired ability of the body to utilize them.

A number of other physiological systems and agents have been implicated in depression and have been reviewed elsewhere (Hicks, Okonek & Davis, 1980). These include beta blockers, especially propanolol, and GABA (gamma-amino butyric acid). The adrenergic system, as opposed to the cholinergic system, has also been implicated because typical responses triggered by these agents include increase in heart rate and heart muscle contractility, relaxation of bronchial muscles, and the inhibition of insulin secretion.

Two problems have presented major obstacles to the progress of research in this area. The first problem is that of measurement. Levels of norepinephrine (and other neurotransmitters such as serotonin) can only be inferred from measurement of the by-products of the breakdown of these compounds in peripheral body fluids. Therefore, actual brain levels may only be inferred. An additional measurement problem is that homeostatic mechanisms may operate to keep levels of certain compounds within a fairly narrow range. For example, circulating levels may be nearly fixed while levels of the same compound bound in cells may vary substantially. Measurements of peripheral fluids would only capture by-products of circulating levels. Furthermore, measurements of norepinephrine taken from urine samples are only weakly correlated with plasma samples.

The remaining major problem of neurobiological research is that almost all of the data on humans are correlational and descriptive in nature. For ethical reasons, true experiments cannot be conducted to determine the causal role of depleted norepinephrine on depression in humans. Since the data are essentially correlational, it is equally logical to infer that depression produces depletion of norepinephrine.

Neurobiological hypotheses lend themselves naturally to pharmacological interventions. However, psychotropic treatment has numerous side effects and associated risks, as will be demonstrated in chapters 3 and 4. A number of contraindications for prescription limit the use of these agents in therapeutic treatment. Individuals with kidney problems, high blood pressure, or heart disease are typically excluded as candidates for psychotropic drugs. These drugs may themselves produce symptoms of depression if an overdose occurs. Additionally, it is sometimes the case that the effective dose for psychotropic drugs is also extremely close to that of toxic levels (Wetzel, 1984).

SUMMARY

Data on indicators of mental health indicate that gender is a master variable, affecting nearly all measures regarding incidence and diagnosis. However, a number of artifacts may affect these measures, and few studies have examined gender effects regarding prognosis once a diagnosis has been established. Sex differences in the incidence of depression do appear to be valid, and general models of depression appear to be particularly applicable to women.

Further implications of gender for mental health are explored in the following chapters with respect to psychotropic drug use, alcoholism, and eating disorders. Final chapters review general criticisms of psychotherapy and explores other feminist approaches to gender issues.

Introduction to Psychotropic Drugs

3

This chapter was written with Pamela L. Moore

This chapter reviews basic classes of legitimate psychotropes and the risks associated with them. Psychotropic drugs are defined as substances that alter mood, thinking, or behavior and are also referred to as psychoactive, psychotherapeutic, or mood-modifying agents. Legitimate drugs obtained by prescription for medical use comprise a high percentage of psychotropes, including Valium, diet pills, antidepressants, sleeping pills, and a host of others. A second major source of psychoactive drugs are those obtained over the counter from local pharmacies. Over-the-counter (OTC) drugs include agents such as Vivarin, Sominex, No-Doz, and appetite suppressants. Illicit or "street" drugs are a third major source of psychotropes and include cocaine, marijuana, heroin, LSD, hashish, and others.

Analysis of self-reports regarding use of prescription and OTC drugs indicates that women use these categories of mood-modifiers at a greater frequency than men. Studies have shown that 58% to 69% of all psychotropic drug users in these two categories are women (Mellinger, Balter, & Manheimer, 1971; Parry, Bodler, Mellinger, Cisin, & Manheiner, 1973). Men, in contrast, are more likely to use illicit drugs and alcohol than are women (Mellinger, Balter, and Manheimer, 1971; Knupfer, 1967). Sex differences in types of psychotropes consumed exist as well; women tend to use drugs that depress the central nervous system (CNS), whereas men are more likely to use CNS stimulants. This chapter will focus primarily on the use and abuse of legitimate psychotropic drugs obtained by prescription.

CLASSES OF LEGITIMATE PSYCHOTROPIC DRUGS

There are four major types of legitimate psychotropic drugs. The most well-known are *tranquilizers*, subdivided into major and minor tranquilizers. Other psychotropes include *sedative/hypnotics*, *antidepressants*, and *stimulants*. In addition, some psychotropic drugs are found in combination with other drugs. For example, a minor tranquilizer might be combined with an analgesic (pain killer). Finally, some psychotropic drugs are "hidden;" that is to say, the purpose for which they are prescribed does not indicate that they may be mood-modifying. A muscle relaxant is really a minor tranquilizer; that the drug relaxes muscles is merely a side effect. Types of psychotropic drugs, examples of generic and trade names, and likelihood of producing psychological and/or physi-

56

Table 3.1 Summary of Psychotropic Drugs

Drug Class	Generic Names	Trade Names	Potential for Addiction
Major Tranquilizers	Chlorpromazine	Thorazine	No
	Thioridazine	Mellaril	
	Haloperidol	Haldol	
	Prochlorperazine	Compazine	
Minor Tranquilizers			
Benzodiazepines	Diazepam	Valium	Yes
	Clordiazepoxide	Librium	Yes
	Clorazepate	Tranxene	Yes
	Oxazepam	Serax	Yes
Glycerol derivatives	Meprobamate	Equanil	Yes
Antidepressants			
Tricyclics	Doxepin	Sinequan	No
	Imipramine	Tofranil	
	Amitriptyline	Elavil	
MAO inhibitors	Tranylcypromine	Parnate	No
	Phenelzine	Nardil	
Litium carbonate	Lithium carbonate	Lithotabs	No
Sedative/Hypnotics			
Barbiturates	Pentobarbital	Nembutal	Yes
	Secobarbital	Seconal	
Nonbarbiturates	Flurazepam	Dalmane	Yes
	Chloral Hydrate	Noctec	Yes
	Glutethimide	Doriden	Yes
	Ethchlorvynol	Placidyl	Yes
	Methaqualone	Quaalude	Yes
Stimulants	Amphetamine	Benzedrine	Yes
	Dextroamphetamine	Dexedrine	Yes
	Methamphetamine	Methedrine	Yes

ological dependency appear in Table 3.1.

The National Center for Health Statistics divides psychotropic drugs into three categories according to psychoactive effect. Category I includes antianxiety agents, sedatives, and hypnotics; Category II drugs are antidepressants; Category III drugs include antipsychotic and antimanic agents.

Category I Drugs:
Antianxiety Agents, Sedatives, Hypnotics

Category I drugs are prescribed primarily for their effects as sedatives, hypnotics, and antianxiety agents. Often intended effects are determined by doses. A large medication does would be used to sedate a patient, whereas a small dose would suffice to reduce anxiety.

Category I drugs comprise the majority (60%) of psychotropic drug prescriptions. Most of the minor tranquilizers fall within the Category I classification, and most prescriptions are for benzodiazepines (75%). Valium (generic name, diazepam) is the most frequently mentioned psychotrope. Dalmane (flurazepam) and Tranxene (chlorazepate) are psychotropes in the same class and are ranked third and fourth in frequency of prescription of all psychotropes.

Minor tranquilizers were introduced during the early and middle 1950s and quickly replaced barbiturates as drugs of choice in treatment of anxiety, due to their comparative safety. However, the term "minor tranquilizers" is probably somewhat of a misnomer, since recent evidence has revealed dangerous and addictive properties of these drugs (Peturrson and Lader, 1981).

Prescriptions of Category I drugs are frequently for the reduction of anxiety. Anxiety usually manifests itself in signs of psychic and somatic distress. Psychic symptoms of anxiety have been summarized as excessive worry, tension, irritability, and inability to concentrate (Greenblatt and Shader, 1977a). Somatic symptoms include restlessness, difficulty in falling asleep, breathlessness, palpitations, headache, vague abdominal or chest pain, sweating, nausea, and diarrhea. Ideally, minor tranquilizers should reduce symptoms of anxiety without causing side effects of drowsiness, reduced motor coordination, or slowed reflexes. However, most minor tranquilizers, to a greater or lesser extent, cause such side effects.

Six guidelines have been suggested for prescription of antianxiety agents (Hollister, 1982b). First, it should be recognized that anxiolytic drugs induce merely symptomatic relief; ideally, they should be used in conjunction with psychotherapy or alteration of the anxiety-producing environment. Second, anxiety is usually episodic; treatment, therefore, should be short-term. Third, doses prescribed should never be standard or routine; different patients vary widely in their response to treatment. Fourth, efficacy of the antianxiety drug should be continually assessed. Fifth, use of anxiolytics should be avoided in patients with a history of alcohol or drug abuse. Finally, if treatment has continued longer than 1 month, or if high dose has been used for less than 1 month, discontinuation should be gradual, so as to avoid any possible withdrawal effects.

Sedatives and hypnotics are also classified as Category I drugs. Sedatives are usually prescribed for their calming effect and reduction of anxiety, and hypnotics are used particularly for alleviation of sleep disturbances. It has been asserted that far too often, hypnotics are prescribed for insomnia without determining the underlying causes (Greenblatt and Miller, 1977). Pain, pulmonary congestion, hypoglycemia, anxiety, or depression may cause insomnia.

Long-term use (greater than 2 weeks) has not proven effective for treatment of insomnia and indeed may exacerbate symptoms. Moreover, barbiturates (the most common sedatives/hypnotics) are metabolized very slowly and repeated nightly use could cause drug accumulation and cumulative effects. In fact, slow drug metabolism is responsible for a "hangover" side effect that commonly occurs. Many users experience drowsiness and impairment of reaction times, motor coordination, or intellectual performance the morning after a bedtime dose. Since physical addiction can occur with daily doses only three to four times the usual therapeutic dose, dispensing small numbers of pills without refill permission has been suggested to ensure frequent follow-up (Greenblatt and Miller, 1977). A final caution is that barbiturates are notoriously dangerous if consumed with alcohol since both substances have a depressive effect on the central nervous system.

Category II Drugs: Antidepressants

Prescriptions for antidepressants account for 25% of all psychotropic drug mentions. Elavil (amitriptyline) is the second most frequently prescribed psychotropic drug. Antidepressants are classified as either tricyclic antidepressants or monoamine oxidase (MAO) inhibitors. Tricyclics are more effective drugs and are less toxic than MAO inhibitors (Greenblatt and Shader, 1977c). Marked interaction between these drugs resulting in death has occurred when tricyclics and MAO inhibitors have been given concurrently.

Sometimes called "the great imitator," symptoms thought to be indicative of depression may be signs of underlying medical disease, for example, malfunction of the adrenal or thyroid glands, anemia, or cancer (Hollister, 1978a, 1978b, 1982a; Greenblatt and Shader, 1977c). Additionally, drug-induced depression has been implicated with some heart medications, diuretics, and minor tranquilizers. Therefore, physicians should consider a physical etiology for depression before assuming a psychic origin of symptoms.

However, it is more likely to be the case that physicians will perceive numerous vague somatic complaints as indicative of psychological conditions rather than a disease process. In fact there is a strong press for physicians to locate the cause of apparently anomalous conditions within the psychology of the patient. This attribution of cause to intrapsychic events relieves the physician of the need to find a medical diagnosis and at the same time allows for a course of treatment.

Partly as a function of their training, physicians are likely to adopt a neurobiological model of depression, locating symptoms as the product of faulty levels of neurotransmitters. Physicians are also likely to believe they have discharged their professional obligation by relieving women of the bothersome symptoms and incapacitating effects of depression. Since physicians are seldom fully aware of community resources in dealing with essentially social problems, they have little recourse but to offer palliative, although temporary, relief through pharmacology. However, physicians are cautioned that patients with depression clearly related to problems of living do not need drug treatment, and in fact, tend to tolerate it poorly (Hollister, 1978a).

To the extent that physicians prescribe psychotropic drugs to women without further referral when depression is produced by role stress, social inequity, or abusive relationships, they are contributing to the oppression of women. Not only does such a pattern tend to deprive women of potential resources for problem solving, but additionally it tends to increase the probability that women will see their problems as the result of some personal failing. Under such conditions women tend to engage in self-blame. Hiding dependency and denying anger become primary goals.

Category III Drugs:
Antipsychotic and Antimanic Agents

Only 14% of all psychotropic drug mentions are for antipsychotic and antimanic agents. *Major tranquilizers* are most often used for their antipsychotic effect and, therefore, are prescribed for treatment of thought disorders in schizophrenia. However, clinical use of these drugs is not limited to psychiatry. Several major tranquilizers have potent sedative effects and may be used to treat confusion, delirium, or alcohol withdrawal syndrome.

This class of psychotropes also have antiemetic properties, which make them effective in alleviating nausea and vomiting. Since major tranquilizers impair thermoregulatory mechanisms (that maintain body temperature), they may be used concomitantly with cooling techniques in case of life-threatening fever or heat stroke. Though they do not have addictive properties, major tranquilizers do have several main side effects, including extrapyramidal symptoms (involuntary muscle movements or dyskinesia) and postural hypotension (low blood pressure upon standing) (Greenblatt and Shader, 1977b).

Other Psychotropic Drugs

Stimulants, including amphetamines and anorexiants (appetite suppressants), constitute a drug type not included in the NCHS category system but are nevertheless frequently prescribed. Amphetamines obtained from legitimate sources are almost exclusively "female" drugs. "Thin is in" and many women seek prescriptions for diet pills from their physicians to help them fit society's image of the ideal woman. Excess weight is deleterious to good health, but risks involved in the use of stimulants may prove to be more hazardous.

Infrequently, stimulants are used to combat depression, but as a rule, antidepressants are prescribed for this disorder. When taken in large enough quantities, stimulants can induce a psychotic paranoid state. In addition, psychological dependence and minor physiological dependence have been demonstrated (Imlah, 1970).

"Hidden" psychotropes and combination drugs also account for a significant portion of psychotropic drug use. Examples include anticonvulsants (used to treat epilepsy), antispasmodics (for menstrual cramping or spastic colon), analgesics, muscle relaxants, and other combination drugs, which include a psychotropic agent.

Estimates of the extent of psychotropic drug use are probably grossly underestimated because of the hidden nature of these agents. For example, mixed psychotropes with more than one function (e.g., tranquilizer *and* antispasmodic) may not counted as psychotropes (Cooperstock, 1978). Combination drugs may contribute to overdose problems if not considered when prescribing or taking another psychotrope.

RISKS OF PSYCHOTROPIC DRUGS

Experience has revealed a number of hazards associated with psychotropes, including numerous pharmacological side effects, toxic effects due to overdose, and drug dependence.

Side Effects

Side effects are undesired pharmacological effects associated with the normal range of drug dose taken according to physician directions. For example, muscle tremors are associated with long-term use of major tranquilizers; risk of hypothyroidism occurs with prolonged lithium intake, and loss of muscle coordination accompanies minor tranquilizer use.

Side effects are commonly observed in many patients, but idiosyncratic effects may also occur. Idiosyncratic and hypersensitive effects include unpredictable responses occurring only in some individuals and may include blood disorders, cardiac irregularities, and paradoxical reactions, all of which may be life-threatening. A summary of some of these effects is presented in Table 3.2.

Table 3.2 Adverse Reactions to Psychotropic Drugs

Drug Category and Name	Symptoms of Toxicity	Idiosyncratic Reactions
Major tranquilizers		
Phenothiazines	Drowsiness, postural hypotension, extrapyramidal syndromes, weight gain, restlessness, delirium, convulsions, tardive dyskinesia, atropine-like effects	Potentiation of morphine, barbiturates, alcohol; coma in myxedema
Haloperidol	Hypotension, extrapyramidal syndromes, dystonia, tardive dyskinesia	Neurotoxicity with hyperthyroidism
Minor tranquilizers		
Benzodiazepines	Drowsiness, ataxia, hypotension, extrapyramidal syndromes, hangover	Convulsions on withdrawal, paradoxical excitement
Meprobamate	Drowsiness, ataxia, addiction, arrhythmias, hypotension	Alcohol intolerance, seizures in epilepsy, exacerbation of porphyria
Antidepressants		
Tricyclic Antidepressants	Restlessness, delirium, convulsions, tremor, hypotension, parkinsonism, cardiac arrhythmias, dry mouth, nausea, vomiting, drowsiness	Exacerbation of glaucoma or urinary retention, potentiation of monoamine oxidase inhibitors
Monoamine oxidase inhibitors	Psychosis, hypotension, edema, hypochromic anemia, constipation, impotence, dry mouth, nausea, insomnia, anorexia	Potentiation of sedative, hypnotic, and tranquilizing drugs; potentiation of pressor amines including those in cheese and wine
Lithium Carbonate	Tremor, polyuria, nausea, diarrhea, confusion, lethargy, edema, weight gain	Goiter, leukocytosis, nephrogenic diabetes insipidus, kidney damage, fetal damage
Sedative/Hypnotics		
Barbiturates	Drowsiness, addiction, hangover, coma, ataxia	Excitement, exacerbation of acute intermittent porphyria
Chloral Hydrate	Gastric irritation, hangover, dizziness	Exaggerated effect in liver or kidney disease, excitement
Glutethimide	Hangover, ataxia, dizziness, nausea, vomiting, hypotension, anorexia	Paradoxical excitement, porphyria blurred vision
Ethclorvynol	Hangover, ataxia, dizziness, hypotension, vomiting, blurred vision	Paradoxical excitement, confusion
Stimulants		
Amphetamines	Addiction, psychosis, irritability, insomnia	Increase of hypertension, increase of hyperthyroidism, angina pectoris

Drug Interactions

Drug interactions are another hazard associated with consumption of psychotropes. Women comprise 63% of patients hospitalized for adverse drug reactions and account for a similar percent of drug-induced fatalities (Caranasos, Stewart, & Cluff, 1974). Patients often receive prescriptions from two or more physicians, increasing the risk of negative interactions. Over-the-counter preparations and alcohol may also interact with prescribed medicines.

Additionally, drug interaction effects may be produced by changes in the metabolism of one drug induced during administration of another. For example, oral contraceptives reduce the metabolism of diazepam (Valium) (Abernethy et al., 1982). When both drugs are taken, there is a potential for tranquilizer buildup in the system and a consequent overdose, even though prescription directions are accurately followed.

Overdose

Toxic effects arise when excessive administration occurs and usually manifests itself as an exaggeration of desired clinical effects. An overdose may be potentially fatal, and each year about 29,000 women and 13,000 men are admitted to hospital emergency rooms for poisoning associated with psychotropic drugs (NCHS, 1982b).

Overdose may occur for several reasons. Physicians may fail to monitor prescriptions or other medications a patient is currently taking. In prescribing additional drugs, physicians may precipitate an overdose. Physician-precipitated overdose may also be due to the fact that clinical trials conducted to establish effectiveness, appropriate doses, side effects, and general safety of such drugs are routinely conducted exclusively with male patients. Thus, appropriate safe clinical doses for women are often inferred from data acquired about men.

The physician pathway to overdose was illustrated in an anecdote by Muriel Nellis in her book, *The Female Fix*. During a routine physical exam, "Joan" mentioned feeling some anxiety about beginning her new job. Her internist prescribed a low-dose tranquilizer to help get her "over the hump." During her first week at work, she strained a neck muscle and an office mate referred her to her own neurologist who prescribed a muscle relaxant. A week later, ovary spasms led her to the gynecologist who also prescribed a drug. All three prescriptions contained different amounts of the same kind of tranquilizer. Fortunately, her reaction to the overdose was paradoxical—instead of becoming overly tranquilized, she became irritable and agitated. None of the doctors she consulted inquired about other current medications.

Patients themselves may accidentally overdose. Accidental overdose initiated by the individual may occur because of drug-induced confusion or simply lack of information about prescribed medication. In a study of patients hospitalized because of drug-induced illness (all drug types), only 40% of patients could correctly identify their prescribed medications (Caranasos et al., 1974). Additionally, 60% of patients felt that the drugs prescribed them were completely safe, perhaps contributing to the belief that "if one pill is good, two are better."

Intentional overdose and suicide attempts are additional hazards. Approximately 67% of deliberate drug overdoses requiring hospital admission involve one or more psychotropic drugs (Skegg, Skegg, & Richards. 1983). Antidepressants and minor tranquilizers are associated with the highest rate of deliberate overdose. Statistically, women are somewhat more likely than men to overdose with tranquilizers.

Dependence

Minor tranquilizers were initially preferred over barbiturates in treatment of anxiety, based on an assumed lower risk of drug dependence. However, evidence has indicated otherwise.

Recognition and treatment of dependence is complicated by the fact that withdrawal symptoms experienced by the addict mimic symptoms of anxiety the tranquilizer is designed to eliminate (Fidell, 1981). Unfortunately, addiction may occur gradually over a period of time in such a way that the individual may be unaware of it. This is especially likely to happen when legitimate use has been prolonged. A vivid autobiographical account of this type of addiction is described by Barbara Gordon in her book, *I'm Dancing as Fast as I Can* (1979).

Another source of confusion for both patients and practitioners is associated with early symptoms of alcohol withdrawal. Symptoms of alcohol withdrawal include jitteriness, tremors, palpitations, and sweating, symptoms also indicative of anxiety (Khantzian, 1978). Thus, women attempting to manage alcohol dependence without guidance may report symptoms mimicking anxiety. If physicians fail to detect alcohol dependence, it is likely that a psychotrope will be prescribed, establishing the potential for a fatal interaction.

A summary of limitations and potential hazards of psychotropic drugs includes the following:

1. Psychotropes are palliative, not curative.
2. Most psychotropes carry a risk of psychological and/or physiological

dependence; abrupt discontinuation may result in withdrawal symptoms.

3. Adverse reactions and undesired side effects are common.
4. Psychotropic drugs involve a special risk of overdose and attempted suicide.
5. Many psychotropes interact with other drugs, including alcohol.
6. Standardization of dose and determination of side effects are typically established through experimental trials with male patients, placing women at potential risk for undetermined side effects and overdose.

SUMMARY

The most common psychotropes are major and minor tranquilizers, sedatives and hypnotics, and stimulants. These are classed as Category I (antianxiety), II (antidepressant), or III (antipsychotic). Additional effects, such as antiemetic and relaxant qualities, make psychotropic drugs useful in the treatment of conditions in diverse body systems (musculoskeletal, cardiovascular, etc.). Because of their broad range of effects, psychotropes may be prescribed in combination with other medicaments for conditions unrelated to mental illness. Risks of psychotropes are serious and generally fall into four classes: side effects, drug interactions, overdose, and dependence.

Psychotropic Drugs: Treatment Issues 4

PATTERNS OF DRUG USE

Diagnostic Conditions
Patient Characteristics
Prescriber Characteristics

EXPLANATORY HYPOTHESES

System Level Variables
Medicalization of Stress
Research Methodology
Economic Incentives
Chemical Comforts

Person-Centered Variables
Morbidity Hypothesis
Role Stress
Wellness Consulting
Reporting Hypotheses

Intervening Variables
Signs and Symptoms
Diagnostic Strategies
Attribution Bias
Gender Stereotypes
Acceptance of Chemical Comforts

FEMINIST ANALYSES

Liberal Perspectives
Radical Perspectives
Socialist/Marxist Perspectives

SUMMARY AND COMMENTS

This chapter was written with Pamela L. Moore

This chapter outlines patterns of drug use in terms of diagnostic conditions and patient and prescriber characteristics. Explanatory hypotheses for sex differences are presented and feminist analyses are examined. These are critical issues because, as illustrated in chapter 3, psychotropic drugs are prescribed for a wide variety of conditions and have potential for serious health effects. The fact that the majority of prescriptions are for women suggests that women's roles are particularly stressful and that alternative methods of resolving the stress are not readily available to women. Indeed, some feminists would question whether or not society has a vested interest in maintaining women's roles as they are, regardless of the psychological costs incurred.

PATTERNS OF DRUG USE

The National Center for Health Statistics (1983) estimates that 62% of all visits to physicians are drug visits, that is, prescriptions for one or more drugs are provided. Ten percent of these drug visits involve one or more psychotropic drugs. A wide variety of diagnostic conditions, in addition to mental disorder, may be treated by psychotropic drugs. Sex differences are so large as to warrant careful attention to those factors that may differentiate the sexes in terms of morbidity, utilization of health care services, and wellness and illness behavior. Further analyses that examine social frameworks are considered briefly in this section and in more detail later.

Diagnostic Conditions

Over half of physician visits where patients are given a diagnosis of mental disorder result in a psychotropic drug prescription. This is most likely to be true for those mental illness diagnoses associated with mental anguish, such as depression or anxiety reactions, which are most common among women.

Another group of conditions appear, on initial examination, to have a somatic basis but are found to involve a psychological or mental disorder as well. Symptoms most likely to result in such a diagnosis include somatic complaints such as stomach pains, headaches, insomnia, palpitations, etc. A large percentage of these patients are also women, partly because women's reporting styles tend to be comprehensive. Thus, women may report neurological, cardiovascular, and gastrointestinal symptoms during the same office visit. In addition, women are likely to engage in more self-disclosure with respect to negative thoughts or emotions. When confronted by such a confusing array of symptoms, the likelihood of a mental illness diagnosis is increased. In contrast, the reporting styles of men are more terse and tend to be focused on a primary complaint.

Psychotropic drugs are prescribed for a wide variety of symptoms and conditions in addition to those indicative of mental disorder. A number of physiological conditions can be managed with partial success through the combined use of psychotropic drugs and other medicaments. A variety of chronic conditions and illnesses fall in this category, for example, cardiovascular diseases, diabetes mellitus, and multiple sclerosis. The muscle relaxant qualities of some psychotropes make them a preferred choice in the treatment of a variety of musculoskeletal strains, sprains, and traumas. The antiemetic qualities of other psychotropes make them ideal in the treatment of some types of poisoning. Psychotropic drugs also are prescribed to diminish stress reactions, which may exacerbate a physical illness and to facilitate adjustment to the illness itself. In some cases, such as extreme hypertension, normal stress reactions might prove catastrophic by precipitating stroke. Problems of adjustment to an illness may also be somewhat relieved by psychotropes.

Symptoms or disorders in any of the systems listed below may result in prescriptions of psychotropes for the purposes of managing primary physical symptoms, reducing the risk of complications brought about by failure in related systems, or in the psychological stress of adjusting to a serious illness.

Disorders involving biological systems, including:

digestive	skin/cellular tissue
circulatory	CNS sense organs
genitourinary	bones & organs of movement

Conditions or symptoms related to any of the following:

accidents & poisoning	senility & related symptoms
respiratory conditions	allergic/metabolic/nutritional

The distribution of specific types of psychotropes over conditions is predictable and revealing at the same time. Major and minor tranquilizers and antidepressants are prescribed for mental disorders, senility, and related conditions (Parry et al., 1973). Stimulants (amphetamines) are prescribed primarily for metabolic and nutritional conditions. Sedatives are prescribed in essentially equal rates for mental disorders, circulatory disorders, and senility. Hypnotics are prescribed about equally for mental disorders, senility, and special conditions without sickness.

Sex differences in the use of psychotropic drugs are partly related to treatment for mental disorder but are also related to sex differences in other types of symptoms and illnesses. For example, since women outlive men, more women than men are likely to receive psychotropes to treat symptoms of senility. The extent to which the labeling of older women as senile is shaped by negative stereotypes about women and aging is a matter of speculation. Women also tend to have more genitourinary problems than men, and part of the treatment regimen for these conditions may include psychotropes.

Table 4.1 indicates the distribution of psychotropic drug prescriptions by diagnostic condition, functional action, and pharmacological classification. Over half of prescriptions for major tranquilizers are associated with mental disorder and approximately one third of the minor tranquilizers are prescribed in conjunction with this diagnosis. Sedatives are most likely to be prescribed in conjunction with circulatory disorders in addition to mental disorders. Hypnotics are prescribed in essentially equal rates for mental disorders, senility and related symptoms.

Patient Characteristics

Data acquired from health diaries on all types of prescription drug use reveal general characteristics of patients most likely to receive and comply with drug prescriptions (Verbrugge, 1982). An increased use of preventive and curative drugs of all types is associated with increased morbidity, age, nonemployment, stressful life events, self-ratings of poor health, and feelings of helplessness. Compared to men, women take more kinds of preventive and curative drugs of all types.

Table 4.1 Psychotropic Drug Mentions Per Thousand Office Visits
by Major Clinical Problem

Major Clinical Problem	All Psychotropic Drug	Drug Category		
		I	II	III
All visits	69	41	17	11
Mental disorders	527	207	200	120
Diseases of the circulatory system	116	82	24	9
Diseases of the digestive system	81	48	20	12*
Diseases of the musculoskeletal system	74	55	15	5*
Symptoms, signs, and ill defined conditions	123	89	25	9*

*Exceeds a relative standard error of 30%.
Data Source: Advancedata June 15, 1983

Absolute numbers of psychotrope prescriptions, rate of prescriptions per 1,000 office visits, and long-term use patterns all indicate that women are more likely than men to receive psychotrope prescriptions. Approximately twice as many women (31%) as men (15%) will use some type of psychotropic drug during a given 12-month period (Parry, 1968). However, both women and men are most likely to receive Category I prescriptions.

As indicated in Table 4.2, there are approximately 1 billion office visits annually, with substantially more visits by women than men. In comparison to men, women receive more absolute prescriptions of psychotropes (53 million for women versus 26 million for men). In addition, women receive a higher *rate* of psychotrope prescriptions than men (8% versus 6% of office visits). If 100 women visit a physician, approximately eight will receive a prescription for psychotropic drugs, whereas for a similar number of office visits by men only six will receive psychotropes. That is to say, sex differences in psychotropic drug prescriptions are not simply due to the fact that women go to the doctor more often than men.

Insurance records from one Canadian province indicate that sex differences may be even larger when examined over time. During a 5-year period, long-term follow-up revealed that 15% of women receiving a psychotrope in 1970 also received one in 1974. This was true for only 7% of men (Cooperstock, 1978). These data indicate that once women receive psychotropic drugs, there is a tendency for prescriptions to be continued and use patterns to be extended over periods of several years. Apparently the pattern among men is to receive psychotropes for more limited periods of time.

Personal characteristics of users of psychotropic drugs were recorded in telephone interviews with nearly 1,200 women (Pihl, Marinier, Lapp, & Drake, 1982). Women were asked to rate themselves on health status and practices, psychological well-being, use of psychotropic and analgesic drugs, and alcohol and tobacco use. Over 25% of women surveyed had taken psychotropic drugs at some time.

Table 4.2 Number of Office Visits & Psychotropic Drug Mentions by Sex of Patient

Sex	Number Visits	All Mentions	Category I	Category II	III
		(Numbers in Thousands)			
Female	699,718	53,409	31,972	14,398	7,039
Male	461,204	26,173	16,076	5,897	4,200
Total	1,160,922	79,582	48,048	20,295	11,239

Data Source: NCHS Advancedata, June 15, 1983, no. 90.

Pihl and his colleagues also classified women in terms of the extent of drug use, high consumers, moderate consumers, or abstainers. High consumers were most likely to describe themselves as being in poor health and to report feelings of unhappiness. Additionally, high consumers were likely to report physician visits for undefined problems, but seldom for preventive care. High consumers were also more likely to be married, have children, and unemployed outside the home.

Sex differences in the use of psychotropic drugs are partly related to differences in morbidity, mortality, and life-style. Compared to men, women are more likely to be classified as suffering from depression, anxiety, and psychoneurotic reactions. Hospitalization for these conditions is likely to be more lengthy than those conditions most associated with hospitalization among men. Thus, the length of exposure or treatment is likely to be longer for women than men. Therefore, sex differences in the nature and incidence of mental illness, as well as length and course of treatment, contribute to higher levels of psychotropic drug use among women. The fact that men are most likely to be hospitalized for drug dependence probably also contributes to a lower prescription rate for psychotropes. Additionally, women are more likely than men to desire to lose weight and to seek assistance in weight loss, with the consequence that more women than men receive prescriptions for amphetamines. Further, because women outlive men, they are more likely to experience symptoms of senility and related conditions of aging, placing them once more in a category of increased psychotropic drug use.

Although morbidity and medical conditions might account for a substantial amount of the variance in sex differences, other patterns of sex differences present anomalies. As Figure 4.1 illustrates, there appears to be a sex and age interaction. The prescription rate for psychotropes is quite similar for both sexes until age 45; after age 45, women have a substantially higher rate than men. Thus, prescription patterns of physicians appear to be gender neutral until patients reach older ages. The probability of receiving a psychotropic drug prescription is essentially equal for females and males during the preteens, teens, and young adulthood.

The sex and age interaction is in some ways a surprising pattern because the incidence of formally diagnosed depression tends to decline among women after age 45. If psychotropes were administered primarily in the management of mental disorder the lifespan prescription pattern for women should follow diagnoses of depression.

One must begin to question what it is about women at age 40 and beyond that is not related to mental disorder but does require psychotropic drug prescriptions. It is worth noting that the increase in prescription rate among women coincides with major life events, including meno-

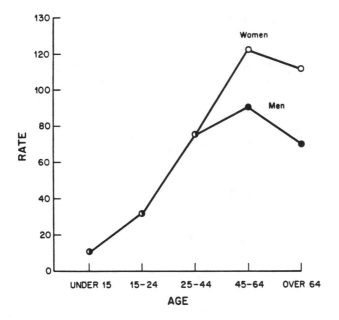

FIGURE 4.1   Psychotropic drug prescriptions as a function of age and sex. Source: NCHS, H. Koch (1983). Utilization of psychotropic drugs in office-based ambulatory care: National ambulatory care survey, 1980–1981. *Advancedata*, June 15, No. 90.

pause, retirement (of spouses as well as the women themselves), and, in many cases, widowhood. These represent a mixture of role and life events stress. Much of the stress, however, may be based on economic and financial hardship associated with loss of employment income and limited community resources dedicated to assisting individuals in need. Increases in violent crimes against older people also limit opportunities for socializing, which might supply emotional support. However, except for menopause, these are conditions which men of similar age also experience.

A radical analysis of this prescription pattern suggests an additional hypothesis. The general thesis is that psychotropes are one way of allowing women to adjust to their lot in life and represent in one sense a form of social control. It has been suggested, for example. that women do not reach adulthood until age 40, and come into their maturity at age 50. That is, it is at these ages that women become psychologically free to contemplate the direction of their lives and to recognize their own anger derived from foregone choices, selfless nurturance of others, and lack of reward for their sacrifices. Therefore, it is not depression that is being treated but rather anger, which is ameliorated by psychotropic drugs.

Prescriber Characteristics

Among physicians of differing specialty, psychiatrists prescribe psychotropic drugs at the highest *rate*. The distribution of prescriptions by physician specialty is presented in Table 4.3. However, in sheer number of mentions, general practitioners and internists far exceed psychiatrists in prescription of Category I drugs, are twice as likely as psychiatrists to prescribe Category II drugs, and equal psychiatrists in prescription of Category III drugs. The high incidence of prescriptions for psychotropes among general practitioners stems partly from their management of diagnostic groups other than mental disorders that can be treated by psychotropics, for example, ill-defined conditions, and circulatory, digestive, and musculoskeletal disease groups (NCHS June 15, 1983). In fact, drugs acting on the central nervous system are prescribed by general practitioners more often than any other drug type (18.5% of all drug mentions).

EXPLANATORY HYPOTHESES

Patterns of psychotropic drug use and abuse represent interactions of numerous complex phenomena. Explanatory hypotheses are almost limitless and have been structured according to several theoretical perspectives (Smith, 1977; Verbrugge, 1982). A simple approach is to classify explanatory hypotheses into those based on system level variables and those emphasizing individual characteristics. This classification and subsequent intervening events and conditions are illustrated in Figure 4.2.

System level explanations focus on the medicalization of stress, research methods, economic incentives, and social acceptance of chemical comforts. Explanations that focus on individuals include prevention and fitness activities, wellness consulting, illness reporting, and compliance. Both sets of variables may shape and be shaped by diagnostic strategies, signs and symptoms of illness, attribution processes, and gender stereotypes. The phenomenological experience of signs and symptoms by the

Table 4.3 Psychotropic Drug Mentions per 1,000 Office Visits
by Physician Specialty

Physician Specialty	All Psychotropic Drugs	Drug Category		
		I	II	III
All prescribers	69	41	17	11
General/family practice	84	55	21	9
Internal medicine	115	75	28	12
Psychiatry	441	122	171	148

Data Source: NCHS Advancedata #90 June 15, 1983

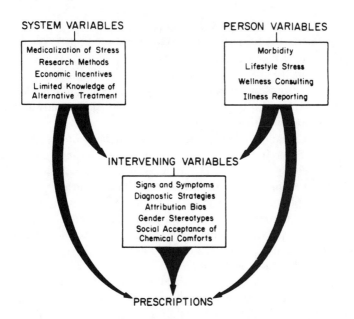

FIGURE 4.2 Causal model of factors influencing psychotropic drug prescriptions. Arrows indicate direction and strength of relationships.

individual, as well as medical interpretation and diagnosis, may also be modified by attribution biases and gender stereotypes. All may contribute to a complex set of conditions leading to psychotropic drug prescriptions.

System Level Variables

Medicalization of Stress. Stress is no longer viewed as simply an inconvenience of pressured life-styles but is now classed as a potential precursor to serious health conditions, for example heart disease, high blood pressure, etc. Thus, diffuse aches and pains (headaches, backaches, and some types of gastrointestinal disturbances) are now viewed as warning signs of disease. Repeated challenges (stress) to the *general adaptation syndrome* (initially described by Selye, 1946) may lead to an exhaustion of body defense systems, especially immunological processes, resulting in a variety of illnesses.

The growth of the field of health psychology is partly a product of the medicalization of stress and the search for social/psychological predictors of stress responses. Thus, understanding and managing stress is now a major goal in wellness behavior and the prevention of illness. Research on *type A* personality and cardiovascular signs is one product of the changed concept of stress (Friedman & Rosenman, 1974; Glass, 1977; Rosenman et al., 1976; Vlachakis et al., 1974; Whitehead et al., 1977).

To the extent that women's complaints are seen to be a response to stress, they are likely to be treated with psychotropic drugs. Medical management of these conditions with psychotropes is a logical response, especially when tranquilizers or sedatives are seen as a means of preventing more serious health problems.

The medicalization of stress reflects a general preference to locate causes for events in individuals rather than situational factors. Once stress was acknowledged to have real biological consequences, it was only a short step to focusing on medical treatment. The medicalization of stress also reflects a philosophy of natural monism that smaller units of analysis drawn from the natural sciences are basic to science and the understanding of more complex phenomena. In some ways, the medicalization of stress contributes to a perception that problems can be strictly delineated and treated within a set prescription. Beyond these factors, medicine, and the pharmaceutical industry in particular, is a multimillion dollar business with substantial resources devoted to bringing these products to the attention of physicians. Koumjian (1981) has outlined a scenario of the medicalization of stress and the consequences of this phenomena.

1. Definition of social problems as medical problems
2. Search for medical solutions of such problems
3. Dependency on medical solution, because the social problem is not addressed, and symptoms recur.

Research Methodology. Research methodology is problematic because women are underrepresented in premarketing clinical trials of new drugs (Kinney, et al., 1981). The intention, which seems reasonable at first, is to eliminate women of childbearing years from studies until potential teratogenic effects of drugs can be determined.

However, gender differences in efficacy and toxicity of drugs have been noted for many drugs (Goble, 1975). Thus, the effectiveness of a drug and side effects associated with it frequently are found to vary across sex. Reasons for these findings are unknown but may involve sex differences in several factors listed below.

1. Hormonal status
2. Differential excretion by liver and kidneys
3. Amount of body fat
4. Percentage of plasma proteins
5. Body weight

Optimal drug dose is usually determined among male patients, who weigh more on average than females. Thus, women are at risk to experience overmedication.

Though some researchers exclude women from drug studies on ethical grounds, others avoid including them for reasons of expedience. For example, compared to men, women tend to report more adverse symptoms. Other researchers have indicated they want to avoid difficulties in assessing drug action due to women's continual hormonal fluctuations.

Economic Incentives. The profit nature of medicine forms a basis for the economic hypothesis. This hypothesis suggests that pharmaceutical corporations cultivate images of women among physicians and among women themselves designed to improve sales.

Content analysis of advertisements and frequency of advertising provides some support for this hypothesis. Advertisements for psychotropic drugs in medical journals often depict a female patient (Seidenberg, 1971). These advertisements illustrate women as suffering from anxiety, sleeplessness, and depression. Symptoms and conditions represented in advertisements are often vague and nonspecific. Such symptoms require extended time and repeated appointments to search for physiological dysfunction, a commitment physicians may resist. Diagnosis and appropriate treatment are only vaguely defined. Tranquilizers bearing different trade names, though they belong to the same pharmacological class, may list different conditions as appropriate indicators for prescription.

Women in these advertisements are often portrayed in a chauvinistic, stereotyped manner. The "bored housewife" is a common image. Captions imply that women have less serious physical health problems than men; that women are bothersome to their spouses, families, or physicians; or are unreasonable, emotional, and shrewish.

A few examples will help to illustrate the basis for the economic hypothesis. One advertisement depicted a woman seated in a chair with her head and arms fading into the back and arms of the chair, while the caption asks, "Is this patient becoming a fixture in your office?" Advertisements also refer to the adaptation of women to traditional female roles and responsibilities. For example, one advertisement illustrated a harassed housewife encased behind bars made of brooms and mops. The caption reads, "You can't set her free, but you can make her feel less anxious." Another advertisement stated that the physician could help an entire family by tranquilizing the mother because she would then be able to cook and serve their meals. The caption for this jewel: "Treat one—six people benefit."

A variety of studies of differing research designs lend support to the economic hypothesis and criticisms of drug advertisements on which it is based. A tabulation of advertisements in medical journals classified sex of patient depicted and the organic or psychogenic origin of symptoms (Prather & Fidell, 1975). Fifty-nine percent of women were classified as having symptoms of a psychogenic origin, whereas 59% of men were seen as presenting organic symptomatology. Prather and Fidell (1975) concluded that impressions fostered in drug advertisements might promote misdiagnosis of both women and men. That is, women may be misdiagnosed as having psychogenic symptoms when in fact an organic condition exists, and men may be misdiagnosed as having an organic complaint when an emotional problem is present.

Advertisements depicting males or females do foster different impressions. A laboratory study presented student subjects with 10 advertisements for psychotropes depicting a male or female patient (King, 1980). Compared to advertisements depicting female patients, those with male patients fostered impressions that the patient was more independent, active, coping, and rational. In a questionnaire survey, a majority of psychiatrists reported they were more likely to give their attention to advertisements depicting attractive women patients (McRee, Corder, & Haizlip, 1974). Thus, advertisements for psychotropes that depict women may have special salience or psychological "pull" for physicians.

An overrepresentation of female drug users also exists in advertisements for over-the-counter drugs. A substantial percentage of television advertisements for analgesics (relief of tension headaches, etc.) and other drugs occur during daytime television, usually daytime dramas and other shows likely to attract a female audience. When a drug product purchaser is shown, the purchaser is likely to be a woman in the large majority of cases. Thus, advertisements not only shape physician perceptions, but self-image may be shaped by these messages as well.

Chemical Comforts. Social system variables have contributed to the effective medicalization of stress in the form of a general acceptance of chemical interventions. If stress is defined as a disease, then it can be treated as any other disease, with medication. However, defining stress as a disease may reduce attention to the social/psychological conditions that produce it. Attacking social conditions that foster these reactions is a formidable task; however, management of symptoms through chemical comforts is an acceptable alternative.

Acceptance of chemical interventions has grown among the lay public and also among physicians. The following commentary by Silverman and Lee (1974) illustrates the nature of the problem.

> To some clinicians and pharmacologists the utilization of psychoactive agents represents a highly satisfactory if temporary solution . . . (These

drugs) enable many patients to live with such problems as an unhappy marriage, a frustrating job, the fear of getting a tooth extracted, a snub at the country club, the generation gap, racism, pollution, and war. They help frantic mothers cope with young children who insist on behaving like children. They let many individuals stay awake all day and sleep all night. They serve as an antidote to emotional tension—as if emotional tension always calls for an antidote. They alleviate depression. In some cultures or subcultures, their use serves as a mark of belonging. They can bring peace and tranquility to a household, a schoolroom, an old people's home, a psychiatric institute, an entire hospital ward. Such a result may be viewed as a blessing by parents, teachers, nurses, hospital attendants, and other caretakers, but the value to the children or parents concerned may be seriously questioned. . . . (Silverman & Lee, 1974, p. 271).

The problem Silverman and Lee refer to is the mistaken belief that chemical treatment of these conditions will actually solve the woes of living. Chemical assuagement, however, is only palliative and not curative (Stimson, 1975). A serious shortcoming of chemical treatment of social problems is that drugs may actually serve to perpetuate malignant patterns and social arrangements (Lennard, Epstein, Bernstein, & Ransom, 1970).

Person-Centered Variables

Morbidity Hypothesis. The morbidity hypothesis argues that sex differences in aches and pains is a major factor in patterns of drug use (Dunnell & Cartwright, 1972). A major indication for prescription of psychotropic drugs is the management of pain. For example, sex differences in endocrine function probably are involved in the etiology of arthritis and related pain, conditions experienced most frequently by women. Chronic pain from these conditions constitutes a recognized organic condition that may be treated by several drugs, including psychotropes. Thus, women receive more psychotropic drugs because they truly may have greater physiological need.

Role Stress. Role stress has been hypothesized as a major factor in symptoms amenable to treatment by psychotropic drugs. Among women, stress associated with traditional roles is thought to precipitate many of the symptoms psychotropic drugs are designed to relieve (Gove, 1972, Gove & Hughes, 1979; Gove, Hughs, & Style, 1983). Gove and Hughes (1979) reported that when marital status, living arrangements, psychosomatic symptoms, and nurturant role obligations were statistically controlled, general health differences between women and men disappear.

This hypothesis is supported by the fact that marital status is a strong predictor of psychological symptoms. Compared to single women, married women are twice as likely to use tranquilizers on a daily basis (Chambers, Inciardi, & Siegal, 1975). The majority of women who use psychotropic drugs on a daily basis are married with children in the home (Pihl, et al., 1982). Further, as the number of children in the home increases, there is a tendency for the percentage of mothers using psychotropics to also increase (Parry, 1968).

Cooperstock (1980) conducted extensive interviews with women who had used tranquilizers from 4 to 18 years. Asked why they used tranquilizers, many women admitted that drugs allowed them to remain in a role that they found difficult or intolerable without drugs. One woman made this comment:

> Now I am in a situation which I cannot get out of. There is no way I will drop my responsibilities to my husband who is a very fine man, or my children. My husband's and my interests have gone different ways. The communication has diminished, but he's still a very good husband, and he's an excellent father to the children. . . . I can't leave them and because I can't leave them I'm sticking to the Valium. That's my escape (Cooperstock, 1980).

The function of psychotropes as a means of securing a nurturant female for the male at the expense of her own mental health is a major issue from feminist perspectives. The tendency for women to "deself" in order to protect fragile men may be furthered by the use of psychotropic medications. Repeatedly, women find themselves in the role of providing the nurturant energy on which male-female relationships exist. The fact that women may be better able than men to cross between public and private spheres of activity also means that women may bear greater psychological costs in relationships. These costs evidence themselves in lower self-concepts, lower aspirations, more anxiety, and more somatic signs.

Wellness Consulting. In addition to life-style variables, wellness variables also play a part in the incidence of morbidity and prescription patterns. One proposal suggests that sex differences in prescription patterns are due to the increased exposure of women to medical care. Women are more likely than men to consult physicians in the management of a wide variety of conditions, to monitor symptoms, seek immunizations (precautionary measures encouraged by reproductive roles), and receive screening. In addition, women often gain access to physician opinion and treatment by virtue of the fact that women, not men, see to the health care of their children. Therefore, women may consult with pediatricians or pediatric nurses about their own problems. Thus, women receive more drug prescriptions because they are more likely to consult physicians.

Support for the consulting hypothesis is provided by the fact that women are more likely to report "not sick" visits to physicians (Verbrugge, 1979, 1980). Sex differences in the use of nonprescription medication provides additional support for the consulting hypothesis. Women receive more prescription medications of all types, but sex differences are greatly minimized when nonprescription, over-the-counter (OTC) medications are measured.

Sex comparisons in prescriptions and OTC medications suggest that women and men simply have differential access to health services. No sex difference has been found in the use of OTC medications, equally available to women and men. Results of one survey indicated that, regardless of the number of symptoms reported to interviewers, 14% more women than men reported having received a prescription medicine (Dunnell & Cartwright, 1972). However, when use of nonprescription medications were examined, sex differences were much smaller. Given the same number of symptoms, sex differences in use of nonprescription, OTC medications dropped to only 3%.

One explanation for differential consulting behavior is based on the relative inconvenience and cost of office visits. This approach refers to the fixed roles of men and the relatively flexible roles of women (Dunnell & Cartwright, 1972). Men obligated to fixed work roles must often take sick leave or have their paycheck docked if they consult a physician. Although many women also experience the same constraints, women are more likely to be in positions that make office visits less costly or inconvenient. This is a case where wellness behavior interacts with features of the medical system and life-style patterns.

Reporting Hypothesis. The reporting hypothesis has often been employed to suggest that sex differences are artifactual; that is, prescription differences are not due to true morbidity. The argument is that women report a large number of vague, diffuse, and nonspecific symptoms to their physicians. Fatigue, sleep disturbance, anxiety, headaches, and abdominal discomfort are examples of symptoms that are thought to fall in this category. Women may also report marital dissatisfaction, financial difficulties, and worry over child discipline problems. In contrast, men tend to have more stoic patterns of reporting, to focus on a single problem for which they seek treatment, and to decline to comment on life-style stress (Verbrugge, 1979, 1980).

Intervening Variables

Signs and Symptoms. The recognition and classification of indicators is an important step in the sequence of "events" leading to the prescription of psychotropic drugs. The nature and justification of treatment is often based on an assessment of signs, symptoms, and functional capacity. In circular feedback, treatment efficacy is evaluated against improvement in these same indicators.

The recognition and classification of signs and symptoms is partly a product of social and medical convention and, as such, is somewhat arbitrary. Typically, signs are viewed as objective indicators of possible dysfunction, disease, or pathology. Examples of signs include elevated blood pressure, bile cholesterol, enlarged nodes or glands, and so on. Symptoms are generally viewed as indicators of subjective conditions requiring patient interpretation. Examples of symptoms include fatigue, pain, dizziness, and nausea.

Functional capacity represents a third class of health indicators that serves as an interface between signs and symptoms. Functional capacity refers to ability to perform normal activities and is sometimes used as a reference point to evaluate the seriousness of signs and symptoms. Sleep disturbance and an inability to work due to fatigue or pain are examples.

Basic judgments of signs and symptoms include a distinction between those having an organic etiology and those that are psychogenic in origin. Conditions that cannot be linked directly to objective indices of disease are more likely to be classified as psychogenic in origin. For example, when a patient visits a physician, a particular diagnosis may be specified, or the physician may acknowledge an organic basis for complaints but be unable to specify a diagnosis. As a third option, the physician may classify complaints as psychogenic in origin.

A national survey of patient records transcribed from office visits indicated that physicians are more likely to be uncertain of the proper diagnostic classification of disease among female than male patients and that for some types of symptoms, for example, headache, physicians are more likely to specify psychogenic etiology for women than men (Verbrugge, 1980).

Physicians determine whether conditions are acute (temporary) or chronic (requiring long-term care and follow-up). Physicians may view psychologically based conditions as chronic and likely to lead to an unwarranted consumption of resources in time and money with little hope of a reduction in symptoms. Thus, prescriptions of psychotropic drugs may be partly a result of intuitive cost-benefit analysis on the part of physicians.

Diagnostic Strategies. Diagnostic strategies associated with many signs and symptoms are well recognized by the medical profession. That is, given a particular set of signs and symptoms, any professionally competent physician would request a more or less standard set of diagnostic tests. However, complaints commonly associated with psychological problems may be analyzed with varying degrees of meticulousness. One hypothesis is that physicians are more likely to underdiagnose women than men.

A true example will help to illustrate the problem. "Jane" went to a gynecologist in January for a Pap test. She was asked to return for a second test the next month because abnormal cells were observed in the first sample. After the second test, Jane was told she had cervical cancer, and the gynecologist proposed to treat it by in-office cryosurgery. Surgery was performed the following month, in March. Jane was told the surgery was a complete success. The pathology report indicated a benign condition, that is, the initial diagnosis of cancer was incorrect. Jane was admonished not to worry about cancer.

For 2 months after surgery, Jane failed to have a menstrual cycle. She consulted her gynecologist, who declined to conduct an examination and again told her not to worry. During the summer, Jane once more consulted her gynecologist, reporting abdominal pain, discomfort, and unusual fatigue. The gynecologist insisted that the condition was produced by anxiety and that if she relaxed her body would function normally. In November, Jane returned to her gynecologist and reported that she still had not had a menstrual cycle since March and that pain and discomfort had continued. She insisted her condition was more than a case of nerves. Although he did not conduct another Pap test or pelvic examination, he prescribed steroids to induce menstruation. However, a menstrual cycle did not result from this treatment.

Jane's discomfort increased, and upon palpating her own abdomen, Jane discovered a large mass. After consulting another gynecologist, Jane was diagnosed as having a uterine fibroid tumor approximately the size of a term fetus, consisting of 10 pounds of fibrous tissue and fluid. Her condition was resolved by surgery, after nearly a year of signs and symptoms mistakenly diagnosed as psychosomatic.

Attribution Bias. Attribution bias refers to the tendency to focus on personal traits, dispositions, and behaviors in explanations of cause and to ignore environmental or nonpersonal causes. In a medical context, this bias may be evidenced in cases where stress reactions are explained on the basis of personality rather than social circumstances.

Attribution bias has been researched extensively by social psychologists and demonstrated in a number of experimental studies. A typical research design requires subjects to make judgments of cause and responsibility for the actions of an individual described in a story protocol. There is a clear preference for attributions that allocate cause and responsibility to the individual rather than the environment (Ross, Amabile, & Steinmetz, 1977).

This phenomenon is often termed "blaming the victim." Individuals who have suffered some misfortune or hardship and who are in effect innocent are nevertheless often held accountable for their misfortune (Lerner & Simmons, 1966; Lerner, 1970). Blaming the victim has been demonstrated in many circumstances, including rape (Jones & Aronson, 1973; Adleman, 1976), career and work (Laws, 1978), and mental health (Ryan, 1971).

Ostensibly, judgments of responsibility and cause are partially based on consensus information, that is, the behavior and experience of other people in the same setting. When all individuals in a similar setting behave in a similar manner, attributions are usually made to environmental factors. When an individual's behavior differs significantly from that of others in the same setting, attributions of cause are made to the individual. However, this principle is often violated (Major, 1980; Fiske & Taylor, 1983). Apparently judgments regarding women often locate responsibility and blame within personal disposition.

It has been suggested that one explanation for this attribution bias is a norm of internality (Jellison & Green, 1981). Another not incompatible explanation is that individuals like to feel they have control over significant life events, particularly, that individuals can secure, with reasonable certainty, rewards and avoid punishment. This belief is the basis for a "Just World Hypothesis" (Lerner, 1980).

Rhoda Unger (1979) succinctly diagnosed the great appeal to classify adaptation problems as problems reflecting shortcomings of the individual women involved.

> A member of a socially powerless group who manifests behavior that is defined as being somehow undesirable may be viewed as responsible for that behavior. Thus any change in that behavior is the responsibility of the individual rather than of society. The origins of the behavior are perceived as safely in the past or in biology—beyond the need for any effective social change (Unger, 1979, p. 463).

Because medical practice has traditionally focused on the individual as a unit of analysis, rather than the social system in general, this type of bias is probably more prevalent in medical settings in general. Obviously, if a physician attributes the cause of anxiety, sleep disturbance, fatigue, etc. to some psychological condition as opposed to inequitable family arrangement or other social condition, psychotropic drug prescriptions would seem an appropriate treatment.

Gender Stereotypes. Gender stereotypes actually represent a combination of influences, reflecting general societal views and expectations, as well as stereotypes of women fostered specifically within the medical context, and have been more fully discussed in other chapters. Medical students learn that basic elements of the female personality consist of narcissism and masochism (Weiss, 1977, 1984). Contemporary psycho-analytic theorists continue to espouse this position (Hare-Mustin, 1983). Women are seen as existing under a handicap of raging hormones and unresolved psychological complexes and are emotionally fragile at best. Physicians may thus expect that many of the physical complaints de-scribed by women have an underlying psychological etiology, best treated by tranquilizers or other mood modifiers. Given these stereotypes, it is not surprising that women are more likely than men to be classified as members of the "worried well."

Acceptance of Chemical Comforts. Public opinion has come to support a favorable attitude toward both prescription and over-the-counter medi-cines. The alleviation of pain by analgesics is readily accepted. Stresses and strains of daily life are viewed as unnecessary and unacceptable. Television advertising reiterates these values and supports the expecta-tion that relief is readily available for headaches, backaches, nausea, indi-gestion, sleeplessness, drowsiness, and a host of other ailments. There is also an implication that the worry and anxiety underlying some of these conditions can be resolved by similar treatment. There is a general intol-erance for these inconvenient conditions. Since the life events seen to precede them are often judged to be unavoidable and beyond control, treatment of symptoms rather than causes becomes the order of the day.

There may even be a certain prestige quality about taking psychotropic drugs, especially when they are associated with the demands of business and career. Although life in the "fast lane" is seen to have some associ-ated costs, it is nevertheless taken as indicative of competence, success, and upward mobility. Not only does one acquire a larger name plate, or bigger car, but a therapist as well.

FEMINIST ANALYSES

Several concerns regarding psychotropic drug prescriptions have been presented by feminists. As in feminist criticisms of childbirth practices, some arguments call for increased medical intervention, but others advo-cate a decrease. The approach calling for more intervention is based on the position that because women are not taken seriously, their complaints tend to be underdiagnosed. Even when mental illness is the appropriate diagnosis, psychotropes are often administered indiscriminately, without appropriate adjunctive therapy or attempts to remediate underlying problems. In the case of underdiagnosis, women's complaints are trivialized, and a psychotropic drug is prescribed to 'cure" them. Thus, general health is ignored and perhaps is even threatened by risk of adverse reactions and potential addiction.

Other problems arise because of the limited nature of training found among general practitioners, the group of physicians most likely to make the initial diagnosis of mental illness. This limited training may contribute to a delay in seeking help from appropriately trained professionals. For example, general practitioners have extremely limited training in crisis or marital counseling, yet without additional consultation, may undertake a prolonged course of treatment of these types of problems. General practitioners are also often unaware of community referral agencies or support programs. Alternate treatment methods (counseling, referral to a psychiatrist, change in life-style, etc.) are virtually ignored.

Another set of concerns reflects the orientation that too much medical intervention is a problem. This orientation is held by critics of the medicalization of stress and the interpretation of social problems as mental disorders. Too much intervention has the effect of continuing the oppression of women, by undermining their confidence in their understanding of their own life experiences. When treatment is primarily based in pharmacology, women receive the message that their experience is a personal failing, and they lack the power to initiate problem solving. Feelings of helplessness are engendered in such scenarios and dependency on psychotropes is a possible consequence.

Liberal Perspectives

Liberal feminists tend to locate the problem of psychotropic drug abuse in both medical and social systems. These problems can best be summarized as limitations of training and a pervading sexism and reliance on stereotypes. Suggested strategies for change are multifaceted within this perspective. Social system variables center around sexism. stereotypes, and their consequences. In particular, social segregation is judged to contribute to a belief that women and men are vastly and categorically different. There is a tendency to see women as closer to their biology and victims of raging hormones. Women's self-experiences, therefore, are viewed as independent of the social framework in which they occur, contributing to a belief in the efficacy of medical-biological solutions.

Medical school education may also contribute to sexist treatment. It is well known that humorous and anecdotal examples given during medical school lectures often insinuate that female patients are "crocks." This may lead to trivialization of women's somatic complaints; women are treated as if they were hypochondriacs or malingerers. Thus, it quickly becomes apparent that treatment with psychotropic drugs may be a means for the physician to rid himself/herself of a patient whose trouble cannot be readily diagnosed.

Other aspects of medical education contributint to problems simply involve limited training and an acceptance of general sex stereotypes. It has been suggested that practitioners may misdiagnose many cases of drug and alcohol problems in women because of an expectation that women suffer from depression. Likewise, they may misdiagnose depression among men who are self-medicating with alcohol or other drugs (Khantzian, 1978).

Some critics argue that physicians are ill-prepared to cope with emotionally disturbed patients whose problems are barely, if at all, medical (Melville, 1980). One proposal is to expand teaching of behavioral sciences in medical and nursing schools, including particular problems regarding drug and alcohol abuse. Other training limitations include the fact that physicians may also be ill-informed regarding prescription of psychotropes. A greater understanding of toxicology, the psychology of addiction, clinical sophistication, and sensitivity are necessary to deal with emotionally disturbed patients (Khantzian, 1978).

Professionals devoted to reducing unnecessary psychotropic drug prescriptions stress that attention should be directed toward nonmedical solutions to social problems. However, referral to social agencies requires that doctors and health professionals be aware of available options. Seldom does medical school curriculum include a course on community resources as alternate solutions to social problems. Several British general practitioners (Marsh and Barr, 1975; Cohen and Halpern, 1978) have used a marriage guidance counselor in their practices.

Communication among members of the health care team has been emphasized by Fidell (1981) as a means of detecting potential psychotropic drug abusers. She states the psychologists should know what drugs their clients are taking and both psychologist, physician, and patient should confer on expected benefits, potential side effects, and duration of treatment if decision to employ psychoactive drugs is made.

Liberal feminists additionally encourage women to assume more responsibility for the quality of health care they receive as a means of reducing unnecessary psychotropic drug prescriptions. They urge women to ask names of medications prescribed to them, to inquire about hazards associated with use of psychotropic drugs, and to consult their physician about the possibility of drugs interacting with those they are currently consuming. Well-informed patients acting as critical consumers will probably begin to reduce excessive prescription of psychotropes to women.

Liberal perspectives also suggest several research issues appropriate for study. One set of problems, for example, concerns the prescription practices of physicians, particularly the treatment circumstances and types of individuals who are most subject to problems of substance abuse. Other research problems simply involve the need for a more complete information base. The literature lacks information about numbers and characteristics of women receiving treatment for the abuse of legitimate psychotropes, the rate of recidivism in treatment, and whether psychotropic drug use leads to alcohol abuse and vice versa. Liberal feminists also encourage improving research methodology in the development and testing of new psychotropic drugs, by including women in clinical trials.

Radical Perspectives

From a radical perspective, status differences and power conflicts contribute to the high numbers and rate of psychotropic drug prescriptions for women. The problem is not simply one of changing medical education or research. Status differences operate in a direct fashion by imposing on women the secondary and support roles of society. Because these roles are seen as requiring only limited skill, individuals who perform them are judged to have few admirable qualities, achieving more by natural inclinations than skill or ability. These roles and the individuals who perform them receive few rewards and little acknowledgment, conditions that tend to promote lethargy, indifference, and depression.

Power conflicts operate on mental health and its treatment by virtue of who has precedence in the definition of reality. To the extent that men control resources, hold status, and receive rewards, the masculine definition of what is real and legitimate prevails. Thus, the emotional/psychic protest women evidence is really a product of social context but is identified by their dominant role partners (husbands, boyfriends, etc.) as an indication of personal neurosis. Women are socially defined to be creatures who are happiest in their support functions and who actually have a psychological need to be nurturant to others, especially men. Experiences, desires, or responses not consistent with this image are denied legitimacy. Under such circumstances, women are reluctant to contradict the accepted world view of those in dominant positions. There is even a strong press to internalize this vision of self. When socially established world views are in conflict with self experiences, protest and anger are natural responses. However, expression of either may be threatening for people in subordinate positions. and depression is likely to follow.

Radical perspectives on how to deal with these issues within the health care arena are consistent in advocating that women should assume responsibility for their own health care. A women's health care plan as outlined by radical feminists is primarily a wholistic approach—exercise, good nutrition, meditation, etc. There is a concern for physical and spiritual fitness and health especially as it is defined and resolved by women themselves.

Socialist/Marxist Perspectives

The economic, social, and political features of medicine and health care are prominent in socialist/Marxist perspectives. The general thesis is that a capitalistic social structure leads to a greater incidence of mental illness among women, and subsequently, to greater psychotropic drug use. Therefore, altering the social structure is the only means of resolving these issues.

The position of women as nonpaid workers in the home is seen to be a particular problem, and indeed it is the case that nonemployed home-makers are more likely to receive psychotropic drug prescriptions than employed women. Physicians do exhibit a selectiveness in prescription patterns along class and employment categories. Hollingshead and Red-lich (1958) found that physicians were reluctant to administer major tran-quilizers to persons of higher social status or to men operating heavy machinery. However, housewives are generally thought to perform work requiring minimal skill; therefore, psychotropic drugs may be perceived as allowing for satisfactory performance of these low skill activities. That is, it is acceptable for women to be somewhat drowsy or less than fully alert because their activities do not require much mental acuity.

Socialist/Marxist perspectives also point to the profit making nature of the medical industry as a major factor in the overmedication of women. The plethora of advertisements designed to promote psychotropic drug sales certainly goes beyond the necessities of simply informing physicians of available medicaments. Pharmaceutical manufacturers create their own generic equivalents and market them as having unique or special qualities that make them superior to others. Furthermore, pharmaceutical manu-facturers often challenge research and development regulations imposed by the federal Food and Drug Administration.

Strategies for change include personal and social frameworks. One recommendation is that women join the paid work force. Beneficial re-sults are predicted to follow: Women will gain in a sense of self-esteem and will have the financial resources appropriate to greater choice among life-style alternatives. Other recommendations involve removing profit incentives from medicine and medical care. However, these latter recom-mendations are seldom developed in detail.

SUMMARY AND COMMENT

Gender appears to be a master variable in the use patterns of psycho-tropes. Compared to men, women receive greater numbers of prescrip-tions for psychotropes, eventually higher rates of prescriptions, and are likely to use psychotropes for a longer duration, extending over several years in many cases. This pattern does not become marked until after age 45. Physicians most involved in contributing to this pattern are general practitioners, who as a group prescribe more psychotropes than any other physician class. Explanations for this pattern include both system and individual level variables. System level variables include such factors as economic incentives, limited knowledge of alternative care, and medicalization of stress. Individual factors include role stress, and wellness and illness behavior. Sex stereotypes and a general attribution bias also contribute to a tendency to limit the search for causes of symptoms to the intrapsychic events of women.

Feminist analyses define the problem as simultaneously too little and too much medical intervention. Strategies for change involve personal and social frameworks. Attention to social stereotypes, gender roles, medical education, and research is advocated from several feminist perspectives. Alternative health care options, increased consumerism, and paid employment for women are also advocated.

Awareness of differential prescription of psychotropic drugs and the associated social psychological implications is relatively recent. Much information remains to be obtained regarding this phenomenon. The potential association with alcohol and other addictive behaviors has yet to be explored. Furthermore, treatment issues have not been addressed to any great degree. Unfortunately, the problem is in danger of receiving less attention in the future, due partly to the fact that in naming the problem, researchers and funding agencies may come to think the problem is solved. Additionally, creative insights involved in the initial recognition of the problem will be difficult to duplicate in the less spectacular, but nevertheless valuable, work of clarification and delineation. As will become evident in the following chapters, some of these same issues prevail with respect to alcoholism.

Epidemiology of Alcoholism

5

This chapter was written by
M. Marlyne Kilbey and Joanne Popour Sobeck

Women's use and abuse of alcohol is a topic of concern to the general public; to workers in the physical and mental health fields; and to those people, regardless of their professional affiliation, whose activities impact upon the social, political, and economic aspects of women's lives. Among concerned people there is a perception that alcohol use and abuse is increasing in women. It is generally thought that a significant number of undetected women abuse alcohol and/or suffer from alcoholism in addition to the large number whose problems are recognized. Also, the physical and social consequences of alcohol abuse are believed to be more severe in women than men. This chapter reviews the epidemiology of alcohol consumption, demographic correlates, and health consequences of alcohol use with respect to these beliefs. In so doing we first define alcohol use and abuse and related terms such as alcoholism.

DEMOGRAPHIC PATTERNS

The goal of epidemiological studies is to present an accurate description of how often something happens in a certain area within a specified time. Thus three aspects are crucial: defining the event, identifying the area, and specifying the period.

General Considerations

When one is interested in alcohol use and abuse the problems of definition are formidable. One problem is to define the amount of alcohol consumed. This is generally inferred from data on the production or sales of alcoholic beverages, the number of alcohol-related deaths, or based on self-reports obtained in surveys. Each method has its problems.

Consumption of alcohol can be inferred from data on sales and/or production of the various types of alcoholic beverages, but these data do not give one any information about who is drinking alcohol or about the pattern of use. Consumption can also be inferred from the number of alcohol-related deaths, but this figure omits deaths in instances where alcohol played an undetected role. Moreover, fatality information obviously does not identify people at a point where intervention is possible. Large scale surveys are useful in identifying patterns of use and characteristics of users. However, household surveys have several problems. Consumption reports do not reflect accurately the amount of alcohol sold (Pernanen, 1974; Johnson, Armour, Plidi, & Stambul, 1977), leading one to infer that either reports are inaccurate or a biased sample is being reached.

Accuracy of self-reports of alcohol intake seems to vary, depending on the circumstances, the level of consumption being reported, and, no doubt, personal characteristics of the person making the report. When people are responding to questions of an interviewer perceived as disinterested, validity is reported as satisfactory (Kolonel, Hirohaba & Nomerra, 1977), but reports to a physician are of questionable validity (Little, 1976; Russell & Bigler, 1979). It also appears that the more distant the event reported, the less valid the report may be (Little, Mandell & Schultz, 1977). With regard to bias, household surveys do not include people who are institutionalized (including those being treated for alcoholism) or incapacitated (including intoxicated persons) and may oversample homemakers. In so doing, the pattern of women's drinking inferred from household surveys would be skewed toward that of homemakers, which may differ from that of women who are employed outside the home.

Since 1969, several surveys in which the respondents were chosen to represent the demographic characteristics of the nation at large have been conducted. Most of these have been prevalence studies in which people reported their alcohol use for a lifetime or for a period of time varying from several months to a week. Asking people to describe their alcohol use highlights additional problems in epidemiological work. These involve the need to categorize and describe the patterns of alcohol use and to formulate standard definitions of heavy drinking, excessive drinking, alcoholism, alcohol abuse, etc. In most studies reporting alcohol use, terms representing excessive use reflect roughly similar levels of intake within a sex. However, between men and women, similar terms indicating extreme intake refer to vastly different amounts of imbibed alcohol, with women being labeled as heavy drinkers on the basis of much lower levels of consumed alcohol than men so labeled.

Sex Comparisons

Surveys have shown vastly different patterns of alcohol consumption for women and men. According to a survey describing drinking practices of Americans (Calahan, Cisin, & Crossley, 1969) 77% of men and 60% of women drink at least once a year. Of those who drink, 28% of the men and 8% of the women are classified as heavy drinkers. Estimates of the ratio of heavy drinking men to women vary from a low of 2 to 1 to a high of 5 to 1 (Terrance, 1980). In general, women are more likely than men to be abstainers or light drinkers. In a 1981 survey, the National Institute of Alcohol Abuse and Alcoholism (NIAAA) found that 40% of the women but only 25% of the men abstained. Of those women who drank, most were light drinkers, and only 4% were heavy drinkers. However, 36% of the men were moderate drinkers, and 14% were heavy drinkers. Regardless of methodological biases across the various studies, men report more daily drinking, more drinking binges, and more frequent drinking than women (Braiker, 1984).

In general, women drink less often and in smaller quantities than men. This is illustrated in Table 5.1. However, weight and percentage of body weight present as water are factors that must be taken into consideration when describing the effect of a given dose of alcohol. In comparison to men, women weigh less and have a higher portion of their weight present as water. The former results in women having a higher blood alcohol concentration (BAC) than men if alcohol consumption is equal, and the later results in women having a higher BAC than men if the ingested alcohol per unit of body weight (mg/kg) is equal (Jones & Jones, 1976a, 1976b). These factors result in equal amounts of alcohol (absolute, or in terms of mg/kg body weight) in men and women producing a higher blood level of alcohol in women. It is not surprisingly, then, that equivalent doses of alcohol have been found to impair women's function in memory and reaction tasks more than men's (Jones & Jones, 1976a, 1977). This effectively higher dose per drink might be thought to contrib-

Table 5.1 Sex Differences in Consumption and Problem Drinking

| | Percent Drinkers | Percent Drinkers in BAC categories | | | | Avg | Expected No. of Hvy. Drinkers |
		Lght.	Mod.	Hvy.	(n)	BAC	per 100 Drinkers
Age Group							
Females							
18–20	79	68	41	22	(74)	.027	17
21–34	69	44	44	14	(310)	.027	10
35–49	63	41	40	21	(236)	.023	13
50–64	45	56	31	13	(231)	.018	6
65+	32	78	13	9	(208)	.010	3
Males							
18–20	93	35	30	34	(65)	.035	32
21–34	87	30	37	33	(317)	.046	29
35–49	80	26	45	29	(224)	.041	23
50–64	68	32	40	28	(217)	.036	19
65+	41	56	29	15	(143)	.016	6

From Johnson, 1982

ute to the consistent observation that although women alcohol abusers begin drinking at a later age than men, they enter treatment at approximately the same age (NIAAA, 1983a; Beckman, 1976), a phenomenon that has been referred to as a "telescoping effect." An effectively higher dose per drink may relate also to the observation that the transition from social drinking to problem drinking appears to occur over a shorter period of time in women than in men (Corrigan, 1980). However, as can be seen in Table 5.1, men's average consumption of alcohol is sufficient to overcome the physiological differences that would result in a higher BAC in women so that on the average, men's BAC in Johnson's study (1982) was 1.7 times that of women. Thus, women's more rapid transition from social drinker to problem drinker to patient must relate to factors other than the relationship between amount drunk and the level of alcohol found in the blood.

Another reported sex difference in alcohol use is that women tend to drink alone and at home more often than men (Beckman, 1975; Corrigan, 1980; Lisansky, 1957). This might be thought to reflect a difference in life-styles, as, over the lifespan, up to 50% of women may not work outside the home and, thus, may spend more time alone. However, skid row women and skid row men share a common pattern of unemployment and homelessness (Garrett & Bahr, 1973). Yet, skid row women exhibit solitary drinking patterns to a greater degree than skid row men.

Review of the epidemiological studies that include housewives report them to be no less at risk for alcoholism than other groups of women (Terrance, 1980). However, women not employed outside the home are not easily identified in the typical systems that refer people to treatment, and, thus, any existing drinking problems might escape detection. For this reason, literature in the alcohol abuse field often refers to women as hidden drinkers, protected from discovery by their families and suffering from isolation and stigmatization. On the basis of clinical findings, women have been described as hiding their drinking more than men (Gomberg, 1976), but this suggestion was not supported in a study in which no sex differences were found in the percentage of heavy drinkers who conceal their drinking (Johnson et al., 1977). The notion that women alcoholics are protected by their families and, thus, do not receive treatment was not supported by Mulford (1977) who found no difference between housewives and other women in the length of time that elapsed between the onset of heavy drinking and entry into treatment.

Life-Span Trends

In epidemiological studies, cohort analyses are done to separate trends associated with age from those that reflect the myriad factors associated with cultural changes across time. Fillmore (1984) presents a cohort analysis of alcohol use based on national surveys done in 1979 (Clark, Midankik & Knupfer, 1981), 1964, and 1967 (Calahan et al., 1969). Heavy-frequent drinking was defined as drinking daily or almost daily and drinking five or more drinks on some occasions. Comparisons of women born in 1925 with those born in 1945 showed that during their middle years (i.e., 35 to 45) 7% of women in both cohorts were labeled as heavy-frequent drinkers. When data of women born in the 1950s are compared to age 21 to 29 to women born between 1905 and 1943 at an identical age, the percent classified as heavy-frequent drinkers rises from 3% to 7% (Fillmore, 1984). If this trend remains constant across the life span for these women born in the 1950s, one would expect to see a doubling of the number of heavy-frequent drinkers in mid-life (35-45) with the percent going from 7% to 14% or more. Since women born in the 1950s began reaching these middle years in 1985, any increase of alcohol problems in women should be discernible before the decade is over.

Cohort analyses of women born between 1905 and 1943 show that approximately 66% of women in their 20s drink alcohol. This decreases to 60% of women in their 40s, 50% in their 50s, and 33% in their 60s (Glenn & Zody, 1970). While drinking, per se, shows a steady decrease with age, heavy-frequent drinking first rises, peaking in middle age, and then falls. This peak, however, is only apparent in women employed outside the home, among whom 10% are rated as heavy-frequent drinkers. In comparison, heavy-frequent drinking remained at 3% for women not employed outside the home during their middle years. As noted previously, there are some indications that the proportion of heavy drinkers among middle-aged women may increase in the next decade as a larger percentage of women born in the 1950s are heavy-drinkers in their 20s than earlier born women. More women from the 50s cohort are employed outside the home than from the earlier born cohorts. Employment is also associated with heavy drinking in the third decade of life for women born before 1943. Thus, increased employment outside the home may also lead to an increase in the proportion of heavy-drinking women in the next decade or so. The finding that alcohol abuse problems in mid-life may be more prevalent in those who are employed outside the home warrants careful scientific scrutiny. If this relationship is found to be robust, it has clear implications for the prevalence of alcohol problems considering the fact that working outside the home is rapidly becoming the norm rather than an exception for adult women.

The life span trends identified in Fillmore's analysis (1984), are apparent also in Wilsnack, Wilsnack, & Klassen's (1984) comparison of a national survey data obtained in 1981 with that obtained between 1971 and 1979. The decrease in number of drinkers as a function of age is apparent in each year's survey going from 71% (age 21-34) to 26% (65 and over) in

1971 and from 70% to 33% for these age groups in 1981. In this analysis, heavy drinkers were defined as those who drank an ounce or more of alcohol per day. In most years the greatest percentage of heavy drinkers was found in the 35- to 49-year-old age range, and in 1981 this group included 9% of women born between 1930 and 1944. This represents a 2% increase in heavy drinking among women in this age group in comparison to the cohort born between 1925 and 1943 discussed by Fillmore (1984). However, Wilsnack et al.'s (1984) youngest group (21-34) born between 1945 and 1960 showed a slight decrease in the number of heavy drinkers compared to the 21- to 29-year-old cohort born in the 1950s (6% vs. 7%, respectively). Overall, however, these data support the idea that for women born after 1945, heavier drinking may continue to be more common throughout their life spans than it was for women born before 1945.

Recent studies (Fillmore, 1984; Wilsnack et al., 1984; Rachal et al., 1980; Rachal et al., 1975) indicate that 73% to 77% of 10th through 12th grade girls have drunk alcohol; and Johnston, Backman, and O'Malley (1984) implicate an even greater percentage (i.e., 82% to 84%). Surveys of high school aged girls, which asked about drinking over a one-week period, found that 9% of 10th through 12th grade students drank five or more drinks per occasion at least once during the period (Rachal et al., 1980). When the time interval surveyed was lengthened to 2 weeks, 31% of 12th grade girls were included in this category (Johnston et al., 1984), with 40% of these heavy drinkers reporting that they got moderately or very high on each drinking occasion. There is no way of knowing if these data reflect a change in drinking practices of high school girls since similar data from earlier periods are not available.

Race and Class Patterns

Heavy drinking practices vary according to race (Rachal et al., 1975). Among girls aged 13 to 18, heavy (1/week, 5-12 drinks/occasion) drinking was highest in Indian (11%), and lowest in black (3%) girls, with white (6%), Hispanic (5%), and Asian girls (4%) being intermediate. Among teenagers, male/female ratios for heavy drinkers were: 2.5 for whites, 3.0 for blacks, 3.6 Hispanics, 2.0 for Indian, and 55.0 for Asians (Rachal et al., 1975). Male/female ratios for adult heavy drinkers are 4.2 for whites, 2.0 for blacks, and 4.3 for Hispanics (Clark et al., 1981). These data confirm those given earlier that show a preponderence of men to women among heavy drinkers. The finding of racial differences must be looked at closely. Classification by race often encompasses class, cultural, and economic differences, which may relate to the behavior in question. In this case, the data suggest the presence of unique factors associated with race that operate to diminish the number of young Asian-American and black women who are included in the heavy-drinking category.

One of the first studies of alcohol consumption among urban American women (Bailey, Haberman, & Alksne, 1965) estimated that 4.13/1000 women experience problems of living associated with excessive alcohol use. Zaix, Gardner, and Hart (1967) analyzed the public records of Monroe County, NY and found that 0.56/1000 white women and 4.78/1000 non-white women had received a medical diagnosis of alcoholism, had been treated for alcohol problems, or had been arrested for intoxication. The extreme racial difference found in these data could reflect an over representation of lower socioeconomic groups, which tend to have a higher composition of nonwhite, in the data listed in public records. Extreme racial differences were not found in a national sample, which placed 5% of white women, 7% of black women, and 10% of Hispanic women in the heavy drinker category (i.e., 60 or more drinks per month) (Clark et al., 1981). The percentage of adult heavy-drinking women is higher than that found for teenagers (Rachal et al., 1975), and in the case of Hispanic and black women, the percentage increase is great enough to raise the question of whether there are unique economic, social, or cultural linked factors that place these women disproportionately at risk for alcohol abuse as adults.

Schuckit and Morrissey (1976) assert that social class may be a more important characteristic than gender for predicting differences in drinking patterns. They hold that drinking patterns and problems seen in women of lower socioeconomic status are likely to resemble those of the average alcoholic male. Recent data, however, do not support this contention. Women's socioeconomic status is correlated with the use of alcohol, and higher status persons are more likely to use alcohol than those with lower status, as 70% of higher status women use alcohol in comparison to 42% of lower status women. The percentage of women who drink that are included in the heavy drinking category is very similar for lower status (14%) and higher status (17%) women (Johnson, 1982). Since the number who drink differs, however, this means that 6 per 100 lower status women versus 12 per 100 higher status women are in this category. The association between heavy drinking and higher economic status is strengthened when a woman has a nontraditional life style (Johnson, 1982). This will be discussed more fully shortly.

Social Roles

Women's changing roles in the post World War II era have resulted in more visibility for women in the public and private arenas. As women have become more active in social and political organizations over this 40 year period, they have gained more influence in defining problems that affect their lives. Finally, over this period the conception of alcoholism has changed so that it is being seen as a disease or behavioral problem rather than a moral weakness. All these factors, along with a general increased sensitivity to the role of life-style on health, have contributed to a heightened awareness of the existence of alcohol problems among women. This awareness may contribute to the widespread perception that alcohol abuse has increased greatly in women in the recent past when, in fact, the data indicate that the percentage of heavy drinking women has remained relatively constant for women born between 1900 and 1950. There is the chance that the perception of increase is based on observations of young women born since 1950, among whom heavy drinking is twice as frequent as it was in earlier-born women during their youth. There is also the chance that these women born since 1950 will maintain the pattern of increased heavy drinking in mid-life seen in the earlier born women. They may also maintain this pattern after they reach age 40, the age at which heavy drinking began to diminish in the earlier born women. Were this to happen, we would truly have the "drinking epidemic" often reported by the media for contemporary women. The epidemiological data of the 1980s will settle this question. At this point, an examination of women's social roles may identify some of the possible correlates of increased drinking in younger women.

The importance of social roles in understanding drinking patterns was shown by Johnson (1982) who compared demographic variables obtained from a national sample of 2,000 persons in which men and women were represented approximately equally. Divorced and unemployed people of both sexes consumed the most alcohol. Daily BAC for divorced women was estimated to be .052 and for unemployed women .034. For auto operators, a BAC of 0.1 defines intoxication. Thus, the BACs reported by Johnson (1982) are substantial. In her sample, 75% of the males and 56% of the women used alcohol, and 29% of the men and 16% of the women were categorized as heavier drinkers (i.e., BAC greater than .04). Table 5.2 shows the relationship between certain demographic characteristics and drinking, as well as the number of heavy drinkers one can expect in each category per 100 drinking men and women. For both sexes, drinkers who are of higher socioeconomic status, single, divorced or separated are at greater risk to become heavy drinkers.

A group of national surveys have examined the association between variables, such as marital status, education, income, employment, religion, and drinking in women (Wilsnack et al., 1984). Both education and income were positively related to drinking and inclusion in the heavier drinking (1 oz. or more ethanol daily) category. Among women over age 21, 38% of widowed women; 60% of married women; 72% of divorced,

Table 5.2 Demographic Differences in Consumption and Problem Drinking

	Percent Drinkers	Percent Drinkers in BAC categories			(n)	Avg BAC	Expected No. of Hvy. Drinkers per 100 Drinkers
		Lght.	Mod.	Hvy.			
Employment Status							
Females	62	44	40	16	(303)	.019	10
Employed	49	43	39	16	(46)	.034	8
Unemployed	53	53	36	13	(635)	.017	7
Not in force							
Males	79	29	41	30	(672)	.036	24
Employed	78	37	17	46	(51)	.114	36
Unemployed	48	50	33	17	(156)	.023	8
Not in force							
Marital Status							
Females	67	40	43	16	(125)	.025	11
Single	61	46	38	15	(655)	.019	9
Married	57	47	28	26	(112)	.052	15
Div./Sep.	44	52	20	5	(197)	.012	2
Widowed							
Males	91	32	25	43	(125)	.046	39
Single	71	32	44	24	(748)	.034	17
Married	91	5	46	48	(28)	.110	44
Div./Sep.	46	59	15	28	(35)	.029	13
Widowed							
Socioeconomic Status							
Females							
Lower	42	57	29	14	(543)	.025	6
Higher	70	43	40	17	(546)	.021	12
Males							
Lower	63	37	33	30	(490)	.049	19
Higher	86	29	42	28	(496)	.032	24

From Johnson, 1982

separated, or never married women; and 100% of cohabiting women used alcohol. Heavy use patterns were reported for 20% of cohabiting, 8% divorced or separated, and 9% of never married women. In these data, employment of married women was not related to heavy use, as 4% of the full-time employed as well as the part-time employed women were included in this category along with 6% of the full-time homemakers.

The relationship between demographic variables and drinking in female adolescents has also been studied (Thompson & Wilsnack, 1984). This recent work failed to support earlier work showing a relationship between parental socioeconomic status and drinking. Studies of religious differences yield results that follow those found surveying adults, with fundamentalist Protestant and Jewish youth being less likely to drink and Catholic youth more likely. Additionally, religious commitment regardless of denomination is negatively associated with adolescent alcohol use (Jesser & Jesser, 1977).

Summary

In summary, epidemiological data show that a large number of women drink, and a significant proportion drink frequently and consume large amounts of alcohol. The number of women who drink has increased slightly over the past 30 years, and there are indications that younger women are more likely to be heavy drinkers than their foremothers were. The ratio of men to women who drink has remained fairly constant and indicates that somewhere between 10% and 40% more men than women drink, with heavy-drinking men estimated to outnumber heavy-drinking women by between 2 and 4 to 1. Over the life span, both the percentage of women who drink and the percentage who abuse alcohol decreases. Data on race and class factors as they relate to drinking are less clear, although there are indications that American Indian, Hispanic, divorced, and single women, as well as women in higher socioeconomic groups, may be disproportionately represented in the heavy-drinking category.

HEALTH EFFECTS

Epidemiological data point out that most women use alcohol at some point in their lives, usually beginning in their teens and continuing through their 40s and that the vast majority of these women control their drinking. However, the large group (1 woman in 10 under age 50) who are consuming excessive amounts of alcohol (1 oz. or more/daily) are at risk for numerous health problems. A recent review (Hill, 1984) makes a strong case for considering the health consequences of alcohol use and abuse independently for men and women and suggests that women may be more vulnerable than men to physical damage and death from alcohol.

Mortality

Alcoholic women seem to be at greater risk for death than alcoholic men when each is compared to a same-sex nonalcoholic population. Alcoholism increases the mortality rate for men by a factor of from 2 to 3, whereas the death rate for alcoholic women is 2.7 to 7 times greater (Nicholls, Edwards, & Kyle, 1974; Medhus, 1974). This differentially greater increase in death rates for alcoholic women holds across a number of diseases associated with alcoholism: circulatory disorders, cirrhosis of the liver, and digestive disorders. Similarly, alcoholic women are 10 to 70 times more likely to be involved in a fatal accident than nonalcoholic women, but for alcoholic men risk is increased by a factor of 2 to 15 (Medhus, Edwards & Kyle, 1975; Dahlgren & Myrhed, 1977; Nicholls et al., 1974). In two studies, the increased risk of death from suicide was greater for alcoholic women than alcoholic men (Schmidt & de Lint, 1972; Dahlgren & Myrhed, 1977), but another study showed essentially the same increase for both sexes: Alcoholism increased the mortality rate due to suicide by a factor of 22 for men and 23 for women (Adelstein & White, 1977). As a result of the differentially increased rates of death from disorders associated with alcoholism, women's biological advantage for longevity is lost, and alcoholic men and women have approximately the same life expectancy.

Several investigations have been carried out to determine the drinking patterns of men and women who develop cirrhosis of the liver and hepatitis to determine why the risk of death is so greatly increased in women. In one study, men and women had abused alcohol for similar durations and consumed similar amounts, yet 86% of the women versus 65% of the men suffered from liver disease (Morgan & Sherlock, 1977). In other studies, women with cirrhosis reported much shorter histories of heavy drinking (13 years) than did men (20 years) (Wilkinson, Santamaria & Rankin, 1969; Ashley et al., 1977).

The mechanism underlying the apparent vulnerability of women to alcohol-induced liver damage is not clear, although one cause of cirrhosis may be direct toxic effects of alcohol on the liver (Williams & Horn, 1977). As discussed earlier, when men and women imbibe similar amounts of alcohol in terms of numbers of drinks or mg/kg body weight, the BAC is higher in women. Thus, women's organs would be exposed to higher levels of toxin than men's. The proportionally smaller liver in women versus men would also predict exposure to a more concentrated toxin. Both these relations would predict more hepatic damage in women alcoholics than men given similar alcohol-ingestion histories. However, as we established earlier, men and women do not drink the same amount. When average BACs are compared, men's are much higher (Johnson, 1982). For this reason, another factor, genetic susceptibility related to autoimmune reactions (which are more common in women) directed towards the liver (Bell & Nordhagen, 1980; Krasner, Davis, Portmann, & Williams, 1977) has been suggested to underlie the differential rate of death from cirrhosis seen in alcoholic men and women. Another aspect of this problem concerns the effect of diet. It has been suggested that free radicals stimulate lipid peroxidation which, in turn, results in alcohol-associated hepatotoxicity

(Videla & Valenzuela, 1982). Uric acid is a powerful scavenger of free radicals and, thus, protects against alcohol-associated hepatotoxicity. Dietary fats will increase free radicals and dietary proteins will increase uric acid levels. Deaths from cirrhosis have been shown to be lower in countries whose populations have high serum uric acid levels and animal protein consumption (Nanji & French, 1986). Thus, high consumption of fats would potentiate alcohol-associated hepatotoxicity and high protein intake would protect against it. Women have serum uric acids that are lower than those of men (Boss & Seegmiller, 1979). It is possible that women, in their concern for weight control, limit their protein intake. They may, while drinking, also increase their consumption of "junk foods" high in fat. These possibilities need to be examined for their relationship to cirrhosis. The extent to which women engage in these behaviors (limiting protein intake while dieting and snacking on high fat foods while drinking) more than men may be related to the differential vulnerability to alcohol-associated hepatotoxicity.

Morbidity

One method of assessing the health consequences of alcohol abuse is to determine the morbidity rate among persons classified as alcoholic in comparison to those not so classified. Sick days and health insurance services may be compared for male and female alcoholic and nonalcoholic groups. These indices have been used in a series of investigations carried out in Sweden (Asma, Eggert, & Hilker, 1971; Lokander, 1962; Medhus, 1974), which found that both alcoholic men and women used more health insurance benefits and had more days off work due to illness than did nonalcoholic members of their sex. Impairment, which may initially be moderate when measured by disability rates and sick days, typically shows marked increase over a 4 to 5 year period preceding an initial compulsory treatment period for alcoholism. Physical impairment remains higher in these women than in a nonalcoholic control group throughout a 4 year posttreatment period (Medhus, 1974). A comparison of health insurance use rates showed that alcoholic women were more impaired than alcoholic men over a 6 year period preceding onset of alcoholism treatment and that women continued to have higher disability rates, more sick periods, and longer illnesses than men after receiving treatment for alcohol abuse (Dahlgren & Idestrom, 1979). Data are needed to determine if the posttreatment hospitalization utilization rates for formerly alcoholic women are increased over women who have not had the problem.

Other investigators (Ashley et al., 1977) compared health consequences in male and female inpatients being treated for alcoholism. For women, a shorter duration of drinking preceded the occurrence of fatty liver, hypertension, obesity, anemia, malnutrition, gastrointestinal hemorrhage, and ulcers. Also, the duration of drinking for women (14.1 years) preceding admission to the hospital for treatment of alcoholism was shorter than that for men (20.2 years).

Brain Damage. Increased incidence of brain damage in alcoholic men is well established on the basis of neuropsychological test batteries (see Parsons & Liber, 1982 for review). Alterations in brain structure or pneumoencephalography functions have been indexed using electroencephalography (Brewer & Perrett, 1971; Allen, Wagman, Tallaici, & McIntosh, 1971) and computerized transaxial tomography (Bergman, Borg, Hindmarsh, Idestrom, & Mutzell, 1980). Brain dysfunction varying in severity from subtle cognitive impairments to severe chronic organic brain syndrome has been estimated to be present in 50% to 70% of detoxified alcoholics (Lee, Moller, Hardt, Hauber, & Jensen, 1979; Parsons, 1977). However, a similar fund of information for women does not exist. Comparisons of alcoholic and nonalcoholic women's performances on abstracting tasks have shown alcoholic women to do more poorly (Hatcher, Jones & Jones, 1977; Silberstein & Parsons, 1979; Fabian, Jenkins & Parsons, 1981), as do alcoholic men when they are compared with nonalcoholic men. These findings suggest that women may suffer the same types of alcohol related brain damage as men, but the data to evaluate this supposition have not been gathered.

Cancer. The contribution of alcoholism to the risk of various forms of cancer in men and women has been studied (Williams & Horn, 1977). This study attempted to separate the risk attributed to smoking from that attributed to drinking and determined that drinking increased the risk of cancer of the lip, tongue, pharynx, and esophagus in women. These authors suggested that alcohol may induce cancer in proportion to its concentration at the tissue site, with the risk being greatest in the oral cavity; lower in the esophagus and liver; and still lower in the stomach, colon, and rectum. Thus, the risk varies with the concentration of alcohol, which when swallowed becomes diluted by the stomach's contents and then further diluted as it enters the circulatory system.

Reproductive Consequences. A little over a decade ago, a group of researchers at the University of Washington (Jones, Smith, Clelland, & Streissguth, 1973) reported a characteristic pattern of malformation in eight children born to alcoholic mothers, which they termed fetal alcohol syndrome (FAS). FAS involves growth deficiency, facial dysmorphology, central nervous system involvement, developmental deficiency, and kidney and cardiac abnormalities of prenatal onset. FAS appears to be the end point of a broad spectrum of disorders of prenatal origin, and for this reason the term fetal alcohol effects (FAE) has been suggested (Smith, 1979). The amount of alcohol to which the fetus is exposed correlates with the severity of FAE, and FAS has been established only in children whose mothers consume at least six drinks per day for some portion of the pregnancy (Little & Ervin, 1984). Children whose mothers had consumed four or more drinks per day during pregnancy show a dose-related deficit in infant mental and motor development (Streissguth, Barr, Martin, & Herman, 1980).

Although current thinking attributes alcohol's deleterious effects to its toxicological and teratogenic actions, the child's genetic makeup may influence the outcome of in utero exposure to alcohol, as there are reports of fraternal twins who were affected differentially even though they were clearly exposed to the same level of alcohol in utero (Christoffel & Salafsky, 1975). Other factors, such as placental vasculature, organogenesis rate, and fetal rate of ethanol degradation and elimination, which may modify the effects of in utero exposure to alcohol, have not been measured. In humans, a general dose-response function for alcohol's prenatal effects, which identifies a safe level of alcohol use during pregnancy, remains to be established. Identification of an alcohol dose response function for FAE and FAS is further complicated by general issues concerning self-reports and retrospective data (Little et al., 1977; Little, 1976; Russell & Bigler, 1979). Since no dose of alcohol can be guaranteed to be safe, the U.S. Surgeon General in 1981 began recommending abstinence for pregnant women. It should be noted, however, that children born with FAS or FAE realize their potential in a complex psychosocial environment as do all children. For example, dizygotic twins, one of whom was born with FAS and the other with FAE, exhibited marked delay of mental and motor capabilities through 18 months of age, at which time they were removed from an abusive parent's home. By 24 months of age, under the care of adoptive parents, both children's mental and motor capabilities were in the low normal range, and by 4½ years of age Stanford Binet intelligence scores were well within the normal range (Chasnoff, 1985).

Alcohol has deleterious effects for pregnant women in addition to FAS and FAE. Stillborn deliveries were 2½ times more common among French women consuming three or more drinks daily (Kaminski et al., cited by Little & Ervin, 1984). Although a U.S. study failed to replicate the finding of increased stillbirths (Sokol, Miller, & Reed, 1980), the risk of spontaneous abortion in the second trimester was doubled for California women who drank one to two drinks daily (Harlap & Shiono, 1980). Similarly, it is estimated that approximately one woman in four who drinks two drinks per occasion, twice weekly during pregnancy, will experience a spontaneous abortion (Kline, Shrout, Stein, Susser, & Warburton, 1980).

Considering the toxic effect of alcohol for the developing fetus, it is fortunate that alcohol is less appealing to pregnant women and, in pregnancy, consumption is sharply curtailed. About 86% of women drinking two or more drinks daily before conception decrease their mean intake by more than two thirds during pregnancy. However, women who drink the most before pregnancy tend to consume the most during pregnancy (Little, Schultz, & Mandell, 1976; Little & Streissguth, 1978), and, as seen, consumption remains high enough in some women to effect adversely the development of their fetuses. Whether or not a specific mechanism depresses the appetite for alcohol during pregnancy is unknown. However, decreased use of alcohol does not appear to depend on the existence of nausea related to pregnancy (Little et al., 1976). In an experiment to determine whether high levels of estrogen play a role in decreased alcohol ingestion during pregnancy, estradiol or placebo was administered over a 1-month period to experimental groups who drank approximately two drinks (1 oz. alcohol) daily. Although the estradiol elevated serum estrogen levels, it did not lead to a decrease in drinking (Little, Moore, Guzinski, & Perez, 1980). However, the 1 month trial may not have been long enough to reveal effects of estrogen. It would seem important to intensify the efforts to determine whether a specific mechanism underlies this aversion, as its manipulation might prove useful in treating alcoholic women.

Sexual Function. Studies of the relationship between alcohol abuse and sexual dysfunction in women are plagued by a number of methodological problems. In common with all alcohol investigations, the definition of alcohol abuse/alcoholism varies from study to study. Many of the studies are small clinical investigations carried out on patients in treatment for alcoholism and in whom the cause and effect relationship is impossible to separate. Furthermore, control groups are seldom included. Nevertheless, a review of 19 studies published between 1937 and 1982 indicates that alcoholic women experience a high degree of sexual dysfunction (Wilsnack, 1984). The review suggested that for these women, alcohol ingestion may be a form of self-medication (Wilsnack, 1984), as has been suggested to be the case in depression. Orgasmic dysfunction affected between 15% and 64% of the women studied, and lack of interest and frigidity was reported for 28% to 50%. Vaginismus was a problem for 2% to 12% of the women. Kinsey (1966) attempted to sort sexual dysfunction caused by alcoholism from sexual dysfunction as a consequence of alcoholism and asked women their opinion about the sequence of events. In 72% of the cases, women reported that frigidity preceded and contributed to alcoholism. Two other unpublished retrospective studies that attempt to sort cause from effect are cited by Wilsnack (1984). Sholty (cited in

Wilsnack, 1984) found that sexual dysfunction led to alcohol use in some cases and that the reverse also occurred. In this study, 43% of the women reported that sexual inadequacy and/or dissatisfaction contributed to their drinking, and 77% of the women reported that sexual satisfaction deteriorated after they began drinking. Only 17% reported an improvement in sexual satisfaction or adequacy after they began drinking. Two thirds of the previously alcoholic middle-class women studied by Covington (cited in Wilsnack, 1984) who reported sexual dysfunction attributed its onset to a period in which they were actively drinking. Covington's study (cited in Wilsnack, 1984) is also one of few to use a control group, so that the incidence of sexual dysfunction in previously alcoholic women can be compared with that existing in a nonalcoholic group. In this study 35 white, middle-class, previously alcoholic women were matched on age, education, marital status, and religious preference with women for whom alcohol use had not been a problem. In the postalcoholic group, 85% reported sexual dysfunction during their drinking period compared to 59% of the nonalcoholic group. Control women also reported orgasmic difficulties (27%), lack of arousal or pleasure (30%), and lack of interest (44%). For alcoholic women these rates were 64%, 61%, and 64%, respectively. These findings parallel those of Beckman (1979) who queried alcoholic women and nonalcoholic women and found significantly lower ratings of sexual satisfaction among the alcoholic group.

SUMMARY

The studies reviewed in this chapter clearly represent a fraction of the literature on women's use of alcohol. One area, multidrug use, has been omitted entirely. However, there are a few conclusions that one can draw. In our culture, the vast majority of men and women use alcohol socially, at least during their early adult years. A small portion, which nonetheless is a large number of people, experience problems in social relationships, in life activities, or with their health as a result of failing to control their alcohol intake. This is a problem for a much smaller proportion of women than men. Nevertheless, the consequences for women in physical, emotional, and economic terms are enormous; and there is some evidence that women are especially susceptible to alcohol's physically debilitating effects. Furthermore, alcohol use during pregnancy can result in the birth of a physically and mentally impaired child, a consequence which for most women engenders profound and prolonged psychological distress.

Etiology and Treatment of Alcoholism Among Women

6

This chapter was written by
Joanne Popour Sobeck and M. Marlyne Kilbey

Feminist concerns regarding women and alcoholism center on three issues. First, the recognition and identification of alcoholism among women
historically has been of little interest to researchers in the area. Most
theories regarding etiology and treatment have been developed with respect to males. Second, the etiology of alcoholism among women may be
different from that for men, and theoretical explanations need to be crit-
ically analyzed to determine their applicability to women. This is particularly true where causal models have implications for treatment. Treatment strategies and issues of particular significance to women patients is
the third area of concern. For example, life events stress likely to trigger
episodes of alcohol abuse among women are often quite different from
those that impact men. Thus, treatment may require special tailoring to
issues that selectively affect women. Additionally, access to any kind of
treatment may be problematic for women with children; therefore, treatment programs need to address aspects of women's lives and their gender-
based responsibilities, which may exist independently of their alcoholism,
if they are to deliver treatment effectively.

ETIOLOGY

Although there are numerous theories about the causes of alcohol abuse
and dependence, they have not provided satisfactory answers to many of
the questions that are raised. One can easily cite examples of abuse and
dependence that do not conform to any single theory or any combination
of theoretical formulations of the causes of alcohol's misuse. It seems
likely that a unique blend of the factors researchers have identified, as
well as others as yet unidentified, accounts for each specific individual's
alcohol abuse and dependence. In one case, a woman's abuse of alcohol
may relate to ambivalence and doubts about her femininity. In another
case, a woman may drink in response to a specific life situation, and in a
third case alcohol abuse and dependence may mask a severe depression.
No single theoretical framework can explain the variation that seems to
exist in the examples given. The relative strength of any one theory
appears to depend on the particular facet of alcohol abuse and dependence one addresses.

110

Despite proposing the idea that an individual's alcohol misuse and dependence is a multidimensional problem, we will review, nevertheless, several specific models of alcohol abuse and dependence in women. This will highlight the specific contribution of each to our understanding of alcohol abuse and lay the groundwork for a discussion of treatment issues.

Psychodynamic

Psychodynamic theories generally employ an energy model and view psychopathology as a product of the disordered interplay of various psychic forces. Thus, Freud, cited in Royce (1981), held that alcohol abuse could represent a number of psychic disorders. For Freud alcoholism could be viewed as a slow suicide as death instinct forces came to the fore. Alcoholism could also represent fixation at the oral stage of psychosexual development or latent homosexuality, as an individual failed to resolve the Oedipal crisis. These notions not only view alcoholism as secondary to another pathology, they make little contribution to our knowledge of the nature of alcoholism because they are relatively untestable.

Two psychodynamic theories of the etiology of alcohol abuse that have been researched empirically test the ideas that drinking provides gratification of passive-oral dependency needs and that an individual's use of alcohol represents an attempt to enhance feelings of power. Alcohol abuse has been said to satisfy dependency needs that adults are not free to express (McCord & McCord, 1960). For males, the notion has an apparent validity since social stereotypes demand self-sufficiency of men. The discrepancy between men and women's ability to satisfy their dependency needs within their social roles could explain the differences in rates of alcoholism in men and women and increases in alcoholism among women employed outside the home could result from the constraints of employment on their expression of dependency. Since society in general tolerates dependency in women, however, it seems unlikely that failure to satisfy this need motivates a large part of the alcohol abuse that occurs. Furthermore, no one has shown that women who abuse alcohol have greater, or more unsatisfied, dependency needs than women who do not.

The notion that men drink to overcome doubts generated by a conflict between the need to be strong and powerful on the one hand and intrapsychic feelings of weakness on the other has been put forward (McClelland, Davis, Kalin, & Wanner, 1972). These authors demonstrated that men drink to feel stronger and more powerful and that men who value personalized power are more likely to drink heavily. Wilsnack (1974) extended this work to women and found that high power needs characterized women who were heavy social drinkers. Braiker (1984) points out that power may be a special problem for today's younger women whose work roles demand independence and assertiveness while their social roles continue to foster dependence. This is an interesting notion that deserves to be tested empirically.

Social Psychological Theory

Social psychological theories emphasize the importance of social expectations and roles as determinants of human behavior. This perspective points out that men and women who depart from socially accepted behaviors may experience a sense of role confusion. A number of researchers have related drinking problems in women to confusion regarding their appropriate sex role. A number of studies portray alcoholic women as valuing traditional feminine roles (Kinsey, 1966; Lisansky, 1957; Belfer, Shader, Carroll, & Hermatz, 1971). Feelings associated with feminine roles, such as, nurturance, affection, and personal attractiveness, are reported to increase after moderate drinking (Wilsnack, 1974). Wilsnack (1973) contrasted conscious and unconscious sex role identification in alcoholic and nonalcoholic women. At the conscious level both had feminine orientations, but at the unconscious level alcoholic women had a more masculine orientation. Wilsnack's (1976) view is that women drink to enhance feelings of femininity and that for women who have strong unconscious masculine feelings, achieving this goal may engender alcoholism. In this regard, Wilsnack (1976, p. 48) states, "she may manage to cope with her fragile sense of feminine adequacy for a number of years, but when some new threat exacerbates her self doubts, she turns to alcohol perhaps in an attempt to gain artificial feelings of womanliness." Other studies have supported the notion that alcoholic women experience sex role conflict (Anderson, 1980; Beckman, 1977, 1978), although Beckman found major sex role conflicts typical of only one in four alcoholic women. Another study (Schwab-Bakman, Appelt, & Rist, 1981) suggests that alcoholic women may experience sex role conflicts because they hold unrealistic views of femininity as alcoholic women aspired to be more feminine than did nonalcoholic women. In contrast to work that suggests women who value traditional feminine sex roles may constitute a large portion of the women who abuse alcohol are reports that alcoholic women value feminine roles less than controls or reject them (Parker, 1972, 1975).

To date, there are no longitudinal studies to determine what effects women's gender identification and sex role conflict have on alcohol use patterns. It is possible that gender orientation, per se, and/or subjective conflict are not as important as the support one gets from society for one's role. A recent pilot study, for example, found that role conflict was not associated with heavy drinking, but lack of social support at home and at work was (Metzner, 1980). However, the two factors interacted so that women who experienced high role conflict and had low social support were most likely to be found in the heavier drinkers group.

Johnson's 1982 data may speak to this observation also. This study looked at the association between traditional and nontraditional roles and alcohol consumption in women between the age of 30 and 64. Women were classified as nontraditional if three of the following five descriptions applied to them: working outside the home; nontraditional occupation; single, separated or divorced; childless; head of household. More women classified as having traditional roles used alcohol (59%) than women classified as nontraditional (48%). However, among drinkers, 15% of those having traditional roles were classified in the heavier drinker category (i.e., 9/100 drinking women), but 25% of the nontraditional group (i.e., 12/100 drinking women) were so classified. When the interaction of socioeconomic status and sex role is examined, the number of heavy drinkers one would expect to see in 100 low socioeconomic status drinking women is 4 for traditional women and 8 for nontraditional women. In high socioeconomic status women, the expected number is 13 for traditional women and 23 for nontraditional women. Thus, the identification of the process by which high socioeconomic status and nontraditional sex roles interact in the development of alcohol problems in women appears to warrant a high priority for continued study.

Social Learning

A number of studies have attempted to evaluate the relationship between social factors such as family and peer influences and alcoholism. Intergenerational similarities in alcohol problems have long been known. Women alcoholics are more likely than nonalcoholic women to have grown up with alcoholism in the family and are more apt to have had an alcoholic father (Driscoll & Barr, 1972; Lisansky, 1957). Up to 50% of alcoholic women have an immediate family member who also is affected (Sandmaier, 1980). These findings raise the prospect of alcohol abuse as a result of modeling the behavior of a significant other or more generalized social learning processes.

The frequency of drinking problems in spouses has been observed to be greater for alcoholic women than for alcoholic men (Gomberg, 1980). The prevalence rates alone would predict this since male problem drinkers outnumber female by approximately 3 to 1 (Terrance, 1980). Yet when one looks carefully at the association between patterns of alcohol use for women and their spouses, one cannot explain the etiology of problem drinking in women by attributing it to their modeling a spouse's behavior. Although only 10% of alcohol abusing women classified their husband or partner as a nondrinker, 83% of the women classified their husbands as occasional or frequent drinkers. Surprisingly, only 5% of alcohol abusing wives classified their husbands as problem drinkers (Terrance, 1980). A straightforward interpretation of the modeling notion would, of course, expect drinking of marital partners to be highly correlated, and the vast majority of husbands of women with drinking problems would be expected to have drinking problems themselves.

The association between parents' and daughters' drinking, however, does implicate social learning as an important mechanism in alcohol use and abuse. Awareness of drinking by the same-sex parent during girls' seventh and eighth school year is associated with excessive or socially undesirable drinking when young women reach 11th and 12th grades, and drinking by either parent during junior high years is more associated with girls' drinking than boys' drinking during the junior and senior high school years (Thompson & Wilsnack, 1984). A positive relationship between mother's drinking and daughter's use of alcohol has been reported by additional investigators (Widseth & Mayer, 1971; Zucker & Devoe, 1975). Children from one- or two-parent alcohol abusing families have been followed for 20 years (Miller & Jang, 1977). As adults, these offspring, both male and female, drank more than children of nonalcohol abusing parents. Male offspring drank more than females as expected. However, in families where only one parent abused alcohol, daughters of alcohol-abusing mothers were heavier drinkers than daughters of alcohol-abusing fathers. This may indicate a special influence for mothers as a role model or relate to a genetic factor as will be discussed later.

Parental attitudes, as well as examples, are associated with adolescents's use of alcohol with tolerance on the part of parents being associated with increased use on the part of children; a relationship that is reportedly stronger for daughters than sons (Biddle, Bank, & Martin, 1980; Margulies, Kessler, & Kandel, 1977). In addition, the positive association between adolescents' use of alcohol and their peers' use is stronger for girls than for boys (Margulies et al., 1977). Whether or not perceived peer attitude towards alcohol influences girls' use of alcohol and, if so, whether or not girls are more susceptible than boys is not clear, however. The positive relationship between peer endorsement of alcohol use and adolescent use has been found to be stronger for girls than boys (Forslund & Guftason, 1970), not related to girls' use (Biddle et al., 1980), and weaker in girls than boys (Thompson, 1982 cited in Thompson

& Wilsnack, 1984). In the aggregate, studies cited here suggest that family and peer factors may contribute to alcohol use through social learning mechanisms. When family members model drinking behavior, children are more likely to drink and drink heavily as they become older. Peers may support drinking through providing companionship, approval, and a sense of belonging. What is not clear, however, is how social learning mechanisms interact with other factors in predicting alcohol abuse. As we saw in the case of women problem drinkers, problem drinking is not necessarily highly correlated in married couples, which may indicate that earlier social learning takes precedent over later social learning in shaping behavior.

Psychopathology

In addition to psychological theories that treat alcoholism as the product of conflicts around dependency, power, and sex role, or alternatively as a consequence of normal social learning processes, there are other commonly held views. In one analysis, alcohol abuse is seen as a concomitant or result of other psychopathologies. Chapters 1 and 10 discuss psychopathology and the need to modify our theories of their etiology in light of feminist scholars' findings over the past 20 years. This scholarship has not penetrated the alcohol abuse literature, where pathologies thought to relate to alcohol abuse are viewed as resulting from psychic conflicts, or, in the case of depression, a biological anomaly. In this literature, depression and character disorders are the two pathologies most generally linked to alcohol abuse. Since depression has long been thought to disproportionately affect women (Gove, 1979; Weissman & Klerman, 1977) and, in fact, large numbers of women are treated for depression, it is critical to know if depressed persons are at risk for alcohol abuse, regardless of the etiology of the depression itself.

Alcoholic women often report themselves to be depressed (Tamerin, Tolor, & Harrington, 1976), and female alcohol abusers describe their depression as more severe than male alcoholics do (Hoffman & Wefring, 1972). Depression is reported to exist before the drinking problem in 20% of alcoholic women (Sclare, 1970) and to be one of the (Gomberg, 1980) chief determinants of drinking in older persons. One of the first studies to identify depression as an antecedent condition of alcohol abuse showed that a subpopulation of alcoholic women had a larger than expected number of female relatives with affective disorders and familial incidence of suicide (Schuckit, Pitts, Reich, King, & Winokur, 1969). Women in this group constituted 20% to 30% of a sample of women diagnosed as alcoholic, and their alcoholism was considered to be secondary to an affective disorder. These women were felt to have a better long-term prognosis than primary alcoholic women who lacked a family history of affective disorder (Schucket et al., 1969; Schucket & Morrissey, 1976).

Depressive symptoms become progressively more severe as alcohol intake increases in chronic drinkers. This makes it difficult to sort cause from effect when a depressed alcoholic person is seen for treatment. Depressive symptoms in women are related to chronic drinking in contrast to episodic drinking. At least three depressive episodes were reported by 19% of heavy drinkers (1 oz. daily), but only 3% of long-term abstinent women reported similar experiences. Suicidal behavior was clearly related to drinking behavior. A past suicide attempt was reported by 0.2% of long-term abstainers, 5% of women averaging 1 to 2 oz. alcohol daily, 10% of women averaging 2 or more oz. daily, and 24% of the women who report drinking at least six drinks a day at least 3 days a week (Wilsnack et al., 1984). These data, in themselves, do not refute or support the notion that an underlying depression may precede alcohol abuse, but they clearly suggest that rather than relieving feelings of depression, anxiety, or dysphoria, the use of alcohol exacerbates these feelings.

Alcoholism as a correlate of a sociopathic personality was described by Schuckit (1972) in a subgroup of alcoholic women whose antisocial lifestyle antedated their drinking problems. This group had an earlier onset of alcoholism, more marital problems, and a poorer prognosis for recovery than other alcoholic women. Other investigators attempting to link alcoholism and psychopathic deviance, depression, and/or psychasthenia have used the Minnesota Multiphasic Personality Inventory (MMPI) (Curlee, 1970; Zelen, Fox, Gould, & Olson, 1966). MMPI studies, however, have not yielded convincing evidence for either preexisting personality features that predict alcoholism or consistent personality patterns in alcoholic women tested during or after treatment (Rosen, 1960). In an attempt to clarify the relation between MMPI factors and alcoholism, subtypes of female alcoholics have been identified (Mogar, Wilson & Helm, 1970; Klein & Snyder, 1985). The latter investigators identified three subtypes of female alcoholics, each of which had elevated psychopathic deviate scales, which supports earlier findings (Schucket et al., 1969). However, total pathology as measured by the MMPI was strongly related to increasing alcohol consumption, indicating that psychopathic deviance is only one of many psychopathologies that may be associated with alcohol abuse and that severity of pathology may be more closely related to alcohol abuse than the type of pathology (Klein & Snyder, 1985).

Life Event Stress

A final line of psychological studies has identified stress as an important factor in the etiology of alcoholism. A high percentage of both alcohol abusing men and women have experienced family disruptions and childhood trauma. Alcoholic women are more likely than nonalcoholic women to have grown up in an unstable family and to report family disruption such as loss of a parent by death or divorce, economic problems, or placement outside of the home (Curlee, 1970; Corrigan, 1980; Kinsey, 1966; Linsansky, 1957). Alcoholic women recall receiving less approval from their parents than their nonalcoholic sisters (Corrigan, 1980). Adolescent problem drinkers describe their parents as unconcerned, neglectful, and as handling discipline arbitrarily. Heavy or problem drinking in adolescence is related to low parent-child interaction, high family tension, and limited responsiveness to the child's needs on the part of the parents (Williams & Klerman, 1984). Women with alcohol problems often cite marital and family problems as reasons for problem drinking and for seeking treatment (Beckman, 1976; Curlee, 1970; Linsansky, 1957). The studies cited here suggest that disorganized households and nonsupportive family members may place intolerable stress on the individual and, thus, contribute to alcohol abuse.

Other stressful life events are often mentioned in relation to alcoholism and women. Stressful life events are generally defined as a loss of a loved one through death, divorce, or desertion; marked changes in job, health, or financial status; or the experience of violence. Women relate a number of these events to the onset of drinking problems (Plant, 1980). Even though drinking may precede the onset of stressful life events, most alcoholic women relate a specific stressful incident to the onset of heavy drinking (NIAAA, 1983b). This incident is often a loss or a negative event (Homiller, 1977). Thus, a number of researchers have suggested that alcoholism in women is more likely to be associated with the stress of a specific situation than is alcoholism in men (e.g., Beckman, 1975).

Allan and Cooke (1985) have criticized the literature in this area. They point out that the major method used to collect data (i.e., women undergoing treatment for alcoholism are asked to recall stressful events that may have caused drinking) fails to consider that drinking itself may cause stressful events. This is, of course, the perennial problem of correlational data, and readers and researchers must always be mindful of the fact that one cannot infer causality from correlations.

Cooke and Allan (1984) carried out a study of the relationship between stressful events and alcohol use in a population not in treatment for alcohol abuse. Adult women (N = 230) were classified as regular drinkers or heavy drinkers. Heavy drinkers drank more than three times as much alcohol as regular drinkers; yet their reported total life stress was almost identical. Thus, in this sample of women who had not sought treatment for their drinking, there was no relationship between life stress and alcohol consumption. Allan and Cooke (1985) suggest the relationship between stressful life events and excessive drinking described by others may result from the existence of a group of sociopathic females whose behavior provokes stressful life events and who drink to excess. Sociopathic women with alcohol problems have been described by Schuckit (1972) and Klein and Snyder (1985), but these studies did not evaluate stress. A study in which the relationship between drinking and stress was evaluated in sociopathic and nonsociopathic women who were or were not in treatment would further clarify this issue.

Moral/Ethical Model

A moral perspective on alcohol use and abuse has its roots in lay persons' understanding of religious principles. Alcohol use, abuse, and dependence often are viewed as immoral because they defile the body, which is God's creation. For example, a person holding fundamentalist Christian beliefs has an ethical obligation to shun alcohol through exercising will power and by the grace of God. The alcohol abuser, then, is a weak-willed individual who has lost self-control. In this view, the consequences resulting from indulgence are seen as deserved. However, Christian charity encourages one to persuade the person who succumbs to drinking to return to the fold, and missions are established to provide food and shelter for those who have lost their jobs, homes, and families through abuse of alcohol.

Historically, women were among the strongest supporters of the moral perspective. The Women's Christian Temperance movement, an outgrowth of this point of view, sought to redeem males who had fallen victim to alcohol's lure and protect females and youth from the consequences of alcohol use. Levine (1980) provides an interesting brief history of women and the temperance movement. Proponents of the moral perspective used fear as a major technique to discourage alcohol use and attributed a wide range of social problems including poverty, crime, violence, and broken homes to the evils of alcohol. Today, variations of the moral perspective still exist in fundamentalist religious organizations, among whose members alcohol use and abuse is less prevalent than within the general public (Schlegel & Sanborn, 1979; Wilsnack et al., 1984).

The possibility of women abusing alcohol was generally ignored in the 19th century, a period in which the moral view prevailed. When women did abuse alcohol, the social penalties were extreme, and little hope was held for reform (Levine, 1980). A contemporary parallel of this aspect of the moral perspective is found in the widely held view in our culture that alcohol abuse and dependence is a more serious transgression for women than for men (Jones, 1971), which may account for the observation (Gomberg, 1976) that attitudes toward women who drink are harsher than toward men who drink. Today's remnants of these beliefs and attitudes may, in part, account for the fact that women are less likely to use alcohol, but those who do appear to be more reluctant than men to enter treatment when the use of alcohol becomes a health, social, or emotional problem (Dahlgren & Idestrom, 1979).

Possibly, the most far-reaching current formulation of the moral model of alcohol use, abuse, and dependence is its manifestation in Alcoholics Anonymous (A.A.). The program of A.A. holds that the self-proclaimed alcoholic must admit lack of control over alcohol and place reliance in a greater power in order to implement treatment and, thereby, to reestablish the control that allows one to remain abstinent.

Biological/Genetic Model

The role of a biological predisposition to alcohol abuse has received increasing attention as public opinion has shifted from viewing alcohol abuse and dependence as a moral problem to viewing it as a medical problem. Various factors that are thought to result from abnormal genetic expression have been proposed as causal agents in alcohol abuse. One theoretical formulation holds that alcohol may induce a feeling of well-being in persons who are deficient in a substance essential for the maintenance of such a state. In this model, alcohol is used to normalize an abnormal system. Dependence is thought to result from an aggravation of the innate deficiency caused by the withdrawal of alcohol once it has been used to normalize the system. The serotonin neurotransmitter system has been suggested as being related to the maintenance of a sense of well-being. Alcohol produces a small but statistically significant increase in serotonin in normal subjects (Kent et al., 1983). Goodwin (1985) has hypothesized that alcohol induces a biphasic response in serotonin activity, with increased levels being found during intoxication followed by subnormal levels as alcohol is metabolized (Kent et al., 1985). In alcoholic men who have undergone withdrawal, serotonin uptake is 18% lower than that of normals (Kent et al., 1985). This low serotonin activity is hypothesized as representing an innate metabolic error, which places people at risk for alcohol abuse. A prospective study of serotonin uptake and drinking behavior in a representative sample of men and women is needed to clarify this point.

Another biological model proposes that some persons produce a critical level of an addictive substance as a consequence of alcohol ingestion, and thus, these persons are at risk for becoming dependent on alcohol. Work with animals has shown that alcohol produces measurable amounts of an opioid-like compound in the brain (Davis & Walsh, 1970a, 1970b). However, in the decade and a half since the initial work, researchers have failed to convincingly link this finding to humans' use and abuse of alcohol. Recently, however, indirect support has come from prospective studies, which followed narcotic abusers as their treatment dose of methadone stabilized. These people reported less use of alcohol as methadone treatment proceeded (Barr & Cohen, 1979; Jackson et al., 1982; Stimmel et al., 1982). This suggests that alcohol may have been ingested for its ability to satisfy a need for narcotics. On the basis of these data and older retrospective studies that make the same point, a clinical evaluation of synthetic opioid substitution therapy for alcoholism has been proposed (Siegel, in press).

Researchers have attempted to connect the reproductive cycle of women and its inherent endocrine fluctuations to alcohol abuse and dependence, by noting the association between mood alterations and/or physical discomfort and menstrual phases (Smith, 1975; Steiner & Carroll, 1977; Moos, 1969; Wilcoxson, Schrader & Shery, 1976). In this scheme, alcohol use is related to an assumed palliative effect of alcohol on dysphoria and/or discomfort.

Indeed, increased dysphoria and anxiety during the premenstrual or early menstrual phase has been reported (Golub, 1976; Ivey & Bardwick, 1968; Silbergeld, Brast, & Noble, 1971). However, Parlee (1973, 1974) has cautioned that premenstrual dysphoria may reflect social expectancies. Two studies have supported this point (Ruble, 1977; Brooks, Ruble, & Clark, 1977) by showing that women who believed they were premenstrual reported more characteristics associated with a premenstrual syndrome than women who believed they were midcycle, even though all the women were actually at the same stage of the menstrual cycle.

Menstrual cycle effects appear to influence only the timing of negative effect and not the total amount effect. Women, taking or not taking oral contraceptives, and men were asked to report their somatic changes, moods, and stressful and pleasant events over a 35-day period. Surprisingly, total amount of negative affect among the three groups did not differ, although in both female groups the pattern was related to the menstrual cycle. In women taking oral contraceptives, who therefore had stable high levels of progesterone and estrogen, the premenstrual period was related to increased dysphoria. In women not taking oral contraception, maximum dysphoria was associated with the menstrual period. However, the researchers found that for both groups of women, negative mood was more strongly associated with stressful life events than phases of the menstrual cycle (Wilcoxson et al., 1976).

There is evidence that further disassociates dysphoria during the menstrual cycle from estrogen levels. Erickson (1980) reported that maximum dysphoria occurred in different phases of the cycle for women with menstrual periods of 5 days or less and women with periods of over 6 days. Women with shorter periods experienced dysphoria during the premenstrual and the early follicular phases, and women with long periods experienced dysphoria during the ovulatory and midluteal phases. Thus, negative affect was associated in one group (short period) with low levels of estrogen and in another group (long period) with high levels of estrogen.

To assess the effects of menstrual phase on alcohol consumption, patterns of drinking across the cycle have been examined. In one study, significantly more alcohol-abusing women than matched controls reported increased drinking during the premenstruum (Beckman, 1979). Among women being treated for alcohol abuse on an outpatient basis, 46% of the menopausal women and 67% of the premenopausal women started drinking or increased their drinking before menstruation (Belfer et al., 1971; Belfer & Shader, 1976). In a recent study (Sutker, Libet, Albert, & Randall, 1983), normally cycling women showed more frequent drinking to reduce tension or to relieve negative effects, as well as more frequent solitary drinking, during menstrual flow than during the remainder of their cycle.

Although tension is often invoked as a causative factor in alcohol use and abuse, the relatively few studies available have not convincingly related differential levels of stress to specific menstrual phases and that, in turn, to differential use of alcohol. The work of Parlee (1973, 1974), Ruble (1977), and Brooks et al. (1977) points out that social expectation factors must be taken into account to understand the relation between effect and menstrual phase and suggests that expectations indirectly influence drinking patterns. The work of Erickson (1980) underlines the importance of catagorizing women on the bases of the duration of the menstrual period and the menstrual phase if any underlying relation between menstrual cycle and mood is to be revealed.

The response of gonadal hormones to alcohol has been reported to vary across the menstrual cycle (Jones & Jones, 1976a, 1976b). An identical dose of alcohol resulted in a significantly higher BAC at ovulation and during the premenstrual phase than at other times in the menstrual cycle. Differences in BAC were suggested to result from changing gonadal hormonal levels over the menstrual cycle (Jones, 1975). In women taking oral contraceptives, which maintain progesterone and estrogen at high levels, alcohol was reported to be metabolized more slowly than in women not using oral contraceptives (Jones & Jones, 1976b). These findings suggest that women experiencing additional tension during the premenstruum, such as women with short periods (Erickson, 1980), may increase their alcohol consumption at a time of maximum pharmacological effects. However, later work (Hay, Nathan, Hurmans, & Frankenstein, 1984) failed to confirm the earlier work (Jones, 1975; Jones & Jones, 1976a, 1976b) in that women tested in the premenstrual phase did not achieve higher peak BACs or absorb alcohol more rapidly than when tested during other menstrual phases. Thus, at this time, the notion that alcohol's effects vary in response to gonadal hormone level does not appear to be adequately supported by data.

Despite beliefs that women may use alcohol to palliate menstrual psychic and/or physical discomfort, there is little evidence to support the notion that dysphoria experienced as a consequence of the menstrual cycle results in increased alcohol consumption. Moreover, evidence assessing effects of alcohol on mood indicates that alcohol, rather than alleviating feelings of depression and anxiety, in fact, exacerbates them. Numerous studies carried out on men (Mello & Mendelson, 1972, 1978) show that chronic alcohol intoxication increases dysphoria and that social drinkers report increased dysphoria with increased alcohol intake. Female social drinkers also report increased anxiety and depression with increased alcohol intake (Wilsnack et al., 1984; Logue, Gentry, Linnoila, & Ervin, 1978).

Biological models of alcohol abuse become genetic models when they posit that people have an inherent vulnerability to alcohol abuse and dependence, which is specified by their genes and transmissible from one generation to another. Study of the heritability of behavior has long been a part of psychology. Classic studies by Goddard (1921) of mental retardation and Kallman (1946) of schizophrenia are examples of this approach. Although these studies provided familial incidence and evidence of increased concordance as a function of genetic similarity, they were not able to sort out the relative effects of biological and environmental factors because the people studied were raised by their natural parents or close relatives. Beginning in the 1960s, a number of investigators took advantage of the extensive demographic records of the Scandinavian countries to begin testing behavioral genetic hypotheses of alcohol dependence by looking at the incidence of alcohol misuse in persons who did or did not have an alcoholic parent or parents. These people had been adopted at, or shortly after, birth by couples who did or did not themselves experience alcohol problems.

The experimental design shown in Table 6.1 allows genetic factors to be separated from environmental, except insofar as adopting agencies may attempt to place a child with parents similar to the biological parents

Table 6.1 Experimental Design Used to Contrast Genetic
and Environmental Contribution to Alcoholism

		Parents	
		Biological	Adoptive
Alcohol	Present		
abuse	Absent		

on a variety of demographic variables that may themselves be related to alcohol misuse. A number of investigators (Bohman, Sigvardsson & Cloninger, 1981; Goodwin, Schulsinger, Knop, Mednick & Guze, 1977a, 1977b; Von Knorring, Cloninger, Bohman & Sigvardsson, 1983) have employed variations of the "adopted-away" strategy to examine genetic contributions to alcoholism in women.

In these studies, persons were classified as alcohol abusers if they had been registered by the Temperance Board, treated for alcoholism, diagnosed as alcoholic, or identified as having alcohol problems at a young age. The strongest support for a genetic component of alcohol misuse in women comes from a study (Bohman et al., 1981) that found alcohol abuse to be three times more prevalent in adopted-away daughters of alcohol abusing mothers than in adopted-away daughters of nonalcohol abusing mothers. If only the biological father abused alcohol, the increased alcohol abuse in daughters was insignificant. Similarly, alcohol abuse in both biological parents did not increase the risk in adopted-away daughters over that predicted by alcohol abuse solely in the mother. However, the prevalence of alcohol abuse in the adopted daughters reared by nonalcoholic mothers was lower than in their biological mothers, indicating that being raised in an environment free of alcohol problems may have a prophylactic effect on women at risk for alcohol abuse. On the other hand, women whose biological mother plus an adoptive parent experienced alcohol dependence did not show increased prevalence over the group with only an alcoholic biological mother. This suggests that the relationship between genetic and environmental factors are not simply additive. The finding that adopted-away daughters of biological alcoholic fathers did not have an increased risk for alcoholism (Bohman et al., 1981) replicated an earlier finding (Goodwin, Schulsinger, Knop, Mednick, & Guze, 1977a). In another study, these investigators (Goodwin et al., 1977b) found all adopted women to be at risk for alcohol abuse. Daughters of alcoholic biological fathers who were adopted away were compared with those who remained with their fathers. The rate of alcoholism was found to be four times greater in both groups than in the population at large. However, this rate did not differ from that found in women, adopted at birth, whose biological fathers had not used alcohol excessively, which suggests that factors associated with adoption per se increased the risk of alcohol abuse in women.

Whereas a genetic basis of alcohol abuse in men appears to be well established (Swinson, 1980) by the "adopted-away" studies, this relationship is less clear in women. There appears to be no evidence for a paternal genetic contribution to alcoholism in women, and the evidence for a maternal genetic contribution rests on Bohman and co-workers' (1981) work, which appears to have been the only study to consider the mother's role in the genetic transmission of alcohol-abusing behavior. Clearly, confirmatory studies are needed to establish the importance of maternal hereditary factors in alcohol abuse in women. Moreover, there are also data, such as the increased alcohol abuse seen in all adopted women studied by Goodwin et al. (1977b), that suggest the etiology of women's drinking may be strongly related to nongenetic variables.

TREATMENT

Implications and Applications

A person's gender is a primary component of individual identity and determines other's reactions, as well as one's opportunities and responsibilities. The alcohol treatment system has tended to divorce the impact of gender from an overall understanding of alcohol abuse. When gender has been considered, it has tended to be in negative and stereotypic ways. It seems appropriate, then, to conclude this chapter with a discussion of the treatment implications and applications of gender for treatment. Historically, alcohol-abuse treatment issues have been identified in the process of rehabilitation of men. The best controlled treatment studies, those which involved substantial numbers of clients, were conducted in Veterans' Hospitals with male patient populations. Up until the last decade, most studies included few, if any, women. The treatment techniques elaborated through working with male alcohol abusers have been presumed to be equally effective for women, and in some instances they may be applicable to women. However, the different roles men and women play in society and the differences that exist in the relative value men and women attach to various activities suggest that specific treatment issues for women need to be considered to maximize the appropriateness of treatment interventions used for women abusing alcohol.

Each woman will enter treatment with her own complaints and concerns. Some may not be particularly interested in decreasing alcohol abuse but may instead be concerned with meeting the demands of the legal system or family. Other women may wish to cut down on their alcohol abuse only enough to decrease physical problems, regain custody of children, or regain control of other facets of their lives.

Addressing the practical issues that govern these women's lives in an effective manner can produce tangible results. If there are immediate social, environmental, or physical problems that can be resolved, doing so may, in some instances, remove barriers to treatment and, in all instances, should free the female client's energies to concentrate on the alcohol-abuse problem.

A woman's concern for the welfare of her children often motivates her to seek treatment (NIAAA, 1983a). Yet, since women often have primary or sole responsibility for child care, child-related concerns may be a barrier to entering treatment. Some may be afraid of being reported for suspected child abuse/neglect due to alcohol abuse or even losing custody of the children. Other women may not seek treatment due to the lack of child care services or because of the cost of those few services that are available. Assistance should be given in finding adequate day care facilities for clients in outpatient treatment or full-time child care for inpatient or residential programs. If child care is not available, voluntary placement of the children may be necessary, and this necessity may cause women to leave or postpone treatment.

Understanding the patient's responses to treatment is critical in working with female clients. Although all clients entering treatment may show high levels of anger, guilt, anxiety, and confusion, it has been shown that both male and female treatment personnel are more apt to label emotional symptoms in females as psychopathological or indicative of resistance (Broverman, Broverman, Clarkson, Rosenkratz, & Vogel, 1970). This attitude, conscious or unconscious, toward women can result in less effective treatment.

Female clients should be encouraged to view emotional responses, such as anger, guilt, or anxiety, as part of the normal recovery process. Treatment should not focus only on negative aspects of the client's life. The female client, possibly even more than the male alcohol abuser, needs to recognize assets and to develop a feeling of strength and self-confidence.

The client's relationships with others have significant implications for the treatment process. Gaining the support of family and friends in the treatment process emphasizes the importance of the family structure and enlists their efforts in the recovery process. However, family and friends may not be positive influences or willing to work with or on behalf of the female client. Although less than 2% of men reported opposition to their entering treatment, approximately 23% of women experienced the opposition of family and friends during the month that preceded their entry into treatment (Beckman & Amaro, 1986). An examination of the alcohol abuse patterns of the spouse or significant other can reveal some potential obstacles. A woman's commitment to positive change may become weakened when she learns that success in treatment could mean that she may not be able to maintain the same type of relationships with her friends and family. She may experience fear, seeing herself as unable to retain her social network or face the resulting loneliness. It cannot be assumed that a woman will make changes that conflict with the life-style of the person with whom she lives without experiencing a great deal of difficulty. Involving the entire family in treatment can reduce anxiety about a new identity if it is apparent that the whole family is gaining a new identity. The family may focus on a woman-in-treatment's alcohol abuse and, thus, be distracted from another member's substance abuse, serious marital problems, or other behaviors, which the family is less willing to acknowledge. If these problems are left untreated, the alcohol-abusing woman may relapse to drug use once the treatment period is ended.

For many women seeking treatment, low self-esteem and a tendency to self blame is pervasive. Women may enter treatment with a deep sense of guilt about failure at marriage, parenthood, or meeting her own or others' standards of the "ideal" woman. It is important that the female client not be ashamed of herself and see how much she has in common with others—abusers and nonabusers, male and female. Contact with other recovered alcohol abusers, particularly other recovering women, is an important avenue to recovering or developing self-esteem.

In general, alcohol-abusing women have few friends and small social networks (Rist & Watzl, 1983). The female client is often quite isolated, or at least perceives herself to be. The importance of woman-to-woman relationships is great. For one thing, by providing models of competent women, these relationships may break the female's sole reliance on male authority figures. Stressing the importance of the support of women will facilitate recovery. Self-help groups such as Women for Sobriety and Alcoholics Anonymous are invaluable as are groups that foster self-development for women in other life activities, such as the National Organization for Women and many other groups.

The identification and discussion of sexual and sex-role issues and difficulties is also an important consideration for treatment (Mandel & North, 1982). In America's culture, sexuality is intertwined with intimacy, self-esteem, and one's perceptions of relationships with others. The ability to disclose information about intimate sexual matters will emerge at different times in treatment for different women, but for the majority of women it is an area that must be addressed.

A high number of alcohol-abusing women report histories of sexual assault and incest (Beckman, 1979). Women with such histories will often remain silent out of fear, shame, ignorance, or guilt. It is often difficult to help a female client reveal hidden traumatic occurrences because such issues are generally considered taboo and, thus, discussed infrequently. Over the past 15 years, therapists have become more familiar with these problems, and today many therapists are trained to identify incest victims and to help them verbalize their feelings and begin to cope with the consequences of sexual abuse.

In our society, women are subject to pressures to conform to a variety of roles, both traditional and nontraditional. For many women, this has led to greater responsibility for activities in and out of the home (Seiden, 1976). Assuming multiple, conflicting roles leads to overwork, stress, and lowered efficiency (Sandmaier, 1982). Often, alcohol-abusing women have no sense of themselves as a person outside of being someone's wife and/or mother. These women may not be motivated toward, or even aware of, an existence outside the arena of the family. They may harbor deep resentments toward the very people to whom they are attached most closely. Confronting feminist theory and/or recent findings in the psychology of women may be helpful for such women or may make them feel threatened and insecure in the face of new or unfamiliar ideas. Other women in treatment may have rejected the traditional female role and all it represents in a self-destructive manner. They may see normal experiences that arise in the course of treatment for any alcohol abuser, such as interdependency with one's therapist or therapy group, as a relapse to traditional values, which they want to reject. Creating an awareness of many possible role options and alternatives can encourage alcohol-abusing women to move in any direction that feels comfortable and allows them to control their alcohol use behavior.

Alcohol-abusing women are not a homogeneous population with regard to either their problems or their treatment needs. An effective treatment program may provide several service components that can be used at different stages by different individuals. Yet, there are some fundamental program components, techniques, and strategies that may help attract, retain, and treat women effectively. First, the female alcohol abuser must be taken into account when designing community outreach and case identification programs. Second, in order to incorporate gender-sensitive questions, intake procedures may have to be restructured and assessment guidelines reviewed. Third, the staff must be selected and trained with the program needs of women in mind. Last, providing needed ancillary services for the female alcohol abuser is necessary for treatment to be successful.

Casefinding

One of the main reasons for under representation of women in treatment is the lack of effective outreach. Casefinding for women is complicated by several issues. First, because of a perceived harsher public attitude toward women having alcohol abuse problems, women may be more reluctant to seek help openly (Sandmaier, 1980). Women show lower utilization rates for disorders that are incongruent with sex-role stereotypes (Beckman & Amaro, 1984), and they perceive greater social costs to have been associated with entering treatment (Beckman & Amaro, 1986). Thus, women alcoholics may be more apt to seek help for a mental disorder, which is more congruent with accepted stereotypes, than to seek help for alcoholism.

Second, those who come into contact with women (e.g., police, job supervisors, mental health professionals), are often not trained to identify substance abuse problems among women, and they may be reluctant to refer women to treatment. For example, women cited for an alcohol-related traffic violation are less likely than men to be convicted for drunken driving or referred for alcohol treatment (NIAAA, 1983a). Employee assistance programs are the major source of referral for men. However, few women are referred for treatment from such programs. In part, this reflects the employment of women in systems that do not have such programs, and, in part, it reflects the reluctance to ascribe women's dysfunction to alcohol abuse.

Nevertheless, there are other ways to reach alcohol-abusing women. Some women will refer themselves if the information is made available. A program that provides needed services for women should make this known through various places where women go or congregate (e.g., PTA meetings, day care, churches, women's organizations, parents organizations, YWCA, health clubs, schools and universities, and work places that employ women).

By training staff in settings, such as universities and workplaces where women are found, to recognize problems related to alcohol abuse, women can be referred for treatment. Outreach strategies should also focus on community "caretakers" with whom women interact. To our knowledge, although such programs have focused on bartenders as an outreach effort, no program has ever targeted babysitters, wrecker drivers, cab drivers, convenience store clerks, or apartment doormen, all of whom fulfill roles that would expose them to women who may be abusing alcohol. These people could be provided training that emphasizes screening and assessment information along with knowledge of appropriate agencies to which to refer those whom they identify as having problems.

Staffing

It has been stressed that the philosophy and attitudes of staff and their ability to serve as role models are prime factors in treatment success. If a female client is to be engaged in the treatment process she must develop a sense of belonging. This can be enhanced by the presence of staff with backgrounds similar to her own. One way to do this is by providing same-sex counselors. Providing women in treatment with female counselors has several advantages. Women can more easily act as role models for other women. Allowing the client an opportunity to identify with a female counselor may be crucial in helping women see the possibilities for change (Connor & Babcock, 1980). Because alcohol-abusing women often have poor self-images, low self-esteem, poor relationships with their mothers, and problems with their female identity, it is important that these clients be provided with models of women who have control over their lives. Often women identify the women's role as a subordinate one. In coming to recognize the authority of a female therapist as she works with the client herself and/or other clients, the alcohol-abusing woman often gains her first vision of gender-free authority and of women functioning as healthy, mature, and responsible persons.

Assessment Strategies

All important areas in women's lives need to be reviewed to identify barriers to treatment and needs that must be addressed if a woman is to gain from the treatment experience. Information (e.g., cultural, social, economic, familial, physical, psychological, and vocational factors) can be assessed to identify the uniqueness of the individual women's alcohol abuse problem.

Women often enter alcohol treatment programs in a state of physical weakness and cite this reason for seeking assistance. Thus, health assessments to determine the need for medical referral are important. These areas should be taken into consideration (Popour, 1983):

1. Assessment of a woman's basic physical health (e.g., blood pressure, blood tests, etc.).
2. Assessment of use of medication as a means for coping with psychological and physical discomfort.
3. Assessment of the need to consult with medical personnel who have provided such medications in the past.
4. Assessment of obstetrics and gynecological status. Birth control, breast self-exam, and yearly Pap exams should be handled along with assessment of hormonal status (adolescent, premenopause, pregnant, menopause, premenstrual syndrome, postmenopause).
5. Assessment of psychiatric status (e.g., suicidal potential, degree of denial, self-blame, and low self-esteem). Psychological testing may be necessary to provide a more complete evaluation.

In addition, neuropsychological function should be evaluated (Tarter & Edwards, 1986). The intake assessment should also include gathering information on the woman's roles and responsibilities, family background, social support systems, coping patterns, and economic status.

Treatment Components

Many alcohol-abusing women share similar problems, and exposure to an all-female counseling group can be a beneficial aspect of treatment. The group can encourage the development of new support networks for women who are isolated. As women work together to solve problems they provide each other with role models. Both self-esteem and self-acceptance can be enhanced in this matter.

In groups, men and women express different behaviors and concerns. Generally, men tend to dominate a mixed-sex conversation and take a leadership role in problem solving. Often issues salient for women (e.g., child care, health issues, sexuality) fail to be addressed. In a mixed-sex group, women often adhere to the feminine role stereotype of dependence, acceptance, and submission. If lack of self-esteem is involved in the etiology and maintenance of alcohol abuse, mixed-sex group treatment may not be of value.

Some women prefer to be in mixed-sex groups for various reasons. In these groups, women may play secondary roles to men and may not participate in group activities. This nonparticipatory role is familiar and comfortable. Some women may prefer the company of men to that of women, as some women value the approval and attention of men and depend on men for their sense of identity and self-worth. These women may not have a positive regard for relationships with other women. An all-women's group may be a new experience for them, and they may not be aware of the significance of relationships with members of their own sex and the need for support from other women. Thus, not all women will benefit from a women's group initially, although all women are thought to be capable of benefiting from this type of treatment.

Women who are uninterested in women's groups may be introduced to them through exercise, parenting, or stress management classes. Consciousness-raising groups may also be used to address issues of sexuality, self-concept, mother-daughter issues, relationships with others (women, men, and children), sex, and developing an understanding of what it means to be dependent on alcohol. The implementation of a mixed-sex group, supplemented by an all-women's group, is one approach available to treatment programs. With that format, both sexes can improve their understanding of the experiences of their own and the opposite sex.

Skills Training

Treatment programs may be able to retain and treat women more effectively if they provide services that can teach women skills for independent living. Assertiveness training is often needed for building self-esteem and is applicable to many areas of a woman's life. Women may use the training to seek out needed social services. Also, negotiations with banks, stores, utility companies, and legal offices often demand that the consumer be aware of her rights and have the ability to assert those rights when appropriate. Assertiveness can help the client communicate in personal relationships, too.

Parenting is another area that deserves greater attention, especially since women are likely to live with children and be responsible for child care. Parenting training can include learning about child development, examining mother/child interactions, understanding children and their behavior, and exploring different techniques for relating to one's child.

Finally, women should be presented with activities that allow exploration and expression of creative abilities. New or rediscovered skills and talents help to structure sober time, add self-esteem, and promote physical and emotional well-being. Music, art, literature, acting, and physical activities are all believed to have therapeutic benefits in their own rights.

SUMMARY

Although evidence for the role of genetic factors in alcohol abuse for men is relatively strong, the evidence for such a role in women is far weaker. At present, support rests on a single study, which appears to be the only study of maternal influences on adopted-away daughter's drinking behavior. Evidence for psychosocial factors in drinking behavior abound, but no one set of factors has been identified that predicts alcohol abuse. Current trends alert one to the possibility that women with higher socioeconomic status, who work outside the home and attempt to fulfill multiple role expectations, in the absence of sufficient social support for these roles, may be at risk for alcohol abuse. The interrelatedness of these factors comes into consideration as women enter treatment, and programs are well advised to design treatment protocols that systematically address them. Feminist theory and research on the psychology of women have provided a body of data, which is beginning to be incorporated into research on the etiology of alcohol abuse, and whose implications for alcohol abuse treatment programs for women is being integrated into programs.

Overview of Eating Disorders 7

This chapter was written with Bonnie Bailey Bowers

This chapter reviews anorexia nervosa and bulimia, eating disorders characterized by excessive fear of being fat coupled with extreme efforts to control weight. These problems have received intensive study recently, and several national organizations have emerged: Anorexia Nervosa and Related Eating Disorders, American Anorexia and Bulimia Association, Anorexia Nervosa and Associated Disorders, and Overeaters Anonymous. Although this chapter is restricted to anorexia and bulimia, these syndromes can be seen as part of a continuum of eating disorders encompassing obesity as well. Many of the same conditions that promote one disorder are probably relevant to others. Epidemiology, medical consequences, and cognitive/affective correlates are discussed in turn.

We take the philosophical position that the phenomena in question concerns the status and mental health of all women, not only those diagnosed as having clinical dysfunction. The conditions that produce extreme eating behaviors probably influence all women to a certain degree and thus shape the experience of female gender. There is a distinct possibility that these disorders do not represent experiences qualitatively different from those shared by most women. That is, compared to males, the experience of being female includes more awareness of and concern for body image, attitudes about food, special rituals and restrictions about satisfying hunger, and a general sense of overlap between self and body.

EPIDEMIOLOGY

By way of introduction, it is important to remember that methodological problems and issues are associated with any research area, and research on eating disorders is no exception. Anorexia nervosa has an impressively long history within the medical literature (Morton, 1689; Gull, 1868); more contemporary descriptions date from the 1940s (Waller, Kaufman, & Deutsch, 1940). Researchers have applied a variety of definitions to their subject populations, and subject populations have differed in basic characteristics from study to study, occasionally composed only of hospitalized patients and other times of college students. Epidemiological research on eating disorders is of a correlational nature. Therefore, much of the information in this section should be taken as only broadly descriptive, with the distinct possibility that essential features of various syndromes have been overlooked.

Signs and Symptoms

Each year, several thousand individuals receive treatment for eating disorders. The associated behavior patterns have serious personal, social, and medical health consequences. Those who follow starvation eating patterns indicative of anorexia nervosa commonly lose 20% of their ideal weight and are often hospitalized due to the physical effects and risks of starvation. Those who follow a binge/purge cycle typically maintain a normal weight but engage in secret consumption of vast calories in short periods of time, hence the term bulimia, which literally means ox hunger. Anorexia and bulimia are somewhat overlapped, with some anorexics occasionally resorting to purging as a means of maintaining an emaciated body weight.

A generic description of an individual who follows starvation eating patterns (anorexia nervosa) or binge/purge cycles (bulimia) can be developed from the work of several researchers (Halmi, 1974; Halmi, Goldberg, Eckert, Casper, & Davis, 1977; Boskind-Lodahl, 1976; Bemis, 1978; Golden & Sacker, 1984; Casper & Davis, 1977) and is as follows: She is a female in her teenage or young adult years; personally, she is pleasant, obedient, and holds high achievement standards for herself. Academic performance is probably above average. Her personal weight history is likely to include a period in early puberty when she was slightly above ideal weight ranges, perhaps no more than 10 to 12 pounds. The onset of unusual eating patterns is likely to be associated with some significant change in her life-style or support system, for example, loss of a parent, going away to school, etc. Bulimics in particular are likely to be very secretive about their actions.

Ambiguity of definition has been a hindrance to decisive research in the area. However, researchers have consistently required that alternative explanations must first be evaluated and dismissed; that is, the observed conditions must not be attributable to other medical conditions or psychoses (Browning & Miller, 1968). Elimination of physical explanations is important because certain medical conditions produce symptoms of anorexia, and these cases could be misdiagnosed as a psychoneurotic disturbance. For example, brain tumor and regional enteritis may be responsible for weight loss or unusual eating patterns.

Definitions now include beliefs, behaviors, and physical signs. Distorted attitudes about food and body image characterize belief systems of anorexics. Many anorexics perceive themselves as being pudgy or fat even though they appear emaciated to others. Garner and his colleagues have developed an eating disorder inventory (Garner & Garfinkel, 1979; Garner, Olmsted, & Polivy, 1983) that measures beliefs, affect, and behavior associated with eating disorders. Characteristic beliefs and attitudes include thoughts about dieting, a terror of gaining weight, dissatisfaction with body shape and size, and a preoccupation with a desire to be thinner. Anorexics admit they are preoccupied with food, planning of meals, thoughts of food, and so on. However, they often deny feeling hungry, or say they are confused about whether they are hungry or not, and take great pride in being able to satisfy their appetites with minimal calories.

Behaviors and physical signs associated with anorexia may include episodes of bulimia, self-induced vomiting, hoarding of food, and periods of hyperactivity. Physical symptoms of anorexia include weight loss of 25% of original body weight, amenorrhea, vomiting, and a low resting pulse rate (Bemis, 1978). Additional signs may include hypotension and lanugo (a fine, downy growth of body hair), constipation, and cold intolerance. These later signs are thought to be conditions caused by starvation, regardless of etiology (Kirstein, 1981-1982). These and other signs and symptoms are listed in Table 7.1.

Bulimia is considered by some researchers to be a variation of anorexia nervosa (Casper, Eckert, Halmi, Goldberg, & Davis, 1980), but others identify it as a separate eating disorder. The overlap of cognitive, affective, behavioral, and physical signs has led some researchers to propose a general category, such as, dietary chaos syndrome (Palmer, 1979), bulimia nervosa (Russell, 1979), or bulimarexia (Boskind-Lodahl, & White, 1978). The confusion rests partly in the fact that many patients diagnosed as anorexic are not entirely steadfast in their abstinence from food. When they do indulge themselves, they are likely to rely on some form of purging to reduce their weight. Approximately half of diagnosed anorexics will rely on this strategy at some time (Casper et al., 1980; Fairburn & Cooper, 1982; Yudkovitz, 1983). Both anorexics and bulimics are obsessed with a fear of being fat; bulimics typically fluctuate between weight gain and extreme remedies to lose weight, whereas anorexics actually do succeed in losing significant body weight. Individuals who rely on self-induced vomiting and purging to control their weight may fall into any weight class; underweight, normal, or overweight (Orleans & Barnett, 1984). Health risks for anorexia are generally acute, and risks associated with bulimia are more likely to be associated with chronic conditions.

Nevertheless, bulimia is identified as a separate diagnostic condition in the DSM III 1980. Affective components include a fear of being fat, anxiety, loneliness, and feelings of being emotionally unfulfilled (Yudkovitz, 1983). Behaviorally, it is characterized by binge eating and purging in a compulsive cycle involving anxiety-based gorging, attempts to reduce weight by self-induced vomiting, laxatives, or sleep, all compounded by depressed affective states (Yudkovitz, 1983). Much of this

Table 7.1 Diagnostic Signs & Symptoms of Anorexia
and Bulimia

Anorexia	*Bulimia*
Cognition	
Denial of illness	Awareness of abnormal
Preoccupation with diet-	eating
ing and being thin	Self-depreciating thoughts
Distorted body image	after a binge
	Distorted body image
Affect	
Morbid fear of fatness	Morbid fear of fatness
Anxiety fear & depression	Anxiety fear & depression
Food phobia	Powerful urges to overeat
Pleasure in losing weight	Fear of being unable to stop
& being thin	eating
Behavior	
Self-imposed starvation	Inconspicuous binge eating
Self-induced vomiting	Self-induced vomiting
Use of laxatives and	Use of laxatives and
diuretics	diuretics
Hyperactivity and vig-	Impulsive behavior, drug
orous exercise	use
Bulimic episodes	
Physical Signs	
Significant weight loss	Weight fluctuations (10 or
(20%–25%)	more lbs.)
Amenorrhea	Menstrual irregularity
Lanugo	Strong appetite
Bradycardia	Gastrointestinal complaints
Hypotension	Gastric dilation, rupture
Constipation	Dental enamel erosion
Breast atrophy	Headaches, dizziness, aura
	preceding binge

behavior is conducted secretly, and bulimics often report maintaining normal eating patterns in social company, while engaging in secret eating bouts. Periods of binging may last 1 to 2 hours and involve ingestion of 15,000 to 20,000 calories in a single episode (Schlesier-Stropp, 1984). The weight history for bulimics is most likely to reflect a pattern where they have been traditionally heavy for their normal age/height range or have been overweight (Schlesier-Stropp, 1984). While many bulimics maintain apparently normal weight, many obese people also engage in binge behavior, and some researchers have suggested that several subtypes exist (Gormally, 1984).

One subtype may be characterized by neurological signs. For example, patients may report an unusual sensation or aura just before the binge episode, similar to that reported by epileptics (Rau & Green, 1984). Other neurological symptoms include severe headaches and periods of dizziness. Binge eaters who report the occurrence of aura binging also frequently report that binging is followed by somnolence, sleep, or loss of consciousness. These patients also report the feeling that binging episodes are not really part of their true self. They have a sense of depersonalization, as if they were standing outside themselves during the binge episode (Rau & Green, 1984).

Antecedents of binging often involve extremely restrictive diets, for example, fasting or fluid-only diets (Polivy & Herman, 1985). This produces general psychological dysphoria, fatigue, and extreme hunger, making food-related cues also become more salient. The complete cycle, outlined by Orleans and Barnett (1984), is illustrated in Figure 7.1. Binging is followed by efforts to mitigate excessive caloric intake. Self-induced vomiting is a common strategy, as is the use of laxatives. One patient was reported to have used as many as 100 laxative preparations in a single day (Drossman, 1983). Binging may begin as an occasional acute episode and progress to daily frequency. Self-induced vomiting may likewise be limited initially to only those episodes of over indulgence but progress to an incidence of 2 to 10 times daily. One patient is reported to have engaged in self-induced vomiting 30 times a day for 13 years (Fairburn, 1983). Extreme eating patterns and remedies tend to be carefully hidden or camouflaged by bulimics, and the secrecy that surrounds it suggests that it

FIGURE 7.1 The binge-purge cycle may begin with overly strict dieting, but, once initiated, tends to persist.

may be an undetected feature of other psychiatric conditions (Fairburn & Cooper, 1982).

Incidence

In the United States, approximately 9,000 people are hospitalized annually for anorexia; 8,000 of these patients are female. Estimates of the incidence of anorexia in the general population vary slightly, but generally suggest a rate of 4 to 7 per thousand females and may be as high as 10 per thousand among adolescent girls (Nylander, 1971; Crisp, Palmer & Kalucy, 1976; Pope, Hudson, & Yurgelun-Todd, 1984; Szmukler, 1983a). These estimates are variously based on surveys of English school girls, readers of women's magazines, and women at American shopping malls. Data based on hospitalized cases in the United States indicate that incidence rates vary substantially by geographic region. The highest rate of hospitalization for anorexia is in North Central states, followed by Northeast, South, and West geographic areas. Rates of hospitalization in North Central states are nearly three times higher than those observed in the South and West. It is not clear whether these geographic variations in rate of hospitalization are indicative of variation in actual incidence or reflect differing medical opinion about treatment. As will be seen later, there are geographic variations in days of hospital care per patient as well.

Hospitalized cases, however, represent only part of the afflicted population. While there is no preferred method by which to extrapolate from hospitalized cases to outpatient cases, some data suggest how this might be accomplished. Data from a national survey of Japanese physicians revealed that the actual number of cases under treatment on an outpatient basis was roughly three times the number of hospitalized cases (Suematsu, Ishikawa, Kuboki, & Ito, 1985). If this ratio also holds true for the United States, there are approximately 36,000 cases now receiving treatment. Several researchers have suggested that the incidence of eating disorders is on the increase (Bemis, 1978; Garner, Garfinkel, & Olmsted, 1983; Golden & Sacker, 1984). Whether this represents increased sensitivity and screening or an actual change in rates is not clear.

Bulimia is harder to detect and, therefore, estimates of rates are tentative. Surveys of college students indicate that as many as two thirds of women and one half of men report having indulged in binge eating at some time (Hawkins & Clements, 1980), and approximately 13% meet formal criteria for diagnosis by DSM III criteria (Halmi, Falk, & Schwartz, 1981). Among 500 students seeking care at a University of Washington Psychiatric Clinic and receiving a diagnosis, 19 were diagnosed as bulimic, indicating a rate for this specialized population of approximately 38 per thousand (Stangler & Printz, 1980).

Age and Sex

Age at onset is often difficult to determine because individuals may hide their disturbed feelings and unusual behaviors. For example, some anorexics report fasting during the day but eating a normal meal with family members in the evening. Another strategy of concealment is to report having eaten previously with friends as an explanation for refusing to eat at normal family meal times.

Age of onset of anorexia is thought to be before age 25 in most cases (Bemis, 1978; Crisp, Hsu, Harding, & Hartshorn, 1980). Surveys of British school girls indicate that girls over the age of 16 are three times more likely to be diagnosed anorexic compared to younger girls (Crisp, Palmer, & Kalucy, 1976). National data bases for the United States suggest a similar pattern in American girls, and hospitalization for anorexia is most likely to occur between the ages of 16 and 25 (NCHS, 1982a). However, recent reviews indicate that this syndrome is not uncommon among women over 25 (Halmi, 1974; Garfinkel & Garner, 1982; Garner, Garfinkel, & Olmsted, 1983; Crisp, 1983b), with some cases reported among menopausal women (Launer, 1978; Kellet, Trimble, & Thorley, 1976). The distribution of hospitalized cases by age is illustrated in Figure 7.2.

Bulimics are likely to be diagnosed at a somewhat older age than anorexics, with the average age at diagnosis being approximately 23 (Schlesier-Stropp, 1984; Fairburn & Cooper, 1982). However, studies have reported cases ranging in age from 15 to 51. Age of onset for bulimia is probably close to that for anorexia. However, due to the secretive nature of bulimic behaviors, diagnosis and treatment may be substantially delayed (Casper et al., 1980). Furthermore, it is difficult for friends or relatives to detect a problem because the bulimic's body shape tends to remain within normal bounds (Fairburn & Cooper, 1982). Both anorexia and bulimia may have a long incipient or premorbid period of development.

When males exhibit anorexia nervosa, symptoms, precipitating conditions, and physical signs are extremely similar to those observed for females (Crisp, 1983b). The ratio of female to male anorexics is estimated to be 15:1 (Crisp & Toms, 1972); however, among hospitalized populations the ratio is approximately 8:1.

Several possibilities might explain differences in sex ratios for the population in general and sex ratios observed among hospitalized cases. Estimates of general population sex ratios may be in error; male anorexics may be more likely to receive a medical diagnosis, and male anorexics

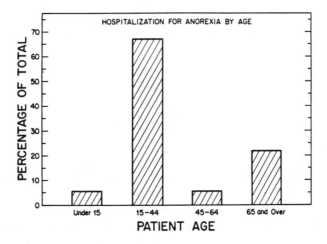

FIGURE 7.2   Hospitalization for anorexia by age. Source: NCHS (1982), Detailed Diagnosis and Surgical Procedures for Patients Discharged from Short-Stay Hospitals. DHHS (PHS) 82-1274-1, Washington, D.C.: U.S. Government Printing Office.

may be more likely to receive hospital treatment. Males may be hospitalized more readily than females for a variety of reasons. There is a tendency for individuals who exhibit mental symptoms more typical of the other sex to be perceived as having a serious problem (Rosenfield, 1982). Thus, male anorexics may be judged as more seriously ill than females with similar symptoms. Issues of individuation and separation may operate as well. Assigning an adolescent to inpatient hospital treatment requires an ability of the parents to relinquish control and accept separation. Socialization in general encourages such separation among male children to a greater degree than among female children. A final possibility for hospitalization sex ratios that differ from those in the general population may involve the tractability or submissiveness of boys and girls. Parents may admit anorexic boys for hospital treatment because they feel they cannot exert sufficient influence to control their eating behavior. Girls, on the other hand, may be perceived as more responsive to influence attempts and thus remain under parental care for a longer period of time.

Sociocultural Features

Eating disorders, both anorexia and bulimia, appear to be phenomena of the middle and upper classes; and parents are typically characterized by professional and managerial occupational status (Garfinkel, Moldofsky, &

Garner, 1980; Yager, 1982; Garner et al., 1983). Estimates are that 75% to 85% of all cases occur in these socioeconomic classes (Bruch, 1973; Crisp et al., 1980). Consistent with these estimates, observed cases of anorexia are more likely to be located among young girls attending private, rather than public, schools (Crisp et al., 1976). However, recent reviews speculate about whether or not eating disorders may become more prevalent among working and other disadvantaged classes (Garner et al., 1983).

Family constellations have been found to hold varying degrees of association with eating disorders. Parents tend to be somewhat older than average; often the patient was born when parents were in their early 30s (Halmi, 1974), as illustrated in Figure 7.3. Other features of family constellation are quite varied, and conflicting results have been reported in terms of presence and number of siblings and birth order of the patient (Garfinkel & Garner, 1982). However, in one study of 102 anorexic patients, nearly 40% were either only or firstborn children (Crisp et al., 1980). It has been reported that anorexic families may be female dominated, that is, a preponderance of female siblings (Bruch, 1977, 1978); however, this observation has not been consistently replicated. General family stability in time and place has often been breached or threatened. A noticeable percentage (30%–40%) of anorexics have a family history

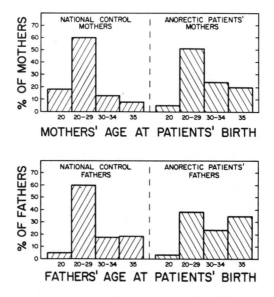

FIGURE 7.3   Parent age at birth of anorexic child. Source: K. A. Halmi (1974). Anorexia nervosa: Demographic and clinical features in 94 cases. *Psychosomatic Medicine, 36*(1), 18–26.

that involves departure of a parent or sibling, or actual or threatened parental separation (Kalucy, Crisp, & Harding, 1977).

Compared to observed rates in the general population, it appears that parents may be somewhat more likely to suffer from one or more illnesses or disorders having somatic expression, for example, migraine headaches. It is not uncommon for parents to have a weight disorder, with approximately 30% involving extremely low body weight and 10% involving obesity (Crisp et al., 1980; Schlesier-Stropp, 1984). When weight disorders among parents are noted, the preponderance of cases occur among members. Obesity is especially frequent among mothers of bulimics (Garfinkel, Moldofsky, & Garner, 1980). When parental obesity is part of the clinical picture among anorexics, they are likely to follow a bulimic pattern to maintain their low weight (i.e., binging, purging, vomiting, etc.) (Strober, 1983). Alcoholism in the parents appears with greater frequency than found in the general population and is most likely to be in the father (Rakoff, 1983).

Implications of these parental maladies are varied. The frequency of weight disorders among parents is compatible with a genetic hypothesis, possibly an inherited biochemical or metabolic imbalance. Neural feedback systems relating to satiety may also be implicated. However, the fact that these disorders occur among mothers more than fathers also suggests sociocultural causes. These possibilities will be discussed more fully later.

MEDICAL CONSEQUENCES

Hospitalization

The history and course of anorexia is likely to be quite long, often 4 to 6 years. Under such circumstances, a wide range of physiological consequences may become manifest. The seriousness of these conditions is highlighted by the number of individuals hospitalized for conditions related to anorexia and the overall time and money expended in care. Approximately 9,000 patients are hospitalized annually for treatment of anorexia and related conditions, the average length of hospitalization is 19 days. The average cost of care for each patient, exclusive of physician fees, is over $4,000; and the national total expenditure ranges upward from 38 million dollars.

Hospitalization is usually initiated in order to effect treatment of acutely dangerous weight loss; in some cases this may be up to 40% of standard body weight. Treatment may involve forced feeding by nasogastric tube or hyperalimentation by vein (Maloney & Farrell, 1980). Additional goals of hospitalization may be to monitor more carefully food intake and generally to reduce calorie expenditure by enforced rest. The administration of psychotropic drugs is also facilitated by hospitalization where a nursing staff can insure regular medication. Additional goals include restoring normal nutrition and body weight and initiating psychotherapy.

Hospital departments to which these patients are admitted reflect medical correlates of eating disorders and theories about etiology. Approximately half of hospitalized patients are admitted to psychiatry departments (Halmi, 1974). Other departments most likely to admit patients with eating disorders are internal medicine and pediatrics.

Determining when to hospitalize a patient is to some extent a matter of subjective judgment. The psychodynamics of eating disorders make the decision to hospitalize particularly delicate. Many patients are psychologically enmeshed with one or both parents, who frequently engage in over-controlling behavior. Within this context, the physician may be subtly induced by the patient or her parents to assume the parental role of unilateral protection and control (Browning & Miller, 1968).

Length of hospital stay varies somewhat according to demographic variables. Average length of stay is equivalent for males and females but varies substantially as a function of geographic region and patient age. For example, the average length of stay in the West and Northeast ranges between 7 and 9 days. However, the average length of stay in north central states is 23 days and is 27 days in southern states. These figures represent dramatic differences and are presented in Figure 7.4. (Geographic differences in average length of stay appears to be independent of the rate of hospitalized cases within a region.) Length of hospitalization

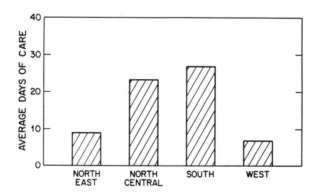

FIGURE 7.4 Average days of hospital care for anorexia as a function of geographic region. Source: NCHS (1982), Detailed Diagnosis and Surgical Procedures for Patients Discharged from Short-Stay Hospitals. DHHS (PHS) 82-1274-1, Washington, D.C.: U.S. Government Printing Office.

also varies by patient age, with patients in the age range of 45 to 64 receiving on the average only 2 days of care, whereas those ranging in age from 15 to 44 and those over 65 average approximately 22 days of care. Explanations for these variations in hospitalization are unclear, and it is somewhat of a mystery at this point as to why anorexics in the South require more than three times the length of care as those in the West or Northeast.

Physiology

Physiological features of eating disorders have been cast variously in causal roles and as natural consequences. Initially, explanations of obesity emphasized social and behavioral causes, but recent analyses have accorded greater significance to physiology, as evidenced by research on set-point theory, genetics, and fat cell production (Foch & McClearn, 1980; Keesey, 1980; Greenwood & Turkenkopf, 1983). Research on anorexia has followed a reverse course. Causal explanations for anorexia initially emphasized physiology and tended to ignore psychosocial features of the illness. Favored hypotheses proposed poor functioning of the anterior pituitary or thyroid. Treatments accordingly included stimulation of the thyroid and implantation of pituitary extract. Difficulty in thermal regulation, lassitude, amenorrhea, and other signs all suggest involvement of hypothalamic-pituitary function, as well as changes in thyroid and adrenal activity.

However, since no prospective studies of anorexia exist, it is equally likely that these conditions reflect consequences of starvation (Rockwell, Ellinwood, Dougherty, & Brodie, 1982). This conclusion is supported by two critical types of data. First, when weight loss is stabilized or when a return to near normal weight is accomplished, most measures indicate normal endocrine function; second, when artificially stimulated by releasing hormones, endocrine glands respond normally (Sherman & Halmi, 1977). Researchers now recognize that psychosocial conditions can significantly affect neuroendocrine function. Indeed, the psychological significance of virtually identical hormonal states may be quite variable, evoking pleasant anticipation or angry tension, as demonstrated in a classic social psychology experiment (Schachter & Singer, 1962).

Regardless of whether physiology is seen as a cause or an effect, there are substantial physiological correlates of anorexia, including changes in menstrual function, gonadotropic hormones, growth hormone, pituitary, thyroid and adrenal function, temperature regulation, and metabolism. There is also evidence that catecholamine metabolism is affected, especially norepinephrine and dopamine (Halmi, 1981-1982).

Physiological consequences of anorexia and bulimia also include conditions produced by dietary measures themselves, not simply weight loss. For example, enlarged salivary glands are often reported among anorexics and bulimics, a condition thought to be induced by habitual vomiting (Walsh, Croft, & Katz, 1981-1982). Other disease conditions that may be initiated or exacerbated by methods of achieving weight loss, include gallstones, kidney stones, gouty arthritis, elevated serum cholesterol, and several other conditions reviewed elsewhere (Polivy & Thomsen, in press).

Menstrual function is closely related to body weight and percent fat. Any condition that significantly affects these two variables will almost certainly have an impact on menstrual function. Menarche is largely determined by body weight and percent fat. The average weight for girls at menarche is around 104 pounds (47 kg.) and is thought to be relatively invariant (Frisch & Revelle, 1971). Percent body fat ranges between 16% and 19% during adolescent growth spurts but increases to around 24% at menarche (Frisch, 1977). A developmental staging of growth spurts, menarche, and stable reproductive cyclicity based on the work of Frisch (1975) is presented in Figure 7.5. Physiological and endocrine mechanisms for these interactions are still largely unknown.

Amenorrhea is so common that it constitutes one of the primary diagnostic indicators for anorexia and is found in approximately 85% of diag-

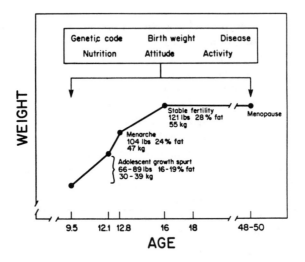

FIGURE 7.5 Relationship of age and weight to reproductive function. Source: R. E. Frisch (1975). Demographic implications of the biological determinants of female fecundity. *Social Biology, 22,* 17–22.

nosed cases (Suematsu et al., 1985). Loss of menstruation is thought to have a biologically adaptive function in that protein and iron losses are minimized. Additionally, it is highly improbable that a pregnancy could result under these conditions, thus preserving other nutritional resources for maintenance of the starving body.

Causes of amenorrhea have been attributed to psychological stress, nutritional disturbance, and severe weight loss. The impact of anorexia on menstruation cannot be directly assessed in some cases because onset of anorexia sufficiently precedes menarche to delay or prevent it altogether (Russell, 1983). However, the complexity of this syndrome is underlined by the fact that in some cases (7%–24%), amenorrhea is reported before any substantial weight loss has occurred (Fries, 1977; Garfinkel & Garner, 1982). Amenorrhea among concentration camp prisoners has been cited as evidence for the weight loss hypothesis. However, the same database of concentration camp prisoners provides contradictory evidence. For example, sometimes amenorrhea occurred during the first month of imprisonment, before substantial weight loss, and in some cases, menstrual function returned before release (Bemis, 1978).

Exactly how body fat and weight influence menstrual function is not known. However, several possible pathways or mechanisms have been suggested (Frisch, 1983). Low body weight may retard the conversion of androgens to estrogen. Low body fat may affect the pathway of estrogen metabolism in terms of most and least potent forms. Body fat may also affect the rate of blood flow to organs critical for reproduction and hormone metabolism. A number of other pathways and concomitant effects are possible as well.

Follow-up of anorexic patients indicates that prolonged starvation may have a lasting impact on menstrual function. A return to standard weight produces regular menstrual cycles in most cases; however, a substantial percentage of women report a continuation of amenorrhea or menstrual irregularity (Morgan & Russell, 1975; Pertschuk, 1977; Crisp, 1965). A 1 year follow-up of 40 anorexic women revealed that 15 had restored menstrual function, but 25 continued amenorrheic (Halmi & Falk, 1983). The primary distinguishing characteristic of those who were menstruating was a general increased participation in sports and other activities, and amenorrheic subjects continued to indicate a fear of becoming fat, emotional lability, fatigue, and social avoidance.

Amenorrhea is not always indicative of anorexia, and a variety of conditions may precipitate loss of menstruation. Strenuous dieting, if only for cosmetic reasons, can result in amenorrhea. A related phenomenon is amenorrhea after withdrawal of oral contraceptives. These latter cases were initially thought to be due to some pervasive change worked on the host endocrine system, with long-term implications for normal function.

However, on investigation of individual cases, amenorrhea appears to be explained by severe dieting and weight loss (often 20 or more pounds) rather than the endocrinological effects of contraceptive withdrawal (Fries, 1977; Fries & Nillius, 1973). Additionally, intense athletic training can delay menarche. For example, one study found that girls who began training at an early age for competitive swimming, running, and other sports reached menarche at approximately 15 years instead of the general population average of 13 (Frisch, 1983).

Amenorrhea has also been reported among bulimic patients, and it has been suggested that any dietary irregularity or abnormal eating habits may disrupt menstruation (Fairburn & Cooper, 1982). Thus, bulimics may also be subject to amenorrhea or irregular menstrual cycles. For example, Crisp (1981-1982) reported disruption of menstrual function brought on by strenuous dieting in an obese woman who weighed 250 pounds.

In conjunction with changes in menstrual function, there are also changes in *gonadotropic hormones*. Luteinizing hormone (LH) is typically low (Nillius, 1983; Golden & Sacker, 1984; Suematsu et al., 1985). Follicle stimulating hormone (FSH) may be normal (Nillius, 1983) or depressed (Drossman, 1983) and shows high variability across anorexic and bulimic dietary strategies (Wakeling & DeSouza, 1983). Lowered LH levels appear to be due to low levels of LH releasing hormone normally produced by the hypothalamus (Nillius, 1983). Anorexic females also differ from normal controls in the circadian rhythms of LH production. Normal females exhibit periodic bursts (in 90-minute cycles during the follicular phase and less often during the luteal phase) of luteinizing hormones throughout a 24-hour period, but anorexics maintain a consistently low level of LH (Drossman, 1983; Gold, Pottash, Martin, Extein, & Howard, 1981-1982). Similar disruption of gonadotropic hormones are observed among male anorexics, with lowered libido, impotence, low urine testosterone levels, decreased sperm motility, and decreased sperm longevity being common (Brown, 1983; Frisch, 1983). These conditions are alleviated with a return to normal body weight.

Other changes are found throughout the *endocrine system*. Growth hormone (GH) is typically elevated, as is plasma cortisol (Frankel & Jenkens, 1975; Vigersky & Loriaux, 1977b; Boyar, Hellman, & Roffwarg, 1977). Higher levels of GH are also found in conditions associated with starvation, malnutrition, and similar diseases. Elevation of plasma cortisol may reflect a stress reaction mediated by the adrenal glands and is also characteristic of depression. Elevated cortisol and associated stress may indirectly affect the production of gonadotropins and thus play a role in menstrual function as well. Elevated cortisol is probably due to increased adrenal activity and also to a depressed rate at which cortisol is cleared from the system (Boyar et al., 1977; Walsh, 1982). The entire body system may be characterized by a general hypothyroidism (Brown, 1983). Finally, the pervasive disturbance of endocrine function may precipitate premorbid diabetic conditions (Vigersky & Loriaux, 1977b).

Substantial changes also occur in the *pulmonary* and *cardiac systems*. Vital capacity is poor, as reflected in lowered oxygen intake. Additionally, cardiac chamber dimensions are reduced, and both systolic blood pressure and heart rate show subnormal responses to exhaustive exercise (Gottdiener, Gross, Henry, Borer, & Ebert, 1978). In fact, most anorexics show some cardiac abnormalities: hypotension, blood pressure less than 90/60 mmHg, (Suematsu et al., 1985; Brotman, Rigotti, & Herzog, 1985) and bradycardia, a resting pulse of less than 60 beats per minute, (Brotman & Stern, 1983). Myocardial degeneration and heart failure due to cardiac arrhythmias are the most common conditions precipitating death among anorexic patients. While there is often improvement or reversal of cardiac abnormalities following weight gain, congestive heart failure is possible when the weakened heart is unable to deal with increased extracellular fluid load brought about by refeeding (Brotman et al., 1985).

Hypothermia, the sensation of continual cold, is partly a product of loss of body fat. In spite of a low resting metabolic rate, patients frequently appear to be hyperactive or restlessly agitated (Golden & Sacker, 1984). Additional physical conditions that accompany starvation are lanugo (a fine, downy growth of body hair on the back), constipation, dry skin, and breast atrophy.

Osteoporosis has also been reported in anorexic patients. One study found that anorexics have significantly lower mean bone density than do controls (Rigotti, Nussbaum, Herzog, & Neer, 1984). In addition, two patients showed multiple nontraumatic vertebral compression fractures due to weakened bone structure. These skeletal abnormalities may be due to the increased cortisol levels associated with anorexia and may not be readily reversible. However, anorexic women who are highly active have a greater mean bone density than less active patients, suggesting that total bedrest may not be the best treatment for anorexia.

Vomiting, laxative abuse, or starvation can all cause acid-base and electrolyte disturbances (Warren & Steinberg, 1979). These disturbances may lead to muscle weakness, arrhythmia, and a number of other serious clinical complications, which may increase the risk of sudden death. Gastric dilation is a rare complication of eating disorders caused by a sudden increase in food intake. If not treated promptly, it can lead to stomach rupture, which has an 80% mortality rate (Brook, 1977).

Medical consequences among bulimics may also be serious. Vomiting and purging lead to loss of body fluids and potential electrolyte imbalances (Fairburn, 1980; Herzog, 1982). These changes have precipitated urinary infections and renal failure in a few cases (Russell, 1979). Chronic vomiting can also cause sore throat, abdominal pain, and tears and rupture of the esophagus (Brotman et al., 1985). Laxative abuse may lead to chronic dehydration, laxative dependency, and rectal bleeding (Brotman et al., 1985). Additionally, deterioration of dental enamel induced by stomach acids can become a serious problem (Herzog, 1982). Tooth structure may be chemically eroded, and there may be increased dental sensitivity due to enamel loss (Peterson & Barkmeier, 1983).

Mortality

Unfortunately, some individuals die from complications of anorexia. This fact was brought to the attention of a shocked public by the death of Karen Carpenter, a successful composer and performer of contemporary music, from cardiac arrest induced by anorexia. Studies indicate that mortality ranges from 0 to 20% (Hsu, 1980; Golden & Sacker, 1984; Suematsu, Kuboki, & Ito, 1985). Most studies report death rates below 5% (Hsu, 1980). Earlier recognition and treatment may contribute to a lower mortality rate. Death rates are somewhat confounded by the length of follow-up, with long-term studies tending to report more deaths (Bemis, 1978). For example a six-year follow-up indicated deaths from anorexia to be 9.6%, but a 15-year follow-up on the same patient population revealed a 12.8% mortality (Theander, 1983).

Unexpected sudden deaths are most likely to occur when body weight drops below 30% to 40% of standard. Death may be precipitated by acute electrolyte imbalances that affect cardiac function. However, postmortem examinations reveal that severely emaciated patients also have a wasted heart muscle (Drossman, 1983). Death may also be caused by infection and generally low immune system resistance. Suicide is not unknown among these groups; the desperation associated with extreme fear of weight gain and struggles for control may become intolerable to some (Golden & Sacker, 1984). The long-term follow-up study (Theander, 1983) previously mentioned found that in addition to deaths due to physical complications, there was a 4.3% suicide rate.

It is not always possible to determine the events most likely to precipitate death because published records often fail to detail this information. For example, one long-term study provided specific descriptions from several patient records but mentioned the death of two patients almost as a passing remark. Whether or not these patients died of conditions brought on by physical consequences of starvation, treatment interventions, suicide, or unrelated causes is not recorded.

COGNITIVE/AFFECTIVE CORRELATES

Factor analytic studies indicate that anxiety, depression, somaticism, obsession, and hysteria are major correlates of anorexia (Crisp & Bhat, 1982; Yudkovitz, 1983). However, they are typically well hidden behind a facade of compliance, tractability, and adherence to social norms. Although these attitudes, beliefs, and inner experiences form a characteristic description of patients with eating disorders, they are not limited to clinical cases. The well-adjusted compliant and orderly behavior characteristic of anorexic females is not unlike behaviors generally inculcated among all females. One may suppose, therefore, that in some ways the experiences of normal and anorexic females differ only in a matter of degree.

Locus of Control

There is general agreement that individuals with eating disorders tend to have an external locus of control. This may be especially true for some anorexics. The outward picture presented by anorexic girls is so well adjusted that parents, teachers, and peers often find it difficult to believe anything is wrong. However, the compliant, eager-to-please attitude is based on serious difficulties in autonomous functioning (Garfinkel & Garner, 1983). This pattern is termed the "perfect childhood" by Hilde Bruch (1978) and is characterized by submissiveness and lack of self-assertion. There is a strong tendency to avoid conflict of any type (Crisp & Bhat, 1982).

Much of the syndrome appears to involve a self-esteem based on adherence to social ideals and the approval of others as opposed to a sense of inherent worth. The balance between self-regard on the one hand and social confirmation on the other is only tenuously maintained. There appears to be a pattern whereby the patient experiences a strong need to do what others expect her to do, to gain the approval of others, and to conform. In accordance with this other-directedness, few anorexics seek treatment, and most hospitalizations occur because of an influential other (Halmi, et al., 1977).

Reliance on others for direction and approval appears to be so pervasive as to produce a general lack of responsiveness to inner needs or even physical sensations indicative of hunger, satiety, low blood sugar, gastric motility, etc. (Bruch, 1973, 1985; Casper et al., 1980; Garfinkel & Garner, 1983; Polivy, Herman, & Garner, in press). Similar features of externality also have been observed among obese individuals; for example, reliance on time of day, or visual signals to cue eating behavior (Stunkard & Koch, 1964; Rodin, 1976; Rodin & Slochower, 1976; Herman, Olmsted, & Polivy, 1983).

The impact of externality on weight fluctuations has also been extended to normal-weight individuals in a study of girls attending a summer camp with abundant food supply. Girls of normal weight but having an external orientation were found to gain more weight relative to internally oriented girls (Rodin & Slochower, 1976). Misperception of internal sensations regarding hunger and satiety have been attributed to obese individuals as well (Schachter & Gross, 1968).

Since girls, more than boys, are carefully instructed with respect to social protocol, obligation, and appearance, this external locus of control is not surprising. One begins to wonder about the extent to which these accounts reflect qualitatively unique diagnostic categories or simply one extreme consequence of socialization experienced by most females. Unfortunately, the externality cultivated as part of a feminine ideal appears to have many vicissitudes, not infrequently resulting in depression, drug dependence, alcoholism, and eating disorders.

Obsessive-Compulsive Patterns

Comparisons of normals and anorexics on various paper and pencil measures indicate that anorexics have relatively higher need for order, are more conscientious, sticklers for precision, and resistant to change (Pillay & Crisp, 1977). Anorexics are characterized in general by obsessive-compulsive traits combined with anxiety and shyness (Halmi, 1974; Bemis, 1978). Additional symptoms involve distortion, somatization, anxiety, introversion, and depression (Strober, 1981). When parents and anorexics are questioned regarding the most troubling symptoms, parents indicate obsessive-compulsive behaviors as most problematic, but the anorexic patients themselves focus on depression and sleep disturbance as most troubling (Halmi et al., 1977).

Intrusive ideas generally have to do with food and body image (Bruch, 1973; Orbach, 1978) and continue even when patients reach normal weight ranges (Crisp, 1981-1982). Efforts to banish thoughts of food often involve compulsive and almost frantic diversions. Preoccupation with fitness and cleanliness is one area where obsessive compulsive patterns are frequently exhibited, as is also true for excessive exercise and work compulsions (Crisp et al., 1980). Bulimics report that their minds are constantly occupied with thoughts of food, eating, and vomiting, and a fear of losing control over eating (i.e., that once they begin to eat they cannot stop) (Fairburn, 1980; Herzog, 1982). Among anorexics, fear of fatness appears to be particularly intransigent, and follow-up at several years posttherapy often reveals these belief systems to remain virtually intact (Crisp et al., 1980).

Body Image

Several forms of body image disturbance are also common among anorexics, including (1) overestimation of body size, (2) disgust for body parts, and (3) special pride in an emaciated body shape. Bulimics and anorexics share a negative body image (Garner & Garfinkel, 1981-82; Johnson, Lewis, Love, Stuckey, & Lewis, 1983). However, anorexics appear to have the greater distortion. They do not see their emaciated bodies as abnormal but rather as larger and fatter than they really are; furthermore, anorexics vigorously protect this delusion. An illustrative case is that of a young inpatient who described another patient as sickly and emaciated, only to find that the emaciated patient was in fact 25 pounds heavier than herself (Crisp, 1981-1982). When asked to estimate the size dimensions of various parts of the body (waist, thighs, etc.) some patients overestimate their actual body dimensions by as much as 65% (Crisp & Kalucy, 1974).

Another distortion is a tendency to be extremely critical of one's body and to view it with general disgust and loathing for body parts. A third form of body image disturbance involves great pride in thinness as evidence of superior will power and achievement in self-control. The anorexic body shape gives evidence of resistance to self-indulgence of all types and is thus viewed as a badge of morality. Denial (objectively of food and metaphorically of self) makes the anorexic feel good, moral, and in control (Boskind-Lodahl, 1976). Patients report feeling enormous, feeling fat, and feeling that most people see them as fat. A negative self-image and sense of repulsion characterizes patient self-descriptions. Weight loss and maintaining subnormal weight are ways to gain relief from anxieties surrounding self, food, identity and control. The self is taken to be unworthy and impoverished; adherence to extreme dietary regimes and other obsessive-compulsive patterns are in some ways forms of self-punishment and means of redemption or compensation for inadequacies of the self.

A variety of techniques has been applied in measurement of body image, including questionnaires, clinical interviews, projective human figure drawings, and various estimates of objective body size. A figure marking technique requires patients to stand before a large paper screen as if in front of a full length mirror; patients are then instructed to mark the paper with a pencil indicating those points corresponding to the outline of their body. Other techniques allow for size judgments based on photographs. These methods appear to have reasonable reliability and to have cross-correlations indicative of convergent validity (Crisp, 1981-1982). In fact, anorexic patients may show more consistency in estimates of their distorted body size than normals who, while more accurate, are also somewhat less consistent (Garfinkel, Moldofsky, Garner, Stancer, & Coscina, 1978).

It has been proposed that body image distortion is related to general perceptual insensitivity with regard to body sensations (Bruch, 1973, 1978). Origins of this insensitivity are thought to involve responses of the mother to infant cues regarding hunger and satiety. In a strict behaviorism, it is only by interacting with others that we learn to interpret our internal body sensations. Thus, when the infant has physiological sensations of low blood sugar, it does not have the formal thought, "I am hungry." Instead, the infant cries, the mother responds with food, which raises blood sugar, body temperature, and internal pressure in the gut. It is this entire sequence of behaviors and internal sensations that comes to be associated with hunger and what to do about it. However, among individuals with eating disorders, it is commonly reported by retrospective recall that mothers ignored infant signs of hunger and satiety, keeping rather to rigid feeding schedules and fixed quantities of food. The fact that body image is distorted is simply another manifestation of an insensitivity to all organic messages.

There are several implications of body image for therapy and ultimate outcome. Bruch (1973) considers adjustment of body image to be a precondition to recovery. Often as anorexic patients gain weight, perceptions of body size become even more distorted. Those patients who most strenuously resist changing their body image are also most likely to revert to starvation or purging as a means of controlling their weight after discharge from inpatient treatment (Garfinkel, Moldofsky, & Garner, 1977). In spite of the importance of body image in maintaining eating disordered behavior, therapists generally do not focus on direct alteration of body image as a therapeutic technique but rather address personal and interpersonal dynamics or modification of eating behaviors. Efforts directed at altering distorted body image, for example, by having the patient view her body in a full length mirror, are seldom effective (Garfinkel et al., 1978).

SUMMARY

Anorexia nervosa and bulimia are part of a continuum of eating disorders, which occur mainly in young women and which partly reflect the experience of all women. Development of these disorders is typically prolonged and involves a wide range of signs and symptoms, including cognitive, affective, physical, and behavioral indicators. A critical point is that these experiences are not unique to women with a clinical diagnosis but rather represent common aspects of female gender in American society. Therefore, eating disorders should not be viewed as interesting but exotic phenomena characteristic of a few neurotic females. Eating disorders represent more than personal events that operate entirely within the dynamics of a self framework; they are very much an aspect of social frameworks as well.

Eating Disorders: Etiology and Treatment

8

This chapter was written with Bonnie Bailey Bowers

Dieting is almost a precondition for female gender in American society. It goes along with the sense of femininity as *being* rather than *acting*. Physical attractiveness determines social standing to a much larger extent for women than men; it shapes how women and men interact and even how women relate to themselves. The message is clear: A woman's body is not acceptable unless it fits a certain ideal; it must be deodorized, shaved, cantilevered, and, above all, slim. A recent survey of female students at a high school revealed that half judged themselves to be somewhat or very overweight, although they acknowledged that their parents and peers would see them as average or below normal weight (Johnson et al., 1983). Further, 69% of these females had engaged in dieting behavior; over half had undertaken their first diet before age 15, and 14% identified themselves as chronic dieters.

These figures reiterate the position expressed in chapter 7, that elements of eating disorders are experienced by most females in American society. Thus, the phenomenon is not simply an exotic clinical diagnosis but reflects broader principles of gender and self-identity worked out against a social backdrop. It is more than the fact that our cultural ideal is for women to be slim. There is an unexamined assumption that it is perfectly normal and appropriate to dictate the body size, shape, and proportions of women in a way that would never be applied to men. The presumed right to impose basically frivolous and trivial expectations on women is indicative of the low status of women in general. The fact that some females get into serious health problems in the process of adhering to these demands is a manifestation of the larger issue.

ETIOLOGY

There is no consensus on a single etiology of eating disorders. Garfinkel and Garner (1983) have concluded that eating disorders are multiply determined; however, the similarity of clinical symptoms has led some theorists to search incorrectly for a single cause. Causal roles have been attributed to neuroendocrine systems, cultural standards, psychodynamic principles, and family systems. These causal hypotheses are not incompatible; and at least one model has integrated biogenetic, psychogenic, social, and cultural factors (Schwartz, Thompson, & Johnson, 1983). Since neuroendocrine correlates have already been discussed, this section

158

will concentrate on cultural, intrapsychic, and interpersonal explanations. We continue here with the thesis that many of the precipitating conditions are operative for women in general and that understanding eating disorders also offers an understanding of female gender.

Culture

Cultural explanations of anorexia and bulimia have both strengths and weaknesses. The major weakness is that many members of the culture are exposed to the same messages, rewards, and pressures without developing an eating disorder. However, a socially idealized body image, economic gains through the propagation of slimness, and the social context of gender-appropriate behaviors all suggest cultural influences. Family influences, early life trauma, and peer influences all operate within a sociocultural context (Schwartz, Thompson, & Johnson, 1983).

Cultural ideals and changing standards in the area of body image are frequently cited as important causal factors in eating disorders (Garner et al., 1983; Polivy & Thomsen, in press). For example, body measurements of Miss America contestants and *Playboy* centerfolds have shown a steady decrease in recent years of overall weight, as well as bust and hip size (Garner, Garfinkel, Schwartz, & Thompson, 1980). Unfortunately, although the ideal body type has become thinner, actual weights of women in the general population have increased, probably due to improved nutrition (Garner et al., 1980). Thus, women are faced with an increasing contrast between their actual body size and the size endorsed by cultural standards.

Clothing fashion probably plays a significant role in establishing idealized body image for women. Styles are often hyped for their purported ability to make women appear closer to the cultural ideal. For example, padded shoulders ostensibly lend height and, by contrast, make the waist appear small. In fact, one could argue that American society has yet to give up the body image captured by the corset. Idealized standards for body shape indicate that waists should be at least 10 inches smaller than hip measurements. Dimensions of mass produced clothes reflect the expectation that waists will be diminuitive. Underweight fashion models emphasize this cultural ideal. The marketing of clothes for large women is limited to "plus size" departments or specialty stores for "stout" women, which emphasize their deviance from the ideal.

There is also an economic component to thinness. The marketing of diets and diet books is big business in the United States, as evidenced by the number of diets with national name recognition. Cambridge, Scarsdale, Beverly Hills, Atkins, Pritikin, and Stillman are only a few. Every major women's magazine routinely carries information on dieting and weight loss. The health spa is another feature of this economic substrate, as is the recent proliferation of celebrity exercise guides. In fact, the desire to look toned, fit, and trim supports a rather large number of businesses. Thus, economic entities have a vested interest in the phenomenon.

The differential distribution of anorexia and bulimia by social class is further evidence of cultural influence. Thinness may serve as a social class marker, and a desire for upward mobility may induce women of lower social classes to emulate this pattern (Polivy & Thomsen, in press). Beautiful people are young, svelte, and rich, a thought echoed by the colloquialism, "You can never be too thin or too rich."

Additionally, cultural analyses seem especially relevant to sex differences in the incidence of eating disorders. In particular, differential access to power and influence strategies among women and men may be pertinent. Women are told they must be agreeable and socially responsive. Good manners, while useful to boys, are absolutely essential for the social progress of girls. Women are encouraged to adopt indirect influence methods and indirect, passive forms of self-expression. Competitive assertion of self is not encouraged. In contrast, it is acceptable to make personal statements by hairstyle and fashion.

To a certain extent, the oral incorporative elements of eating make food a passive form of expression compatible with cultural guidelines for femininity. Thus, one could say that both normative and nonnormative behaviors are shaped by culture. Ironically, for some women, attempts to express independence and liberation from this passive mold may underlie both strenuous dieting toward unisex body shape (Bennett & Gurin, 1982) and obesity (Orbach, 1978). In the latter case, obesity is a means of rejecting the cultural role of women as sexy objects, who must please others (Orbach, 1978). Movement toward either body shape may be a symbolic (passive) attempt to reject culturally defined roles for women. It has been hypothesized that these types of expressions are most likely in societies where womens' roles are rigid, stressful, and have conflicting demands (Selvini-Palazzoli, 1978).

Psychoanalytic Principles

Psychoanalytic approaches generally fall into three categories: those emphasizing drive-conflict, object relations, or the self. *Drive-conflict* approaches characterize traditional Freudian analysis where symptoms emerge because of conflict between the id, ego, and superego. Conflict about and repression of sexual impulse was conceptualized as underlying most symptoms. Early analysis of eating disorders among women formulated an ambivalence about sexuality, simultaneous desire for and fear of oral impregnation, or oral sadistic fantasies. The drive-conflict formulation has little support among current professionals in the field. Self theory and object relations are generally accepted by psychodynamic theorists and are to some extent complementary.

Self theory, developed initially by Kohut (1971, 1977), gives emphasis to the barren quality of the self experience among anorexics (Goodsitt, 1985). Lack of a stable self-concept and secure self-regard is thought to predispose adolescents to eating disorders (Casper, 1983). Anorexics appear to lack integration of self and body, ignoring nutritional needs and remaining indifferent to dangerous changes in physical functioning. They are out of touch with their own experience. When asked about their feelings, patients redirect the question to their parents or respond in a way that indicates they do not own their feelings. In the normal course of development, individuals move from reliance on others to an internalized ability to nurture and comfort the self. When this is interrupted or incomplete, the individual is likely to feel controlled by and dependent on others (Goodsitt, 1985). Such responses appear to characterize the anorexic. The developmental features of this fragmented sef experience can be further understood in the context of object relations.

An *object relations* analysis of eating disorders begins with issues of individuation, separation, and relational identity. Women's experiences are characterized by empathic connection with others and the care and nurturing of relationships, establishing a relational identity. The male experience is characterized by acquisition of a sense of self through separation and agentic actions, establishing contrast between self and other. The male direction of development toward separation reduces risk of an eating disorder, whereas the female direction toward empathic and relational identity increases risk.

Whether this pattern is an invariant feature of human biology, as suggested in classic psychoanalytic theory, or a product of the social reproduction of mothering, as argued by feminists, is a point of debate (Dinnerstein, 1976; Chodorow, 1978). Regardless of whether one takes the classic psychoanalytic or feminist position, the theme remains essentially the same. Boys develop through individuation and separation; girls maintain connection and empathic identity. Women do the socioemotional work of society, and men are assumed to lack the appropriate disposition for developing such skills. (See chapter 1 for a review.)

Implications for the development of eating disorders are multiple and sometimes seem contradictory. Major motivations may be, on the one hand, a retreat to dependency and, on the other, a last ditch effort to regain control. When these motivations are played out within the context of food and physical appearance, any one of several eating disorders may emerge. Thus, the same dynamic may underlie obesity, anorexia, or bulimia. To further complicate the picture, the same diagnostic condition may be precipitated by apparently different dynamics, that is, retreat to dependency or resistance to control. For example, obesity may emerge because of unfulfilled desires for nurturance and also as resistance to control. The complexity of this formulation is illustrated in Figure 8.1.

Anorexia can be approached within the same dual motivational system. Some theorists argue that the basic issue is control and ownership of the body, and most events can best be understood as a struggle for identity, competence, and effectiveness (Bruch, 1973, 1978). The young girl finds much of her life directed and managed by others or shaped by obligations to please others. At some pubescent phase, her very body is drawn into the net of socially constructed identity. It must meet standards of sensuality, without really laying claim to sensual experiences. Breasts must flower, hips must blossom, waists must be willowy. (One would think we were a nation of avid horticulturalists.) Her body is hers but not hers.

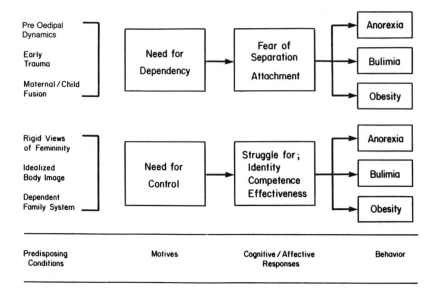

FIGURE 8.1　Variations in object relations theory based on traditional and feminist approaches are illustrated respectively in the top and bottom sequences. Traditional approaches emphasize attachment and dependency needs, while feminist approaches emphasize separation struggles in social context. Both suggest that eating disorders may share a common motivational basis.

Stringent dieting and even starvation may become a way of simply reclaiming one's body. Seen in this light, anorexia (and obesity as well) may be a last struggle to retain a sense of self. However, extreme solutions such as these can only come about because there has already been an erosion of identity.

According to Boskind-Lodahl (1976) the process of identity erosion is initiated by suffocating parental demands for conformity. This produces a child who defines herself in terms of perceived reactions of others. When such girls enter adolescence they typically have low self-esteem and are poorly equipped to socialize with men. When they focus on physical appearance as the key to their problems, they soon engage in dieting, which nevertheless leaves them with the same sense of insecurity. Stringent dieting is followed by depression, binging, anorexia, or obesity, while the basic sense of inadequacy increases and fuels further cycles of dieting. The socialization process may be so pervasive as to leave girls with a sense that in fact they have no identity of their own. This lack of awareness of self may be so complete as to create an inability to recognize basic interoceptive signals such as hunger (Bruch, 1973).

Object relations from the classic psychoanalytic perspective suggests a different set of dynamics regarding anorexia, namely that it is a complaint against separation. This perspective emphasizes the child's fear of breaking away and the associated independence. In this scenario, pubescence and sexuality signal a separation and distancing from parents that is frightening to the girl (Crisp, 1977, 1981-1982, 1983b; Crisp et al., 1980). Starvation and weight loss are a means of concretely demonstrating her psychic childhood, attachment, and dependency. Refusing to eat is a way of capturing and manipulating attention. Periodically, at meal times, the girl becomes the complete focus of activity, while parents alternately entreat and menace. Even if interactions are adversarial, the theme of parental nurturance and care is played out. When anorexia is carried to extreme conditions, amenorrhea develops and further prolongs childhood and dependency. Signs of an adult body are obviated by starvation.

Object relations theory has a certain intuitive appeal mixed with just enough complexity to suggest that the theory captures some part of the real world, and it is conceptually very rich. But this very richness is a serious weakness. The same outcome, obesity for example, may be precipitated by quite different motives. Furthermore, the same motive, resistance to control for example, may give rise to quite different outcomes. Any sound theory needs to have some means of distinguishing when outcome A will emerge as opposed to outcome B. Additionally, since different etiologies imply different therapeutic redress, it would be nice if the theory gave some hint of operational definitions by which one could distinguish anorexia initiated as resistance to control and that resulting from excessive dependency and fear of individuation.

If eating disorders develop as a fear of separation, a number of additional questions must be posed. For example, why do socialization experiences of girls make them feel ineffectual in dealing with a competitive world? Why should love and affection shared with a mother make the world appear such a threatening and dangerous place? Further, why do girls feel that independent action on their part jeopardizes the affection and favorable regard of their parents? To what extent do parents promote dependency in girls, and is this fueled by parental insecurities? These questions arise because traditional psychoanalytic approaches tend to perpetuate the fundamental attribution bias. Individuals are seen as free agents who willfully and purposefully plan and execute eating behavior (obesity, bulimia, etc.) independently of their culture or the families with whom they live. This is especially true in judgmental explanations of obesity (Wooley & Wooley, 1979).

Family Systems

Family dynamics are obviously intertwined with these formulations. However, major confounds cloud all research and causal analyses of family dynamics (Bemis, 1978). First, analyses and studies are initiated after the onset of dysfunction. Information about early relationships are based on recall and subject to editing, distortion, and various other biases. What therapists and researchers observe may reflect adaptation to an illness in the family, rather than conditions which precipitated illness (Kalucy, Crisp, & Harding, 1977). Additionally, many patients are hospitalized because they are in medical crisis, and this also may shape family interactions.

Failure to distinguish between subtypes of syndromes represents another problem. Some authors have proposed that eating disorders that begin before puberty have a qualitatively different etiology than conditions that develop in adolescence or later; however, these subtypes may be inadvertently combined in clinical analysis. There may be multiple determinants of family dynamics and multiple family systems (Rakoff, 1983). Finally, few studies have included analyses of normal control families. Thus, it is difficult to know if observed interactions are unique to patient families.

Most analyses of family dynamics and eating disorders have focused on anorexia; family dynamics associated with bulimia have been discussed only recently (Yudkovitz, 1983; Pope & Hudson, 1984; Schlesier-Stropp, 1984). Initial formulations focused on mother-daughter relationships, describing mothers of anorexics as overly controlling individuals who could not tolerate their daughter's separation (Sours, 1969b). Subsequent formulations of family dynamics have argued that the family must be seen as a system with interactive roles involving all family members (Minuchin, 1974; Rosman, Minuchin, & Liebman, 1975; Minuchin, Rosman, & Baker, 1978; Garfinkel & Garner, 1982).

Perturbations in the family system may be managed by avoidance and denial or threats and entreaties, but the objective is always to return to the status quo. The critical dysfunction may not originate with the child but instead may be within the subsystem of spouse relationships (Kalucy et al., 1977; Crisp et al., 1980; Yager, 1982). Management of the eating disordered child may serve as a displacement activity for parents, and therefore illness becomes a stabilizing element in the family system. At some level, family members are aware of the precarious balance they maintain, and as therapy progresses, other symptoms of family dysfunction may emerge.

Participants in the psychosomatic family system are tightly meshed, and patients are frequently reported as being excessively close with one or both parents (Kalucy et al., 1977). Individuation may be resisted by all family members because it is perceived as a sign of disloyalty to the family (White, 1983). The desire to maintain a fragile status quo within the family, combined with fears of disloyalty, may partly explain why most anorexics are so disinterested in and often violently resist treatment (Halmi et al., 1977). Adolescence is seen, by both the girl and her parents, as dangerous, unacceptable change. Since parental control is cloaked as concern, it cannot be challenged overtly. Thus, the illness may begin as a somatic expression of a larger struggle for control (Bruch, 1977). These intricate patterns are symbolized in day-to-day activities, for example, bedroom doors are never closed, wanting privacy is taken as rejection of others, or there is hypervigilence of the girl's activities even when she is not at home.

Subgroups of family systems may exist, characterized primarily on the basis of conflict resolution strategies (Martin, 1983). Some families rely on the classic mechanisms of denial; that is, they refuse to acknowledge any conflict or anger. Other families deal with conflict by escalation. This is an interesting strategy because it means that even the most minute disagreement, resistance, or confrontation is treated as a major crisis. Thus, the cost of deviating even slightly from the procrustean standards of family obligation is made exceedingly high. A third strategy of maintaining the status quo is to make most communication events ambiguous regarding content and/or intended recipient. Thoughts and feelings may be expressed, only to be negated immediately. Thus, no clear preferences are expressed, no positions are delineated, and no one is held accountable for anything. This strategy was dramatically evidenced by one family that was videotaped while role playing conflict resolution; over 60% of the interaction was not coded because raters could not discern the intended recipient of remarks (Humphrey, 1983).

Another characteristic pattern observed by White (1983) is that anorexic families tend to maintain rigid belief systems about proper role behavior, especially for women. Women are expected to be sensitive, devoted, and self-sacrificing. Often one daughter is selected to specialize in this role, and she may be particularly vulnerable to anorexia. Deviations from this role are viewed as selfish and often associated with guilt. There is an insistence that the girl fulfill a feminine *role* rather than seek self-actualization (Boskind-Lodahl, 1976). The fact that so many of these girls feel they don't have an identity of their own may not be a delusion but rather an accurate assessment of female gender as it is traditionally defined. What they are resisting is the pressure to limit and mold themselves to the veil of femininity. Since families are a prime agent for gender socialization, resistance to stereotypic feminine patterns gets tied up with guilt and feelings of disloyalty. Subconsciously, girls often feel that to retain parental approval they must give up individuation.

THERAPY

Consistent with the complexity of eating disorders, a wide variety of therapies have been adopted, including psychodynamic, behavior, family, and pharmacologic interventions. No single therapy has emerged as the treatment of choice, and most patients are treated with a mixture of approaches (Vandereycken & Pierloot, 1983; Wooley & Wooley, 1985; Lacey, 1985; Kalucy, Gilchrist, McFarlane, & McFarlane, 1985).

Medical management of eating disorders will not be discussed in detail. A variety of procedures may be employed at the time of initial hospitalization to control and manage symptoms. Treatments have included administration of thyroid extract and steroids, as well as surgery (prefrontal lobotomy for anorexia and gastric bypass for obesity). Additionally, psychotropic drugs are prescribed in many cases, primarily to relieve symptoms of depression and poor appetite; these are typically the tricylic drugs (e.g., amitriptyline) and monoamine oxidase inhibitors (e.g., phenelzine also known as Nardil) (Moore, 1977; Needleman & Waber, 1977; Vigersky & Loriaux, 1977a; Pope & Hudson, 1984).

Prognosis and Outcome

Several problems commonly encountered in therapy with anorexics, regardless of theoretical framework, result in poor prognosis, Anorexics frequently come to therapy with the firm belief that they do not have a problem. Rather, someone else, parents or a significant other, insists they receive treatment. Therefore, anorexics may be especially resistant to treatment. In many cases, anorexics feel a sense of pleasure, accomplishment, and control by starving themselves. Efforts to modify these behaviors may be seen as an attack on their last bastion of control. Bulimics also represent special problems because their behavior has been conducted secretly for several years. Thus, the behavior, thoughts, and feelings are well entrenched.

Evaluation of therapeutic techniques is no simple matter. Research designs are often flawed, and confounding variables abound. Case studies may offer considerable appreciation of the phenomenology of eating disorders, but other cases with less satisfactory outcomes or more ambiguous progress are seldom relayed to the professional/scientific community. Even when a consecutive series of cases is reported, a control group is seldom included. There is no way to ascertain how much spontaneous remission may have contributed to successful outcomes. Selectivity in outcome measures may also bias conclusions. For example, evaluation of behavior therapies and pharmacologic treatments can be conducted in relatively straight forward assessment of objective signs. However, the measures taken as indicative of successful treatment, for example, a return to normal weight, may not encompass the wide range of affective and cognitive features of an eating disorder. Furthermore, studies of all treatment methods frequently have a small sample size, making it difficult to generalize results (Bemis, 1978). For example, one therapeutic evaluation featured only two cases (Long & Cordle, 1982).

Other confounds arise from the fact that many hospitalized patients receive a variety of interventions, including psychotropic drugs and behavior management, as well as individual or group psychotherapy. Isolating the effectiveness of any one intervention becomes impossible. A final problem is the length of follow-up in assessing outcomes. Relapse is a common, nearly universal feature of eating disorders, and it is possible that some cases reported as successfully resolved at the end of treatment may not be so 2 or 3 months later. For example, one evaluation of a behavior modification program reported several patients with good or fair adjustment who were subsequently rehospitalized (Pertschuk, 1977).

Despite the difficulty of pursuing experimental procedures in field settings, several studies have reported favorable outcomes. Favorable results have been associated with a variety of therapeutic techniques, including cognitive-behavioral and group-experiential methods (Schlesier-Stropp, 1984). Behavior management procedures have been credited with substantial changes in calories consumed and progress in weight gain (Agras & Werne, 1977). Favorable results with psychoanalysis have been reported for obesity, and it is probably especially valuable in modifying distorted body image and controlling binge eating (Stunkard, 1976, 1980).

However, psychotherapy appears to be ineffective with patients who are below 15% to 20% of their standard body weight (Rockwell et al., 1982). Success rates for family therapy of over 80% have been reported in some clinical case studies (Rosman, Minuchin, Baker, & Liebman, 1977). At this point it is unclear whether or not long-term outcomes differ for family as opposed to individualized therapy, a question currently under investigation (Szmukler, 1983b).

These favorable results, however, are partly shaped by the choice of outcome measure. Selection of immediate or long-term outcome measures can alter estimates of success and final evaluation. Immediate outcome measures typically deal with weight gain and are initial goals of almost all therapy (Drossman, 1983). Most patients (41%-81%) do achieve a standard body weight, but other physical signs may remain problematic, with 13% to 50% continuing to be amenorrheic (Hsu, 1980).

Long-term outcomes involving behavior and psychiatric adjustment are less certain, and many patients (25%–50%) experience a return of the same symptoms, with perhaps one third being rehospitalized (Bemis, 1978; Crisp et al., 1980). A great many (63%-73%) continue to have eating difficulties, including bulimia, vomiting, laxative abuse, anxiety over eating, excessive concern for body shape, depression, and obsessive-compulsive patterns (Hsu, 1980). Although occupational functioning may be adequate, social adjustment is often tenuous.

A variety of factors have been identified as prognostic of outcomes; however, there is considerable difference of opinion regarding the exact role of these factors (Crisp, 1983a; Crisp, Kalucy, Lacey, & Harding, 1977; Garfinkel et al., 1977; Bemis, 1978; Halmi, Goldberg, Casper, Eckert, & Davis, 1979; Drossman, 1983; Schlesier-Stropp, 1984; Suematsu et al., 1985). Poor prognosis appears to be associated with long duration of illness, binging, purging, onset after age 19, prior hospitalizations, and social immaturity. Favorable prognosis appears to be associated with an onset before age 15, a determination to overcome the illness, satisfaction with work and marriage, and higher educational achievement.

Cognitive and Behavioral Therapies

Often initial weight stabilization and control of eating behaviors, (e.g., binging) is seen as prerequisite for other therapies (Mitchell et al., 1985). Therefore, behavior and food management programs are part of most treatment regimens involving hospitalization.

One of the foundation principles of behavioral approaches is that the problem eating behavior is learned and maintained by systems of reinforcement. Second, the same principles that operate to produce eating disordered behavior can be employed to change it, namely, selective positive reinforcement or operant conditioning. Therapists may rely on the rewarding properties of other activities to establish contingency-based eating behavior among anorexics. That is, access to other activities, such as, exercise, use of the phone, or receipt of mail, is made contingent on eating a certain amount of food each day or achieving a certain weight gain each day. If the goal is met, patients attain ward privileges, if not, they are confined to their rooms (Eckert, 1983).

Researchers within this framework specifically reject the notion that eating disorders are due to mental illness, that recovery necessitates years of treatment, or that recovery is contingent on personal insights about causation (White & Boskind-White, 1984; Wilson, 1984). Instead, the focus is on proximal causes and the assumption that anorexia and bulimia are the direct result of beliefs, attitudes, and assumptions about the meaning of body weight (Garner & Bemis, 1985). Patients are encouraged to develop new responses to old stimuli and to focus on the current stimulus field as opposed to past or anticipated future experiences.

Cognitive restructuring gives patients different ways of establishing goals and evaluating experiences (Loro, 1984). Principles of association are hypothesized to operate not only on behavioral acts but on thoughts as well. Conditions that call forth certain thoughts or feelings supportive of dysfunctional behavior are examined. Absolute approaches to behavior and self-judgments are discouraged. Patients with eating disorders do tend to think in dichotomous categories (all-or-none) and to view negative consequences as catastrophic. Perfectionistic demands and expectations are challenged, as is the exaggerated importance of a thin body. Therefore, part of the cognitive restructuring entails decatastrophizing and encouraging patients to evaluate problems and outcomes in gradations (Garner & Bemis, 1985). For example, words like "always," "never," and "forever" are discouraged because they tend to place the patient in an absolutist position where even a slight deviation leads to complete relapse (White & Boskind-White, 1984).

Behavior contracting and *role rehearsal* are often aspects of cognitive/behavior therapy. Behavior contracting allows the patient to participate actively in therapy by selecting goals and objectives of therapy. Role rehearsal provides guidelines for specific ways to meet goals, for example, what to do when feeling out of control. Self-management in normal settings is emphasized. Any cues that tend to elicit or trigger problem behavior, for example binging, are examined. Behavior, especially habitual dieting, is reviewed and patients are informed of some of the negative consequences of dieting. Research suggests that strenuous dieting or self-starvation may make binging and weight gain more probable (Orleans & Barnett, 1984; Polivy & Thomsen, in press). The roles of strenuous dieting and the belief that such diets are almost magically effective are explored. Maladaptive behaviors associated with dieting are outlined and misinformation about nutrition is corrected. Specific skills to deal with interpersonal problems are acquired through modeling, role playing, and assertiveness training (Coffman, 1984).

Fairburn (1983, 1985) describes a cognitive behavioral approach to bulimia that requires about 5 months of treatment and incorporates analysis of behavior, cognitions, and affect. His program is similar to other behavioral approaches, and initially requires only that the patient monitor her eating behavior. Those times of the day when the patient feels most in control are then selected for first attempts at modifying behavior. Self-monitoring is followed by detailed analysis of the stimulus field that triggers binge episodes. Patients are asked to identify conditions that made them feel stressed or anxious; negative thoughts associated with the stimulus field are also identified. Finally, problem solving strategies are developed for implementation during periods of stress or episodes of poor control.

One problem with management programs for anorexics aimed primarily at increased calorie intake and weight gain is the especially high rate of improvement expected, often as much as a half pound or full pound a day. Meeting the standard may require that the patient quadruple her typical daily intake, potentially leaving her with the feeling that the only alternative to starvation is virtual gluttony. Based on standard bioenergetics where one pound is equivalent to 3500 calories, an anorexic (assuming 75 lbs. or 34 kg. hospitalization weight) would have to eat approximately 2,500 calories per day to gain even a half pound (750 calories for maintenance plus 1750). This regimen represents a significant contrast to her anorexic pattern of eating perhaps only 500 or 600 calories a day. A somewhat parallel experience among individuals with a normal intake would be increasing a standard 2000 calorie intake to 6000 calories for days and weeks at a time.

Psychodynamic Therapies

Because distorted body image, fear of fatness, anxiety, and depression may persist long after behavior therapies have brought about a return to standard weight and normal eating patterns, many therapists advocate psychodynamic therapies. Dynamic therapies may include variations on psychoanalytic object relations, self, family or group therapy.

Individual psychotherapy typically focuses on intensive review of life experiences and the grasp of new insights regarding the significance of these events for current cognitions, affect, and behavior. This process is facilitated when emotional attachments previously experienced with significant others are replayed through transference to the therapist. If an object relations framework is adopted, the focus tends to be on the significance of events in the process of separation and individuation. A primary objective must be to assist the patient in discovery of her own abilities, resources, and feelings (Bruch, 1973). Often, psychotherapy proceeds without any special attention to the eating disorder itself, because it is seen as the result of more basic experiences and processes (Garfinkel & Garner, 1982).

Since many patients have a lack of trust in and fear of their affective and other internal states, one goal of therapy is to facilitate genuine expression of inner feelings (Bruch, 1978). When initially asked to convey their feelings, many patients respond with questions such as "How should I feel?" (Garfinkel & Garner, 1982). The therapist helps the patient explore the content of these experiences, working through resistance and defenses against insight, while periodically offering interpretations. However, interpretations must be offered with great caution. If the patient truly doesn't know how she feels, she may be inclined to simply rely on the therapist to tell her what she is really experiencing.

Family therapy also addresses issues of self, separation, and individuation but in the context of a family system. Family systems models suggest that the patient's illness in some way serves to maintain a balance of power and dependency in the family network. Efforts to ameliorate the illness may be subverted by the family or, if this fails, other members of the family may adopt symptoms. Further, a return to the family milieu following inpatient treatment may trigger a relapse. Bruch (1978) indicates that disengagement from the family is an essential part of the therapeutic process.

Individuals with eating disorders often belong to psychosomatic families characterized by rigidity, emotional enmeshment, overprotectiveness, and lack of conflict resolution (Rosman et al., 1977; Minuchin et al., 1978). Departure from family traditions and beliefs is judged to be disloyal, and various strategies may be invoked to elicit feelings of guilt and indebtedness among family members (White, 1983). Frequently focusing on the child's actions is a way of avoiding other conflicts—the child's dysfunction in some way adds stability to the family system (Lagos, 1981-1982). In some families the role of "problem child" is passed across generations (White, 1983). Furthermore, since the child does play an important stabilizing role in the family, there may be secondary gains to the child, which make it more difficult to give up the role.

Goals of family therapy are generally to change the role of the child as the pivot point of family stability, to redefine the eating problem as a relational problem, and to disengage the overprotectiveness and dependency of parent and child (Rosman et al., 1975). Initial stages of therapy typically center on information gathering about the history of the eating disorder, other members of the immediate family, and previous treatment experiences. A common technique of family therapies is to have a family meal, usually a lunch, or "picnic" at the therapist's office (Rosman et al., 1977; Dare, 1983). The authority of parents is often formally examined during sessions, and parents are encouraged to persist in finding a solution to the fact that their child is starving. In later therapy stages, rigid beliefs and overprotectiveness are challenged and alternative relational roles are explored.

All familial relationships are examined, including the parents' relationship, and occasionally marital therapy will also be initiated. In some cases, therapists work with the healthiest member of the family as a potential change agent, on the assumption that change in any part will affect the entire system. Intense methods of intervention are sometimes advocated because the psychosomatic family is typically very successful at avoiding conflict (Lagos, 1981-1982).

Family members may be asked to examine their interaction patterns by a *gossip technique* (White, 1983). One family member is asked to make observations about the interactions of two other family members. These observations are frequently denied or rejected and the tactics used to dissuade the therapist and family members of these conclusions can be instructive. Various types of *gatekeeper actions* may be observed whereby conflict between two members is damped by the intervention of a third family member. Other strategies of avoidance include qualification, ambiguity, and disguise. Family members often find it very difficult to say what they want in the first person singular (Lagos, 1981-1982).

Group therapy may be instituted when family therapy is not practical or desirable. Group therapy, with groups composed only of clinical patients, is conducted under the assumption that frank interchange among group members will energize change. However, such interchange can be anxiety producing and creates potential problems when dealing with anorexics who are already extremely anxious. The group atmosphere must be made especially supportive and safe in order to be effective (Hall, 1985). Potential group members must be selected with care. They must have stabilized weight, with resumption of more normal eating behavior, and must have passed the stage of denial of their need for help. Since anorexics have problems with intimacy and trust, they are often socially withdrawn and emotionally remote. Emotionally restricted patients are not good candidates for group therapy. Another persistent problem tends to be a high dropout rate. Group therapy also has the potential hazard that group members will reinforce each other's eating disorder. In the case of anorexia, this may be a competition to see who can lose the most weight.

Feminist Perspectives

Feminist perspectives on therapy have emerged partly in response to shortcomings of traditional therapies. (Chapter 9 provides a more extended review). First, traditional approaches tend to offer causal models of limited scope, often with an almost molecular focus. This is especially true of treatment approaches based on pharmacologic interventions, which tend to perpetuate mind/body dualism. Additionally, many causal models tend to perpetuate a dichotomy between self and social context. Therapy is directed only to self-understanding, as if self existed in pure form independent of culture, society, family, and so on. A third major problem is that most approaches maintain a traditional model of power: expert therapist helps wretched patient. The legitimacy of the woman's experience and resulting symptoms often tends to be ignored. The woman is not so much a source of information about her own experience as a set of conditions, which must be modified according to methods and timetables set by others. This type of power inequity may contribute further to an already shakey sense of self-esteem, feelings of helplessness, and dependency.[1]

Although particular techniques and theoretical positions show considerable variation among feminist therapists, there are some commonalities. A general goal is to facilitate feelings of agency and control. The validity and inherent self-worth of each individual is a principle characteristic of, if not unique to, feminist therapy. The general objective is to develop a sense of self-awareness, self-direction, and autonomy (Bruch, 1985). Another basic tenet of feminist approaches is that the therapist must accept the patient's beliefs and symptoms as genuine (Orbach, 1978; Garner & Bemis, 1985). The woman is viewed as an expert source of information about what she feels and what she hopes to accomplish in treatment (Orbach, 1985). Finally, the contextual nature of eating disorders is recognized. The experiences of these women are viewed as part of a socially constructed vision of femininity, attractiveness, efficacy, and power. That is, the signs and symptoms associated with eating disorders are not simply the product of poor psychic organization of an individual. Further, eating disorders are seen as reflecting a broad scope of issues pertinent not only to food and eating, but to social definitions of femininity in general.

---

[1]I am especially appreciative of the thoughtful comments on feminist therapy offered by Ellen McGrath.

Feminist perspectives focus on the surplus meaning society has attached to physical appearance and body weight. Physical appearance for women is not just a matter of physical health but has implications for competence, social acceptability, and self-worth. It is especially important because, given the restrictive nature of idealized femininity, it is one of the few areas of self-expression and achievement available to women. Physical appearance also has psychosocial importance because it is a way for women to acquire a certain amount of power, however transient. Attractive women are treated with deference and can hold the attention of others with relative ease. In some ways, this is reminiscent of other choices women must resolve; they can seek to develop an existentially independent sense of self, often paying in negative sanctions and social and interpersonal rejection, or accept the limits of acceptable femininity, with the associated social reassurance and a certain measure of power and status within the role. That is, if they do not struggle too much against their limited roles, society will arrange to let them be magical slaves.

Women's experience of the meaning of their bodies is further hampered by the fact that women are not given authority over their bodies. That which is particularly female in biological function (menstruation, pregnancy, birth) is deemed socially unacceptable, embarrassing, or potentially dangerous. To a large extent, reproductive and contraceptive choices are made by others who have real authority. Additionally, important aspects of female sexuality are feared and denied. The pursuit of physical competence, for example, in team sports and athletics, continues to be available in only limited fashion to women. Thus, although physical appearance holds special significance, it is surrounded by substantial restrictions.

Issues of control, authority, and power regarding physical appearance and weight to a large extent reflect similar issues for women in society in general. Mother-daughter relationships may often be the arena in which these issues become most salient, as suggested by self and object relations theorists (Sours, 1969a, 1980; Surrey, 1984b; Yudkovitz, 1984). Traditional definitions of female gender, jointly reproduced by society and family, contribute to diffrculties in developing an integrated sense of self.

Feminist perspectives on therapy have been pursued with a variety of treatment techniques. Some claim best success rates for extended one-on-one psychotherapy. Individual psychotherapy typically requires 2 to 4 years and is advocated by several feminist therapists. Psychoeducational methods are also advocated, where women are provided necessary facts about nutrition, exercise, metabolism, and physical health.

Other therapies adopted by feminist therapists include self-help and support groups, which differ somewhat from formal group therapy (Enright, Butterfield, & Berkowitz, 1985). Such groups offer a source of safe companionship, especially for bulimics who may feel extremely ashamed of their behavior. Additionally, groups may be constituted not for the patient but for family members or close friends. Most self-help groups rely on co-facilitators, which tends to promote a nonauthoritarian atmosphere. Facilitators may be either trained professionals or lay people. If they exist, fees tend to be minimal. Features considered to be essential for such groups include broad-spectrum goals, accessibility, and confidentiality (Enright et al., 1985). Broad spectrum goals are those that incorporate more than modification of eating behaviors and address personal sense of worth, dependency needs, and so on. Accessibility concerns the necessity of dealing with referrals, maintaining community contacts, and strategies for dealing with emergencies. As the general population becomes more aware of eating disorders and the possibility of self-help programs, it may well be that these groups will increase. Whether they are sufficient in themselves to resolve problems of eating disorders is questionable.

SUMMARY

Explanations of eating disorders encompass culture, the social construction of gender, intrapsychic dynamics, and family systems. Neurological and physiological features of these disorders are generally thought to be consequences rather than causes.

Because anorexia and bulimia typically have long periods of development, treatment is especially problematic. Progress is punctuated by relapse in almost all cases. No single therapy has emerged as the treatment of choice, and most hospitalized patients receive a combination of pharmacologic interventions, behavior management and individual and group therapy. Cognitive/behavioral approaches are often supplemented by family therapy or self-help support groups. Feminist approaches have emerged partially in response to limitations of traditional theory and therapy. These approaches represent a general framework of feminist values and philosophy and have been applied in a variety of treatment formats, including cognitive/behavioral and psychodynamic programs.

Issues in Therapy 9

Several approaches to therapy are examined in this chapter, including psychoanalytic based theory and therapy, as well as nontraditional approaches in consciousness raising and social networks. Psychoanalytic theory, with its emphasis on intrapsychic events, has generally proved unsatisfactory as a means of integrating self and social frameworks. Consciousness raising and social support networks have proved to be valuable alternatives for resolving some issues but have undergone major evolutionary changes.

GENERAL CRITICISMS OF THEORY AND THERAPY

No doubt clinical practitioners often wish for a cessation of feminist "clamorings" about psychoanalytic theory and therapy. A major defense of psychoanalytic theory has been that critics simply do not understand the theory (Mitchel, 1974). Others point out that early assumptions and constructs have been revised or dropped (Fliegel, 1982; Waites, 1982). Nevertheless, narcissism, masochism, and penis envy are still retained as elements of feminine personality. (See Lerman, 1985, for a further review.)

Causal Models

A major criticism of psychoanalytic theory (and others as well) is that it makes a fundamental attribution error. The locus of cause is located in individual mentality, cognition, affect, etc. What's inside is what counts. The individual is viewed as ultimately responsible for her or his own discontent. Problems are personal and, therefore, asocial. A major contribution of feminist analyses is that personal miseries are often reflections of larger social and political practices operating independently of individual personalities.

The attribution error is reflected in a reductionistic or disease model (Tennov, 1975). In a disease model, it is the patient who is sick, and pathology is seen to have an internal origin. In an effort to emulate medical physicians, clinical psychologists look for "syndromes" and symptoms that may go into "remission." Tennov concludes that psychotherapy has a perfect blend of impressive vocabulary, the authority of science, and the incomprehensibility of religion.

Feminists have argued that the focus on intrapsychic events has ig-

178

nored the role of social, political, and economic factors in the life experiences of women (and men as well). Analyses of phobia, depression, and so on might proceed with equal efficacy by attention to these situational conditions. Reliance on a medical model has tended to make mental health providers generally more conservative on social issues.

Normative Male and Deviant Female

The second general criticism of psychoanalytic theory, as well as much general theory in psychology, is the perspective that the male is normative and female patterns represent deviations. This phallocentric view leads to subtle derogation of that which is female or feminine. Further, there is simply a tendency to ignore those experiences and developmental processes most characteristic of women.

Negative traits and characteristics tend to be classified as feminine. For example, masochism, whether apparent in a man or a woman, is defined as basically feminine (Kaplan, 1983). Female development is often described as a metaphor of masochism, for example, fertilization, menstruation, and intercourse are all described as symbolic of masochism for the female.

Artifact and Psychotherapy

A major issue is the extent to which therapists are trained to see pathology in normal behavior (Wright, Meadow, Abramowitz, & Davidson, 1980). Some critics have suggested that therapists have simply created their own patient demand (Frank, 1961), and that psychotherapy is more art than science (Matarazzo, 1965, 1967, 1971). Others have gone so far as to identify psychotherapy as basically the result of placebo effects (O'Connell, 1983). Further, it has been observed that therapy appears to work best with those clients who probably have least need, that is, clients who are young, verbal, well-educated, and middle or upper-middle class.

One of the most outspoken and articulate critics of psychotherapy is Thomas Szasz (1961, 1973, 1976). He has claimed that psychotherapy is at best rhetoric disguised as cure, or in some cases as science. Diagnoses are simply an artificial method for creating the apparent reality of mental illness by giving it a name, and in a sense is like "medical mugging".

One revealing study involved a taped interview of a normal person following a script designed to represent normal responses (Temerlin, 1968). The interview was viewed by groups of psychiatrists, clinical psychologists, and graduate students in clinical psychology. The task was to determine whether the individual being interviewed was psychotic, neurotic, or healthy. However, before viewing, each group was told by a high prestige person that the man in the interview represented an extremely interesting case, because while he appeared to be neurotic, he was in fact quite psychotic. Psychosis was diagnosed by 60% of psychiatrists, 28% of clinical psychologists, and 11% of students. Among control groups, professionals who viewed the tape without prior diagnosis and another group selected from county jury rosters, there was unanimous agreement that the man was healthy.

Social Control

Therapy as a means of social control has been examined by several critics. Szasz (1961) argues that individuals who are incarcerated in mental institutions lose their civil rights and are often forced to perform involuntary servitude. The patient populations of mental hospitals may be viewed in some sense as inmates of POW camps of the undeclared and inarticulated civil wars of society (Szasz, 1973). Other critics have voiced similar opinion.

> In today's rapidly changing world, therapy serves the status quo. It bolsters the power of those who run the country. Therapy distorts reality, and then presents this distortion as the Truth Unveiled, which it presses on people, exhorting them to accept it and adjust to what they cannot change (Glenn & Kunnes, 1973).

Marxist analysis points out that a biased philosophy has exercised a strong influence on the nature of research, construction of new hypotheses, interpretation of scientific results, and the development of theory pertaining to psychotherapy. This philosophy is an integrated rendering of capitalistic thoughts and modes of production (Nahem, 1981). Everything is understood in terms of the individual and "his" subjective feeling state. The dialectics of materialism, economics, and religion are ignored. Thus, psychoanalysis buttresses the ruling class by allowing them to blame working class victims for their own suffering.

A major diagnostic instrument, the Diagnostic and Statistical Manual of Mental Disorders (DSM III), has been acknowledged to have political and economic implications by psychiatrists closely involved in its construction and evaluation (Schacht, 1985). The DSM III is a tool for answering socially important questions, such as, who is entitled to treatment. "It pays lip service to science so that various special interests may acquire a guise of respectability, and its major purpose is to reinforce and expand the health-industrial complex in general, and various forms of professional hegemony in particular." (Schacht, 1985, p. 515).

It has been argued that the political and economic elements of screening and diagnosis are particularly apparent in the case of women and that much therapy ostensibly conducted on behalf of women is in fact structured in such a way so as to control women (Chesler, 1972). It is argued that scientists and clinicians in general have routinely strengthened the myth of the inferiority of women and have directly oppressed them (Barrett, Berg, Eaton, & Pomeroy, 1974).

Among women who have been hospitalized for mental disorders and released, subsequent rehospitalization has been demonstrated to depend partly on whether or not these women adequately perform household duties (Angrist, Dinitz, Lefton, & Pasamanick, 1961, 1968). Husbands were found to be extremely tolerant of helpless dependent behavior on the part of their homebound wives, as long as the wives continued to manage the household cleaning, cooking, and so on. The critical factor appeared to be whether these women conducted themselves in placid acquiescent styles. Women who gave expression to their anger and refused to perform service activities in the home were typically returned to the hospital.

A case reported by Ellis (1974) within the framework of rational emotive therapy is instructive. The case is that of a young adult woman in her late 20s whose primary complaint is that she is anorgasmic. She fears that her boyfriend, with whom she hopes to develop a permanent relationship, will become bored and irritated with her. She is concerned that she does not arouse sexually with ease (although their lovemaking sessions may last 15 or 20 minutes!).

Through rational emotive therapy, the young woman is convinced by Ellis that orgasmic responsiveness is not really important. She is then encouraged to develop a fantasy scene wherein she is sexually assaulted and rendered powerless by two thugs. During intercourse with her boyfriend she is instructed to imagine the thugs to be her boyfriend. Ellis reports this as a successful case because the woman does subsequently report increased sexual responsiveness on her part and apparently receives the approval of her lover.

Thus, the woman is encouraged to accept the definition of sex in general and her sexuality in particular provided by her boyfriend and therapist. Additionally she is encouraged to relate to the boyfriend as completely dominant and controlling. This case clearly illustrates the reason for a strong feminist concern with sexuality and choice. Sexuality is one of the most personal aspects of anyone's experience, and yet women's sexuality is most likely to be defined and controlled by others. In this sense, sexuality and feminism parallel labor and communism; namely, it is that which is most one's own but most exploited by others (Al-Issa, 1980).

Sex-Role Bias

Two forms of gender bias have been outlined with respect to mental health issues: the maintenance of lower standards of mental health for

women compared to men and a greater probability that behaviors expressing either extreme conformity or deviance to traditional gender roles will
be classified as indicative of mental disorder (Angrist, 1961).

Initial research on standards of mental health was reported in a now
classic study by Broverman et al. (1970). Clinical psychologists, psychiatrists, and social workers were asked to described either a mentally
healthy adult, man, or woman. Results indicated that descriptions of a
generic adult and a man were similar, but descriptions of a mentally
healthy woman differed significantly from both.

Additional studies have revealed sex bias in other areas as well. Judgments of masculinity and femininity have been shown to be differentially
affected by mental health classification. Specifically, men identified as
mentally ill are seen to lose masculinity, but mentally ill women are
judged to be as feminine as healthy women. This finding suggests that
mental illness is seen to be compatible with traditional feminine roles
(Westbrook & Mitchel, 1979). Alternatively, mental patients described as
adhering to a highly feminine style are often classified as being more
psychologically impaired compared to masculine style patients (Teri,
1982). Although feminine style patients may be seen to have low levels of
functioning, they are often thought to have a better prognosis, possibly
because ultimate expectations for functioning and mental health are lower
for women than men (Teri, 1982). Sex bias in career counseling has also
been documented (Schlossberg & Pietrofesa, 1973).

General reviews of sex bias in diagnosis and mental health standards
have concluded that initial findings of the Broverman study have been
only partially replicated (Davidson & Abramowitz, 1980; Sherman, 1980).
Debate over the consistency and size of effect regarding sex bias continues (Stricker, 1977; Maffeo, 1979). However, it is also the case that
analogue studies, where hypothetical cases are presented for diagnosis,
have often employed manipulations with questionable face validity and
have seldom incorporated manipulation checks.

More recently, serious questions have been raised about bias in diagnostic instruments, particularly the Diagnostic and Statistical Manual of
Mental Disorder (DSM IH) adopted by the American Psychiatric Association. It has been suggested that individuals are often labeled as disordered, when the true diagnosis should be an unjust society (Kaplan,
1983). Adaptiveness and maladaptiveness are arbitrarily defined by boards
and review panels composed primarily of men.

A particular problem involving DSM III diagnoses is that women who
conform too closely to stereotypic feminine personality styles may become subject to diagnosis as mentally ill. The histrionic personality syndrome is taken as an example by Kaplan (1983). Table 9.1 demonstrates
potential problems. Traits judged by mental health specialists to be indic-

Table 9.1 Gender Bias in Diagnosis

DSM III Diagnosis Histrionic Personality	Traits of Mentally Healthy Women*
Self-dramatization & exaggerated expression of emotion	Being more emotional
Overreaction to minor events	More excitable in minor crises
Angry outbursts and tantrums	Less objective
Vain and demanding	More conceited about appearance
Dependent, helpless, constantly seeking reassurance	More submissive, less adventurous

*Traits of healthy women are those representing opinions of psychiatrists, clinical psychologists, and social workers, as reported by Broverman et al., 1970.

ative of mentally healthy women bear close resemblance to traits and symptoms listed as indicative of histrionic personality by the DSM III.

Thus, it would appear that some women fall into a Catch-22 (Chesler, 1972). Women who don't conform enough to traditional roles may be labeled as mentally ill and those that conform tenaciously are also subject to labeling. "It appears then that via assumptions about sex roles made by clinicians, a healthy woman automatically earns the diagnosis of histrionic personality disorder or, to help female clients, clinicians encourage them to get sick." (Kaplan, 1983, p. 789). Other diagnostic categories of the DSM III also reveal potential gender bias, particularly a dependent personality diagnosis. Diagnostic criteria provide numerous examples of ways in which women might exhibit dependency but ignore examples whereby men do so.

Replies to criticisms of gender bias in the DSM III have included field trial data in an effort to illustrate lack of bias. Additionally, the careful efforts to avoid bias in the construction of categories has been reviewed (Spitzer & Williams, 1983; Millon, 1983). Controversy on these points is unresolved at this time.

Training Limitations

The Task Force on Sex Bias (1975) cited lack of knowledge about processes involving women as a major limitation in clinical training programs. Limitations include little or no training in issues of wife abuse, crisis counseling (especially for rape victims), or information on eating disorders. Training programs seldom provide information about reproductive decision making, for example decisions regarding the timing or termination of pregnancy; problems of aging women are generally ignored, particularly problems involving widowhood and social support.

The Task Force on Clinical Training and Practice (1984) recommended that clinical training curriculum include material on women's identity and development, as well as physical health and life cycle events unique to women. Some of these recommendations were reiterated by the initial review group charged with developing a national agenda to address women's mental health needs (Strickland et al., 1985). This group noted that knowledge about women is not systematically included in many training programs, and opportunities to address this lack through continuing education are shrinking rather than expanding.

A survey of women members of various clinical and counseling divisions of the American Psychological Association revealed additional problem themes:

1. Therapists assume problem resolution and self-actualization for women come from marriage or perfecting the role of wife.
2. Therapists lack awareness and sensitivity to role diversity involving career and work for women.
3. Female clients' attitudes toward childbearing and child care are viewed as an index of emotional maturity.
4. In family or child therapy, the responsibility for successful resolution is located in the mother.

Efficacy and Outcome

Another area of critical analysis has been the efficacy of psychotherapy. Early questions about the efficacy of psychotherapy were posed by Eysenck (1952). He claimed that psychotherapists tend to work from clinical anecdotal evidence with few objective criteria for success or effectiveness and that psychotherapy holds the contemporary status of bloodletting. His initial work was a study of 500 potential therapy patients who were instead treated by sedatives and suggestions. At the end of one year, 45% reported only slight difficulty and generally successful social adjustment; within 5 years 89% had reached criterion measures of success.

Interviews and questionnaires obtained from former patients on their views of psychotherapy constituted the next phase of efficacy and outcome research (Strupp, Wallach, & Wogan, 1964; Strupp, Fox, & Lessler, 1969). In-depth interviews with women who had undergone psychotherapy indicated that in some cases therapy may have had harmful effects (Tennov, 1975). Women reported that therapists encouraged feelings of guilt. Although many of the women were in therapy to manage family-related problems, therapists seldom consulted with other family members, preferring instead to make an individual diagnosis based on the women's personality traits. Some therapists pressured women to stay in therapy longer than the women themselves desired; still other women reported that therapy sessions became the first priority of their lives, leaving them little energy to relate to others or focus on work.

These criticisms notwithstanding, the major impetus for evaluation and outcome research concerning the efficacy of psychotherapy is based on changes in national health care policy. Treatment of mental disorders is now covered by federally based health care programs. The stipulation is that if the government is paying for it, there ought to be some scientific assurance that it works (Jacobson, Deykin, & Prusoff, 1977).

Methodological issues in outcome research are extensive (Gurman, 1977; Bergin & Lambert, 1971; Orlinksy & Howard, 1978; Saxe, Yates, & Newman, 1980). A brief list of methodological issues includes the nature of outcome measures, delivery settings, research designs, and the integration of findings from diverse studies. Outcome measures may include patient self-reports, therapist evaluations, or observations from family and community members. Delivery settings may be outpatient centers, private practice, psychiatric wards, etc. Research designs offer similar diversity.

Research designs have considerable variety, but most fall within three general types: case studies, analogue studies, or clinical trials. *Case studies* involve intensive longitudinal reviews and accounts of individual patients. *Analogue studies* typically involve college students or other normally functioning groups who are recruited to participate in therapy sessions, usually dealing with topics such as stress, test anxiety, etc. *Clinical trials* represent a third approach where therapists are professionals and patients have sought treatment on their own initiative, usually for problems of a more complex and disabling nature than those found in analogue studies.

Even within the clinical trial approach, there are several design variations. In some designs treatment groups are compared to no treatment controls; in other designs treatment groups may be compared with groups receiving a placebo treatment, or groups receiving differing types of therapy may be compared. Unfortunately, failure to make random assignment of subjects to treatment conditions seriously limits the scientific merit of some outcome research.

Evaluating and synthesizing the evaluation research is also problematic. One approach is essentially a *box-score method*. In such reviews scientific criteria are established for inclusion in the review, for example, only clinical trials having random assignment of subjects to treatment. Studies may be differentially catalogued by reviewers, depending on the number and refinement of inclusion criteria. A further problem of this type of review is that results are recorded in broad categories of improvement or no improvement. The degree of improvement or size of effect is not determined. Another approach, following similar initial selection procedures, is termed meta-analysis. *Meta-analysis* is designed to allow for meaningful comparison of studies having diverse research designs and to include an evaluation of effect size (Smith & Glass, 1977).

There have been several major reviews of outcome research in psychotherapy following the work of Eysenck (1952). The number of studies deemed to meet scientific criteria for inclusion and review have varied from 300 to as few as 22. Percentage of studies indicating overall improvement among patients has been reported to be as high as 84% and as low as 4%, with approximately 60% reported most frequently (Meltzoff & Kornreich, 1970; Bergin & Lambert, 1971; Rachman, 1973; Luborsky, Singer, & Luborsky, 1975; Parloff, 1979; Smith, Glass, & Miller, 1981).

Additional issues have been raised about efficacy research. One of the more common criticisms is that research has tended to focus on outcomes, with little evaluation of the therapeutic process itself or of individual therapist and patient variables that contribute to the unique relationship formed in therapy (Bordin, 1974; Kazdin, 1982; Strupp, 1982). Therefore, while there is some evidence that psychotherapy works for some people, there is little evidence to indicate exactly what it is that accounts for these outcomes.

NONTRADITIONAL APPROACHES

Consciousness Raising

Consciousness raising began as a purposeful strategy for political analysis and change. The ideological roots for consciousness raising were that consciousness is a prerequisite for social change (Rosenthal, 1984). This is very similar to the Marxist position that class consciousness precedes political action by the class. It is also reminiscent of grassroots civil rights movements that depended on communal efforts by many individuals.

A key focus in consciousness raising is that problems experienced by women are social rather than individual in origin. Indeed, one of the first things women discover in these groups is that personal problems are political. Individual experiences of shame, dependency, and anger are common to others. These experiences rest on shared conditions characterized by issues of dominance and power. Therefore, the sharing and analyzing of personal experiences becomes a means of raising women's consciousness of their joint status as a class, that the future hopes and destiny of women in general are theirs as well.

A key objective of consciousness raising, therefore, is to establish a class consciousness among women. The degree to which women do or do not see themselves as members of a common class composed of other women is probably a major factor in the progress of women's liberation; however, there are a number of barriers to this awareness. People in general prefer to believe they have control of their lives and that efforts are followed by predictable rewards. While some women may be acknowledged to fall in a subordinate or exploited class, the individual prefers to see herself as unique and, therefore, different from the general class. The belief in uniqueness is psychologically comforting and well entrenched. It is evidenced routinely among students in women's studies courses who recognize that many women have been economically exploited in jobs and abused in personal relationships; however, they see no abuse in their own lives.

The human predilection to view oneself as unique and not belonging to a general class probably explains many apparently anomalous behaviors in other areas as well. For example, masses of individual soldiers often carry out commands where there is a high probability of dying. During the American Civil War and the Pacific campaign of World War II, some battles resulted in more than 70% deaths among fighting units. However, individual soldiers reported that in spite of evidence about the odds of dying, they believed they would survive. Other classes of people, for example, those with poor health habits such as smoking, probably also find ways to psychologically separate themselves from the probable effects of heavy smoking. This resistance to class consciousness might be termed a "Not Me" syndrome.

Barriers to class consciousness among women are socially engineered as well. The fact that "women live with their oppressors" creates a condition unique among minority groups (where minority is defined by limited access to power rather than statistical numbers). Women are encouraged to identify themselves in terms of interpersonal relationships within a nuclear family, that is, as a daughter, wife, or mother, but not in relation to other women in general. The energy and time required to fulfill nuclear family roles typically leaves limited opportunities for interaction with other women. When these interactions do occur they frequently are derogated as frivolous, gossiping, or narcissistic indulgence. Thus, women get the message that connections with other women involve only trivial pursuits and selfish people.

Formal characteristics and goals of consciousness raising groups were initially set forth by Redstockings, a radical feminist group originating in New York (Redstockings, 1970, 1979). Basic philosophical tenets were that women were not responsible or to blame for their status but were instead subjected to daily pressure from men to perform and remain in limited roles. Consciousness raising became an opportunity whereby individuals could review their personal experiences, recognize their common status, and use these personal insights for analysis of their class condition. Understanding the nature of female oppression and sexism in general is seen as essential to the establishment of new goals and alternative programs and strategies for reaching those goals (Kravetz, 1980).

Consciousness raising groups began as political action groups directed toward changing psychological, social, economic, and cultural circumstances of women. They have been significant change agents in developing alternative structures and goals in health care, social services, and so on. Rape crisis centers, abortion counseling services, and shelters for battered women in various communities around the country often started as ideas in consciousness raising groups. Consciousness raising groups also served the function of educating the community at large regarding sexism and discrimination, particularly in the early 70s when society did not generally believe women were subjected to prejudice or discrimination.

Reasons for joining a consciousness raising group range from a desire to share with other women, personal problem solving, search for friendship, and exploration of sexuality, in addition to political awareness. One survey of over 1,600 women in consciousness raising groups indicated that political awareness was not a particularly salient goal (Kravetz, 1978). Common outcomes for participants include an altered world view and awareness of discrimination, changes in self image, more self-acceptance, changes in reference groups, and increased awareness of anger (Kravetz, 1980). Most research on outcomes in consciousness raising groups has involved participant-observer methodology. Those studies employing quantitative measures report a slight shift in profeminist attitudes, whereas those relying on qualitative categories indicate more positive feelings about self and other women (Nassi & Abramowitz, 1978).

The values of egalitarian nonhierarchical structures and cooperative problem solving formed the basis for rules regarding interaction processes in these groups. Common norms of operation are that members can speak without interruption. Participants are encouraged to be tolerant of diverse backgrounds among group members. Often members are asked not to dwell on personal experiences without an attempt to generalize or abstract their experiences in terms of broader principles (Kirsh, 1974). Table 9.2 lists common reasons for joining, principles of interaction, and typical outcomes of consciousness raising groups.

Although initial goals and principles of these groups were political, subsequent developments have been in the direction of personal authenticity and self-awareness. This aspect of groups has led some feminists to

Table 9.2 Motivations, Process, and Outcome
in Consciousness Raising Groups

Motives for Joining	Process	Outcome
Learning experience	Sharing commonalities	Awareness of women
Personal problem solving	Group involvement	Positive self-image
Make friends	Self-disclosure	Positive attitudes on women
Political activism	Political analysis	Changes in job/career
Explore sexuality	Affective discharge	Awareness of anger

propose a therapeutic value for individuals (Kirsh, 1974). Therapeutic possibilities are based on role theory. The construct of role is the mediating link between social structure and the individual. Examination of feminine roles and the sources of conflict inherent in those roles often suggests strategies for change.

Feminist analyses point out that not only are male and female roles established as dichotomies, but the male role is more highly valued than the female role. Roles rather than individuals become the focus of analysis in this context. However, role dichotomies are often so well entrenched that casual analysis suggests they are based on individual characteristics of males and females. Further analysis within the consciousness raising framework makes it clear that role dichotomies are constructed as a means of maintaining differential power between women and men (Kirsh, 1974). Men are highly motivated to maintain role dichotomies and sex differentiation in general as a means of safeguarding their power base. The socialization of submissiveness in women encourages them to accept this differential distribution of power. Locating roles in individuals rather than society promotes a stable status quo.

Others have argued that significant differences exist between therapy and consciousness raising groups (Morgan, 1970; Brown, 1971; Hanisch, 1971; Zweig, 1971). The unit of analysis and change differs in that therapy focuses on the individual, and consciousness raising groups focus on society. In therapy, the level of analysis is interpersonal and intrapersonal events, whereas consciousness raising examines sociocultural context. Further, in therapy settings there is always an assumed hierarchy of expertise and consequently differential power between therapist and patient. Consciousness raising groups work to avoid hierarchical organization, viewing the experiences and analyses of each women as equally legitimate.

Contemporary developments suggest that consciousness raising as a political strategy has been subject to a sort of benign neglect. A number of factors have contributed to this, including psychological resistance, social barriers, and other sources of support. A substantial percentage of women acknowledge their need for nurturant and cooperative relationships with other women but seek association and support for personal strategies in managing stress, making life decisions, and so on. Although these associations may have less political significance than consciousness raising, they nevertheless represent an important strategy for integrating self and social framework.

Social Support and Psychological Function

Perhaps the most pervasive change in models of health and illness in recent years is the inclusion of concepts of stress and social support. That stress or stressful life events are associated with poor psychological function and/or medical impairment has been proposed by several researchers, and is the topic of an extensive literature (Holmes & Rahe, 1967; Harder, Strauss, Kokes, Ritzler, & Gift, 1980; Blazer, 1980; Brenner & Mooney, 1983; Mestrovic & Glassner, 1983). The *stress buffering hypothesis* holds that social support mitigates stressful events and reduces the likelihood of illness, a prevention focus (Cobb, 1976). Other hypotheses suggest that people with good social support networks cope better and recover more quickly when illness does occur.

Recognition of the psychosocial aspects of health has gradually gained status in the medical community, with the result that biological disease models are now often modified to include social support and stress (Cassel, 1976; Kaplan, Cassel, & Gore, 1977; Novack, 1981).

The President's Commission on Mental Health (1978b) concluded that to receive and be able to give social support is essential to mental health. Social support networks have been developed for rape victims, breast cancer patients, single parents, and bereaved spouses, to name only a few. Thus, social support is thought to have beneficial effects in a variety of circumstances.

General hypotheses involve prevention, coping, and recovery (Suls, 1982). Specific pathways by which the beneficial effects of social support occur include health sustaining behaviors, such as diet and exercise; illness behaviors, such as compliance with medical regimens; and stress reduction or coping strategies (Wallston, Alagna, DeVellis, & DeVellis, 1983; Frankel & Nuttall, 1984).

The content of social support can be roughly classified into cognitive, affective, and behavioral components, although some researchers prefer a dichotomy of instrumental and expressive functions (Wallston et al., 1983). Cognitive components involve the interpretation and general identification of an event as stressful. For example, crisis events may be perceived as holding opportunities for creative change, as well as negative outcomes. Other people can influence the interpretation of an event by minimizing negative consequences, offering hope for successful resolution, or suggestions for coping (Sanders, 1982; Suls, 1982; Cohen & McKay, 1984; Cobb, 1976). Social comparison may largely determine whether or not an event is even perceived or experienced as stressful (Cohen & McKay, 1984).

In addition to informational/cognitive features, support may also include emotional and esteem-raising components, as well as tangible assistance. The most beneficial support may vary as a function of the stress situation; thus, different social networks may be more or less effective in buffering stress (Pearlin, 1985). There is even a small body of literature suggesting that if social support is not readily forthcoming, active seeking

Table 9.3 Health Sustaining and Stress Reducing Aspects of Social Support*

Event	Effects	
	Positive	*Negative*
Cognitive:		
Objective assessment of problem, suggestion of coping strategies	Reduced feelings of help-lessness, sense of com-petence	Sense of inadequacy, if models are super copers
Affective:		
Expression of caring, love, concern	Feeling cared for, sense of security	Feeling smothered, de-pendency
Approval, praise, expres-sions of respect	Self-confidence, positive self-esteem	Egotism, over confidence
Behavioral:		
Tangible assistance, money or service	More able to meet de-mands, confidence	Embarrassment, resent-ment
Inclusion in group ac-tivities	Increased perception of number of friends	Thwart development of individual identity

*Derived from Shumaker & Brownell, 1984

after it may be dysfunctional (Gore, 1985). It is also important to acknowl-edge that social support may have both positive and negative conse-quences (Wortman & Conway, 1985). Table 9.3 outlines some general features of social support and potential effects.

Research on social support has suffered from several methodological and conceptual problems (Suls, 1982; Sarason & Sarason, 1984). More attention has been given to prevention and coping than to recovery prob-lems. The effects of social support on the course of prolonged illness, chronic conditions, or life-threatening events have seldom been studied (Singer & Lord, 1984). Specific hypotheses about exactly how social sup-port produces direct or buffering effects on health have not been rigorous-ly explored at this point (Cohen & Syme, 1985).

Definitions of social support have sometimes focused on the quantity of contact, quality of relationship, availability of support, actual utiliza-tion, or satisfaction. Most of these measures rely on self-report and are consequently subject to various types of bias (Gatchel & Baum, 1983). Research designs have varied between prospective tracing and retro-spective recall. Thus, generalization across studies is often difficult (Brownell & Shumaker, 1984; Depner, Wethington, & Ingersoll-Dayton, 1984).

An additional problem, now recognized by several researchers, is that models of social support have often assumed that social support is external to the system under study. That is, social support can affect stress levels and stress management, but these factors do not affect social support (Shinn, Lehmann, & Wong, 1984). However, in some circumstances, life events, such as moving to a new city, may influence the availability of social support. Furthermore, loss of social support may itself be a stressor (Singer & Lord, 1984). It has been recently suggested that the direction of causality and influence is reciprocal (Syrotuik & D'Arcy, 1984) and that these effects can be traced over time (Billings & Moos, 1982). Figure 9.1 illustrates the complexity of social support and health effects.

Research confirming the beneficial effects of social support on physical health has been quite varied (Berkman, 1984). In an extensive long-term epidemiological, study Berkman & Syme (1979) found that mortality rates were significantly reduced among subjects having social support, such as marriage, membership in social groups, participation in a religious group, etc. Furthermore, reduced mortality was observed in all age groups ranging from young adulthood to middle and advanced age. It is interesting to note, however, that the protective effects of marriage were more clearly evidenced among men than women. Other studies have found positive associations between social support and compliance with treatment regimens and health practices (Doherty, Schrott, Metcalf, & Lasiello-Vailas, 1983; Janis, 1983; Levy, 1983).

Of particular interest to women have been a handful of studies examining social support and childbirth. Nuckolls, Cassel, and Kaplan (1972) recruited first-time mothers who delivered their babies in a military hospital. Social resources and recent life events were evaluated against the incidence of delivery complications. Individually, neither variable predicted complications, but social support was associated with a lower relative risk of complications among the group of women having many recent life changes. Thus, social support seemed to operate in a stress buffering fashion. A community-based study measured biomedical risk, life events, family function, and social support (Smilkstein, Helsper-Lucas, Ashworth, Montano, & Pagel, 1984). Psychosocial factors were related to

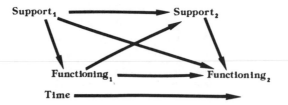

FIGURE 9.1   Social support at time 1 may affect concurrent functioning and social support and functioning at a later time. Additionally, functioning at time 1 may affect the availability and quality of social support at a later time.

both delivery and postpartum complications. Biomedical and psychosocial factors jointly accounted for 11% of the variance in complications.

Among studies relating social support to mental health, little research has specifically addressed the psychology of gender. Potential differences exist as a function of gender in the availability and number of individuals in a support network and network structure, as well as the quality of social support exchanged. For example, gender may influence availability of social support among nonemployed women, who theoretically have relatively more discretion in scheduling their activities, but often work in isolation. Employed women may be a statistical minority in their job, thus having to rely on male peers for potential social support. Additionally, employed women with children often lack the discretionary time to develop social support networks beyond their immediate families. Research has shown that among dual career couples, women continue to assume more responsibility for household tasks and child care (Perrucci, Potter, & Rhoads, 1978; Weingarten, 1978).

Further, it is often assumed that women tend to develop social support networks around a few best friends, whereas men are thought to rely on extended networks of casual acquaintances. Other assumed gender differences in relational style are also relevant. For example, folk wisdom holds that women are more likely to share secrets and express emotional content, whereas men are thought to engage in companionate activities or joint efforts of instrumental problem solving. Whether these assumed gender differences are true has not been determined. Differential functions, stability, benefits, and costs of these social networks have not been assessed.

Nevertheless, a few studies of particular relevance to women and psychological functioning have been reported. In a study of women returning to college in middle adulthood, psychological functioning and mood were found to be associated with cognitive guidance and interpretation of events, and socializing seemed to boost self-esteem (Hirsch, 1980). These findings focus attention on the nature of supportive acts; however, other studies suggest that the social network structure is also important. A community survey of elderly women found that the size and density of support networks were associated with better mood and sense of well-being (Heller & Mansbach, 1984). Professional burnout has been associated with low levels of social support among both women and men (Etzion, 1984).

It is also important to note that social support resources are different for people with and without children. In particular, there seems to be a reduction in the absolute size of social networks among nonemployed mothers in the lowest social classes (Hammer, Gutwirth, & Phillips, 1982). The presence of children also seems to increase one's contact with immediate kin and others having small children (Belsky & Rovine, 1984). It should be noted, however, that presence of immediate family does not insure more emotional or material support, and often close relatives are not regarded as significant others (Belsky & Rovine, 1984).

SUMMARY

Traditional analyses of depression, addictive behaviors, eating disorders, and so on have relied entirely on intrapsychic events, classifying these conditions as essentially belonging to a self framework. This is seen to be a major limitation of psychoanalytic approaches to theory and therapy. Additional limitations of traditional approaches include reliance on a male norm and training limitations among others.

Of the nontraditional alternatives, it appears that several obstacles will prevent the widespread acceptance of consciousness raising, which emphasizes social frameworks. Social structures tend to make it difficult for women to gain a sense of class. In addition some feminist positions, particularly Marxist orientations, tend to downplay the importance of self-relational events. Implications that women must forego these experiences and concentrate on the greater good of social revolution have created a major stumbling block in the growth of feminism. In contrast, the value and efficacy of social support networks, with an emphasis on impact for the individual, appears to have been accepted in scientific circles. However, a number of empirical questions remain to be answered regarding social support and health.

Consciousness raising has political, social, and personal implications. The identification of individual women with the experiences of women as a class has been actively promoted in consciousness raising groups and has created a source of energy for political activism. Consciousness raising has also offered women examples of how people can interact in groups and work effectively to solve problems without relying on strict dominance structures. Nevertheless, there are a variety of sources of resistance to consciousness raising.

Social support represents a contemporary variation on early versions of consciousness raising. Lacking overt political implications, social support has been incorporated in models of physical and mental health. However, research on social support has suffered from methodological and conceptual flaws. Empirical findings give only limited support to the efficacy of social support in prevention, adaptation, and recovery from illness. Although much folk wisdom assumes pervasive differences in social support as a function of gender, gender effects have received minimal attention.

Feminist Alternatives 10

There are two basic tenets of feminist alternatives in theory and therapy. The first concerns a view of the nature of women. Women must be viewed as possessing basically healthy and powerful sources of personal growth and expression. Women's experiences are viewed as important in their own right and not merely as deviations from a male norm. Appropriate development need not occur in the service of fulfilling a role in relation to a man. The second tenet is that the human experience can only be properly understood from the interaction of person and situation variables. Intrapsychic events always occur in a field of social expectations, interpersonal history, and differential access to resources. Thus, while personal events are recognized as a legitimate area of attention and reflection, they are qualified and interpreted within a social context.

This chapter reviews alternatives in nonsexist and feminist therapy and research on gender effects. However, feminist alternatives extend beyond the treatment of pathology, and the second section presents a more general framework based on dominance relations.

FEMINIST ALTERNATIVES IN THERAPY

Three developments led to the emergence of feminist therapy. The first was a recognition that much psychological theory was sexist, based on constructs and methods derived from male experiences, while often ignoring those of women. Additionally, perjorative interpretations and analyses were frequently published without critical review. More important, there was a recognition that the social and economic conditions of women had implications for mental health. Life events commonly experienced by women were acknowledged as stressors, often precipitating mental illness. Poverty, widowhood, pregnancy, and other experiences shared by women were seen to have significant impact on women's lives. A final factor leading to the development of feminist therapy was the collective insight that the status quo of social and political relations was based in part on a psychological oppression of women. That is, women were socialized to accept and feel most comfortable in secondary support roles, submerging their own self-development in the service of promoting esteem in others.

Feminist Philosophy

The goals and principles of feminist therapy are derived from aspects of each of the three major feminist philosophies, incorporating liberal, radical, and socialist/Marxist perspectives (Sturdivant, 1980).

Liberal perspectives have focused on sexist ideas, habits, prejudices, and laws as mechanisms by which women are oppressed. Therefore, liberal approaches to sexism have encouraged the changing of laws and political conditions. Rights concerning community property, access to credit ratings, and the recognition of wife abuse as a crime are all issues having important implications for the mental health of women and their ability to resolve crises that might otherwise result in mental illness and hospitalization. Liberal perspectives have also encouraged and promoted increased flexibility and integration of sex roles. Rights of self-determination in sexual preference, reproductive behavior, and other areas have been of key interest to liberal feminists. These concerns have been incorporated in psychological research on androgyny and changes in the assumption that heterosexuality is the "normal" and most healthy developmental path.

Radical feminists have probably given more attention to the psychological oppression of women than other feminist philosophies. In particular, family and traditional roles of women were identified as arenas where oppression occurred. Radical feminists have often been advocates of the unique strengths of women, arguing that women and men truly are fundamentally different. According to radical feminists, women's experience of self and relationships offer a more constructive and optimal way of interacting than the agentic, competitive model accepted as a social ideal for men. From the radical perspective, women are acknowledged to have personal and psychological power but have failed to recognize it and have given it away. One of the objectives of feminist therapy drawn from the radical perspective is to promote a sense of empowerment among women.

Socialist/Marxist perspectives have consistently criticized conceptions of work and productivity, holding that what is currently considered adult, valuable, and important ought to be structured in a new framework. In particular, hierarchical structures of authority and competition need to be replaced with mutual respect, cooperation, and pride. Individualistic advancement at the expense of others is seen as unethical. It is further assumed that ultimately society and women will benefit from a collective approach to issues of work and productivity. Socialist/Marxist perspectives have also contributed to the belief that instances of political oppression can only be understood initially through personal insight and discovery of the link between that which is personal and the larger social system. The impact on feminist therapy has been to promote egalitarian conduct of therapy and informed consumerism. Both radical and socialist/Marxist perspectives lend support to the value of group therapy approaches.

Nonsexist Versus Feminist Therapy

There has been some discussion concerning whether or not there is such a thing as feminist therapy. Arguments have been that good, sound therapy is nonsexist and therefore feminist. However, others have drawn distinctions between the two.

On some points, nonsexist and feminist therapy overlap. For example, biological determinism is replaced with an interactionist position, incorporating biological, psychosocial, political, and economic forces in shaping individual behavior. Additionally, both recognize that women's social situations play an important role in their mental health, for example, being a single parent, widowed, physically abused, etc. Further, both nonsexist and feminist approaches promote scholarship in the areas of life events experienced in unique ways by women, for example, menstruation, pregnancy, lesbianism. Marecek and Kravetz (1977) have suggested five key elements of nonsexist therapy:

1. Acknowledges the scope and subtlety of sexism, and therapists are encouraged to become sensitive to their own sexism
2. Incorporates knowledge of recent research on sex differences and the psychology of women and the differences in socialization pressures experienced by women and men
3. Acknowledges the close relationship between women's personal problems and social, economic, legal, and political situations
4. Recognizes that the lack of women's social power can generate passivity, submissiveness, dependency, and apathy
5. Involves a commitment to viewing each client as an individual

The task force on sex bias and sex role stereotyping in psychotherapeutic practice has published the following somewhat longer and more detailed statement of principles for nonsexist therapy presented here (Task Force on Sex Bias, 1978).

1. Therapy should be free of gender stereotypes in analysis and solutions reviewed.
2. Therapists should recognize the implications of sex discrimination and should facilitate client examination of options dealing with such practices.
3. Therapists should be knowledgeable about current empirical findings.
4. Theoretical concepts employed should be free of sex bias and stereotypes.

5. Therapists should demonstrate acceptance of women as equal to men by using language free of derogatory labels.

6. Therapists should avoid establishing the source of personal problems within the client when they are properly viewed as situational.

7. Therapists and fully informed clients should agree mutually about aspects of therapy such as time factors and fee arrangements.

8. Therapists should regard all information as privileged, and decisions regarding communication with family members must reside ultimately with the client, not the therapist.

9. If authoritarian processes are employed, they should not have the effect of reinforcing stereotypic dependency.

10. The client's assertive behavior should be respected.

11. The therapist whose female client is subjected to violence by physical abuse or rape should acknowledge that the client is the victim of a crime.

12. The therapist should recognize and encourage the exploration of a woman client's sexuality and should recognize her right to define her own sexual preferences.

13. The therapist should not have sexual relations with a client or treat her as a sex object.

These principles reiterate the emphasis on a need for therapists to be knowledgeable about the psychology of women and gender, to recognize sexism as a significant factor in women's lives, and to adopt a general respect for the client as a consumer. Similar principles have been advocated in counseling settings where career planning and guidance are the primary focus (Fitzgerald, 1973; Vetter, 1973).

Violations of nonsexist guidelines illustrate that the principles reflected by them are not universally accepted. For example, one another, after gently criticizing Freud's male chauvinism, nevertheless agreed that the primary goal of development for women must involve a durable sexual-love relationship with a man (Shainess, 1970). Other violations of nonsexist principles regarding the practice of therapy are difficult to monitor. When professional consciousness was somewhat less sensitive regarding sexism in therapy, approximately 6% of male psychologists admitted that they had had erotic contact with their female clients (Holroyd & Brodsky, 1977). The sexualization of therapeutic relationships continues to be an issue in psychotherapy (Zelen, 1985).

Feminist therapy is distinguished from nonsexist therapy on several points. A general distinction is that in nonsexist therapy, the focus of treatment is individual change and modification of personal behavior, whereas the critique of society and social institutions as experienced in personal dilemmas is a central element of feminist therapy (Marecek & Kravetz, 1977). In feminist therapy, clients are encouraged to identify the effects of sexism in their own lives and the lives of other women. Social change is seen as an important element in personal change. Self-help and collective sharing of resources and power often characterize feminist therapies (Marecek & Kravetz, 1977). The concept of empowerment partially reflects a general goal to not only improve self-esteem, but to change the nature of relationships, both personal and political (Kaplan et al., 1983; Imes & Clance, 1984; Brody, 1984).

Two general principles have prevailed as cornerstones of feminist therapy, the theoretical orientation that the personal is political, and the egalitarian nature of client-therapist relationships (Gilbert, 1980). A validation of the female experience of dependency, anger, and power as shaped by social institutions grows from this theoretical orientation, along with the emphasis on change as opposed to adjustment. Feminist therapy recognizes that there are conflicts unique to women and proceeds to examine gender-specific issues of women.

The importance of situational factors in women's psychological health and the value of social change is a major theoretical orientation in feminist therapy. The emphasis on societal evaluation and social activism establishes feminist therapy as a revolutionary practice.

> We would question here the increasingly accepted notion that changes in inner experience constitute a positive outcome for women in therapy. Given the cultural and institutional prejudices against women, it is not enough that a woman client leave therapy with an increase in self-esteem, regardless of the extent or nature of behavior change. We question whether it can be considered a "successful" therapy when the client "adjusts" to the cultural, societal, and familial contexts in which she lives without an awareness and understanding of their impact on her (Kaplan & Yasinski, 1980, p. 192).

The process of therapy involves a permissive atmosphere in which women can release their feelings of rage, helplessness, and inadequacy, and strive toward healthier assertiveness. Areas that are likely to receive particular attention during therapy include women's discomfort with their own power and fear of the power of others. Fear of anger and negative emotions constitutes another important area normally addressed in feminist therapy, particularly the fear of anger originating from separation anxiety and low status. Problems with sensuality, sexuality, and lack of body awareness are also often addressed. Further, the feminist therapist promotes a reassessment of women's relationships to other women as opposed to focusing on relationships to men (Feminist Counseling Collective, 1975; Gordon, Clance, & Simerly, 1985).

Egalitarian principles of practice involve issues of informed consent and therapist accountability to the client. As part of this egalitarian approach, therapists are encouraged to share their own life experiences as women and to serve in some instances as role models (Feminist Counseling Collective, 1975). The importance of modeling on the part of the therapist is supported in part by laboratory research (Travis & Seipp, 1978).

Beyond basic theoretical orientation and practitioner guidelines, feminist therapy may be conducted in the context of a variety of therapeutic approaches. Feminist analyses of the origin of symptoms include several hypotheses (Sturdivant, 1980). Symptoms may originate from the nature of traditional feminine roles, characterized by limited and vicarious opportunity for recognition or success. Another viable hypothesis is that symptoms arise from role conflict and role overload; that is, the traditional roles of women are inherently contradictory and attempting to perform all aspects of the ideal role leads to mental illness. Symptoms may also be seen as survival tactics and means of exercising power or control behind the facade of male dominance. Finally, symptoms may be recognized as arbitrary labels of society that serve as a means of imposing sanction and social control.

Other hypotheses and theoretical approaches have also been explored by feminist therapists. Obviously, feminist object relations affords a rich conceptual model. Feminist therapists have also worked within the framework of behavior therapy. For example, behavior therapy may be applied with depressed women as an alternative to drug therapy (Blechman, 1980).

Gender Effects

One issue that has affected professional evaluation of feminist therapy has been the question of sex of therapist and whether or not only women therapists should conduct therapy with women clients. Theoretical analyses suggest there may be good reasons for an affirmative answer (Kaplan, 1984). It is argued that women's core relational self structure attunes women therapists to affective connections and to an empathic relatedness essential to effective therapy. Unfortunately, standard training does not focus on the process of building affective connectedness and empathic relations between client and therapist; therefore, male therapists enter professional practice somewhat less prepared than female therapists (Kaplan, 1984).

Empirical studies of the effects of therapist sex on the process and outcome of therapy have revealed mixed results. Difficulties include methodological issues of exactly how to specify therapeutic outcome in a way that allows generalization across studies. Additionally, few process studies based on naturalistic observation have been conducted. Initial reviews suggested that neither sex of patient nor sex of therapist significantly affected outcome (Meltzoff & Kornreich, 1970; Garfield & Bergin, 1978). However, subsequent approaches have indicated that sex of therapist may make a difference under certain circumstances (Howard & Orlinsky, 1979; Orlinsky & Howard, 1980).

In a study of 147 women patients treated by one of 14 male or 9 female therapists, outcomes were evaluated in terms of symptom alleviation and global improvement (Orlinsky & Howard, 1980). In addition to examining sex effects, patients were classed according to age and marital status and therapists were classed according to sex and years of professional experience. Outcomes revealed that most patients were rated as improved or considerably improved, regardless of diagnosis, life status, or characteristics of therapists. Female therapists had a slightly higher, but nonsignificant, percentage of patients improved or considerably improved than did male therapists. Compared to male therapists, female therapists also showed marginally higher rates of improvement among patients diagnosed as anxiety reaction, schizophrenic, or personality disturbance.

While group comparisons of all female versus all male therapists revealed only slight differences, individual performance records indicated that female therapists consistently had high ratings, but considerable variation was found among male therapists. Only one of the nine female therapists received an overall negative evaluation, but 4 of the 14 male therapists received negative evaluations. Further analysis revealed that years of experience was a critical factor differentiating men. Women therapists had an overall improvement rate among their patients of 80%, regardless of years of experience. In contrast, male therapists of moderate professional experience had only a 60% improvement rate, whereas those with 7 or more years experience obtained an 87% improvement rate.

Based on these findings, the authors of the study conclude that young male therapists will probably be relatively safe and helpful with family women and single parents, especially with women who are older than they. However, effectiveness of therapy with young single women tends to be low, and the question is posed, "On whom are male therapists to practice until they become highly experienced?" (Orlinsky & Howard, 1980).

Beyond the already complex question of how gender affects outcome of therapy, the influence of gender on the process of therapy is also critical. In this formulation, the sex of clients, as well as that of therapists, is important. Client gender may influence perceptions of need for and duration of treatment, empathy, intervention style, and affective expression. Research paradigms and methodologies appropriate to the study of these questions have not been rigorously defined, and few studies are available to provide empirical evidence.

Furthermore, findings from such studies that do exist are mixed. For example, a recent review found several studies reporting no difference in length of therapy as a function of patient sex, but the same review also reported several studies indicating longer duration of therapy for women clients (Marecek & Johnson, 1980). Reactions to the affective content of therapy sessions as rated by therapists themselves indicate that female therapists experience and express more feelings in therapy sessions than do male therapists (Howard, Orlinsky, & Hill, 1979). Few studies have examined gender effects regarding the nature of interventions in therapy, that is, comparing reinforcing or extinguishing responses to manifest content presented by clients.

Comment

Many feminists hold the position that therapy of any designation is the wrong approach to liberation. This perspective suggests that women must recognize their status as members of a sisterhood having a shared past and a common future. In this light, therapy is seen as contributing to an illusion that individual actions based on effort or merit will enable them to escape the consequences of social stereotypes, cultural restrictions, and political practices that have led to the oppression of all women.

OLD BEGINNINGS AND NEW DIRECTIONS

Limited acceptance of feminism as a philosophical/political position is partly based on the difficulty of translating principles of macro level events to experiences that are more personal. The merits of feminism have been most easily accepted when elucidated in terms of large, impersonal social system frameworks, for example, equality of educational opportunity and equal pay for equal work. Feminism has seemed most threatening and troublesome when it forms part of the basis for personal and interpersonal frameworks.

The following section attempts to integrate personal and social frameworks, demonstrating the personal relevance of principles typically applied to social systems, dominance relations. The basic thesis proposes that the development and experience of "self" is a social as well as a personal event. Issues of dependency, anger, and power that have been problematic for women as individuals can be restructured in terms of dominance issues. A corollary is that personal events reviewed in the preceding chapters, depression, alcoholism, and other forms of dysfunction, can be understood partly in terms of dominance relations. This final section is designed to establish a basis for the integration of the events of self and social frameworks. Liberal, radical, and socialist/Marxist philosophies have influenced this analysis.

Integration of self and social frameworks in theory and therapy has been a major feature of feminist alternatives. General orientations include the necessity of examining situational variables in models of dysfunction and an egalitarian approach to the process of therapy. Recent theoretical developments have acknowledged the relational identity of self for many women. Being in relation to others is one of the more salient experiences of self. Attending to relationships and valuing attachments formed in relationships are legitimate and worthy enterprises.

This analysis argues that relationships often have a social-political aspect that influences personal experience in three areas: (1) our judgments and theories regarding dependency and attachment, (2) the experience and expression of anger, and (3) the experience and expression of power. The personal experience of dependency, for example, is partly a function of membership in a subordinate class. The willingness to suppress anger or to seek appeasement is partly a function of social sanctions, affiliative needs, and cognitive representations of subordinate status. Understanding the personal significance of this framework may be essential to better mental health, feminist consciousness, and commitment to social change.

Dominance Relations

The feminist principle that the personal is political forms the basis for much of this final analysis. It is the case that, regardless of how they are mothered, women mostly occupy subordinate positions. This is a social condition with psychological consequences; it is not brought about by the psychological traits of women. The importance of remembering this fact has been discussed by other feminist scholars in a variety of contexts (J. B. Miller, 1976, 1982; Unger, 1979). One of the goals of this review is to avoid circular reasoning, whereby the consequences of social conditions are seen to be their cause.

Consequences of status differences are evidenced in generally predictable patterns regardless of the groups or individuals involved (Miller &

Mothner, 1971; Miller, 1983). Dominants tend to engage in all of the following behaviors:

1. Exploit subordinates. Dominants tend to control and use the resources of subordinates. Dominants control expenditure of energy, form of effort, and time and space components of activity. Exploitation may involve labor, nurturance, sexuality, or other resources. Exploitation also entails an inequitable distribution of goods or products based on relative costs or inputs.

2. Limit opportunities. Only certain roles and behaviors are open to subordinates. Violations of expectations are often followed by punishment and further reduction of role options. Limitation of opportunities also mean limits on legitimate access to rewards, feelings of accomplishment, and sense of worth.

3. Ignore subordinates. Since subordinates have limited power and even less status, dominants seldom feel the need to attend to the actions, thoughts, or feelings of subordinates. It is in some ways ironic that while dominants have little sense of the characteristics, needs, or actions of subordinates, subordinates tend to pay careful attention to the moods, styles, and characteristics of dominants. This is how subordinates come to "work the system" without direct confrontation.

4. Characterize subordinates falsely. Subordinates are thought to be happiest in and even psychologically need to perform their service roles. Thus, the status quo is seen to be "natural" and in the best interests of subordinates. Behavior that fails to confirm stereotypes is simply ignored or re-interpreted. Thus, wanting to chair a committee is part of normal achievement striving for dominants, but indicates pushiness in subordinates.

5. Deny the legitimacy of experiences not consistent with the subordinate's role. Reactions to unmet needs, limited opportunity, humiliation, etc. are interpreted not as reactions to an inequitable status quo, but the product of some personal failing in the subordinate, e.g., a histrionic personality. In particular, women's anger is often interpreted, not as a legitimate response to inequity, but as unreasonable demands and dependency needs, indicative of neurosis or a poorly individuated self.

Differences in status or dominance have a number of implications for male-female relationships. Many "sex differences" may indeed simply reflect differences in status. For example, research indicates that women are slightly more likely to acquiesce to social pressure than men (Cooper, 1979; Eagly & Carli, 1981). Although the size and consistency of this finding has often been exaggerated, it can partially be interpreted as a function of status differences (Eagly & Wood, 1985).

Presumed sex differences in group dynamics may also be viewed in the same light. Differential status may lead to different role expectations and consequently differing activity and style within a group. Many women report a common experience of offering suggestions only to be ignored, whereas men easily acquire the attention of their peers. One consequence of this is that men may be perceived to have greater leadership potential, to be more valuable contributors, and hence to merit greater rewards. Even when competent women are accepted in leadership positions, they may not be well liked by other group members (Hagen & Kahn, 1975). Women who behave assertively in groups often are not only disliked but also may be perceived as maladjusted (Costrich, Feinstein, Kidder, Maracek, & Pascale, 1975). Further, it appears that even when women have high needs for dominance, they may refrain from acting on those needs in the presence of a male peer (Megargee, 1969).

Dominance relations continue to be played out by intimate pairs. This is something both women and men would like to ignore. The fact that dominance issues might play a role in relationships initiated on the basis of mutual approval and trust is difficult to acknowledge. However, analysis of a few extreme cases quickly reveals the possibility. The family is a setting for considerable violence (Gelles, 1979; Pagelow, 1981; Finkelhor, Gelles, Hotaling, & Straus, 1983; Russell, 1984). A high proportion of physical and sexual abuse that takes place in families is directed toward girls and women. Additionally, date rape, where couples are well known to each other, has been found to occur with disturbing frequency.

Whether these episodes of violence are labeled as battering or rape by the women involved largely determines help-seeking behavior (Sedlak, 1984). Further, it can be hypothesized that accurately labeling these episodes depends in part on whether or not women appreciate the fact that dominance relations operate even in intimate partnerships.

Episodes of violence are not the only ways in which dominance relations are evidenced among couples. Differing levels of influence are exercised by individuals in the dyad. Decisions about major expenditures of money, childrearing practices, and family schedules are often shaped more by one member than another. Additionally, styles of interpersonal problem solving (confrontive, avoidant, etc.) are probably shaped more by one member. The manner in which dominance in these areas is established and maintained is not well understood.

A working hypothesis for this analysis is that dominance relations may lay the groundwork for placing in social context the psychological experience of dependency, anger, and power. Dominance is not only something observed in experimental studies of social influence or in naturalistic studies of corporate dynamics but also operates in "normal" families and intimate pairs. Dominance can be played out through numerous influence pathways, including strategies of helplessness, guilt induction, selective attention, threats to self-esteem, usurping initiative, and others. Dominance can influence "simple" things like when to take a vacation, as well as more complex events. Dominance has implications for the phenomenological experience of dependency, anger, and power.

Dependency

There are numerous facets of dependency; three that are reviewed here are dependent acts, psychic dependency, and relational identity. Each of these can to some extent be understood in the context of dominance relations. *Dependent acts* include expressions of helplessness, weepiness, frailty, clumsiness, etc. These acts are acquired through normal learning processes; that is, they have been reinforced. They are exhibited because the individual achieves some gain by doing so. The gains might be direct, for example, inducing someone to provide physical comforts, or gains might be psychological, for example, social approval in fulfilling a role. To a certain extent, dependent acts are expected elements of traditional femininity. Thus, by acting dependent, females retain the approval of others and avoid censure for role violations. Acting in such a fashion does not necessarily imply a psychic deficit or lack of individuation.

Dependent actions are characteristic of subordinates and as such are more reflective of low status than gender. Furthermore, dependent acts do not always reflect true helplessness but may instead be an influence strategy. Acting dependent represents one of the few influence strategies readily accessible to women (Johnson, 1974; Raven, 1974; Lerner, 1983). Almost every woman can recount an instance where she presented herself as helpless in order to gain cooperation or assistance. A low status person cannot demand or even directly request aid in many circumstances. However, exhibiting distress and ineptitude will often be effective in recruiting assistance.

However, persistent reliance on dependency as a style of relating can have long-term costs. The presentation of self as dependent may begin as an influence strategy but can eventually shape a permanent self-image of incompetence. Stiver (1984) points out that women are often deeply ashamed of their dependency. Therefore, initial gains may be made by the subordinate but at the cost of long-term psychological damage.

Dependent acts overlap somewhat with psychic dependency because they may be used and interpreted as symbols of attachment or have implications for dependency needs. Marriage celebrations ritualize mutual dependency of partners by the acts of reciprocal handfeeding. Both women and men may gain from acting dependent and encouraging dependent acts by their partner. By acting dependent, some women may feel they are more likely to secure the attachment of their male partner, who cannot leave because it would be so devastating to the women involved. In fact, many active and self-reliant women become very dependent once married (Lerner, 1983).

Although men may grumble about the ineptitude of their women partners, men may also gain by the dependent actions of women. Much dependency probably is supported through the collusion of husbands (Stiver, 1984). For example, it is not impossible to find women of adult years who do not know how to drive an automobile. They manage their households and raise their children by relying on a husband. This dependency reaffirms to the man his own value to the woman and the security of their bond together. If she is dependent on him, he must indeed be competent. Further, she can't leave him (to his own needs and dependencies). Her dependence allows him to play a contrasting role of competent dominance, while at the same time insuring that his own needs for attachment will continue to be met.

Men also engage in acts of dependency and helplessness as a means of influencing women. The politics of housework are such that being helpless is often a good strategy to avoid doing it. He'd be glad to fix the dinner salad, but he doesn't know whether to chop or slice the tomatoes. Failure to learn how to braid daughter's hair will insure that one is never called on to do so. Washing delicate pastel blouses with blue jeans may be one subtle attempt to convince a wife that she really should take over laundry duties.

Women may gain from male dependent acts and may even subtly collaborate to promote them. Men who cannot cook a meal or remove the dirty rings from their own collars are giving visible evidence of needing to be in relation to their women partners. By making themselves indispensable, women are building a sense of security. Furthermore, women may acquire a certain amount of stature or dominance, even if it is within a limited domain. In comparison to these "helpless" men, women can feel particularly competent or dominant in at least one sphere of activity.

Psychic dependency has implications for individuation whereby the individual has remained psychologically merged with another and does indeed lack a differentiated sense of self. Psychic dependency is what Oedipal conflicts and object relations theory are about. Separation and autonomy represent healthy psychological development in this context.

Psychoanalytic theory and traditional object relations theory suggest that women experience more psychic dependency than men because women retain relatively permeable self boundaries, partly because they are mothered by a same-sex person. In contrast, the developmental press for men is to acquire a definitive sense of autonomy with clear boundaries of self. In fact, it probably is the case that both women and men experience psychic dependency, but simply evidence it in diverse ways.

Extreme psychic dependency can produce pathology. An interesting forensic case illustrates what may happen when dependency is threatened. A woman with marginal IQ was arrested for transporting illicit drugs (undoubtedly as a courier for a larger business group). As a result, her young daughter was made a ward of the court and placed in a foster home. Distraught over the loss of her daughter, she claimed to be pregnant and even began to lactate, although medical tests indicated she was not in fact pregnant. The "pregnancy" probably represented an attempt to regain the fusion and sense of self previously invested in her daughter. Other pathologies may be viewed as an attempt to escape psychic dependency. One can speculate that many intrafamilial homicides are based partly on the rages of a fused personality whereby the homicide represents a desperate attempt to psychically separate from the engulfing family. Another forensic case offers an example. In this instance, a teenage boy killed his mother by suffocation, a quite uncommon method of homicide, but probably symbolic of his feeling that she was suffocating him.

Incapacitating jealous rages probably also reflect a certain degree of psychic fusion with the other, whereby the putative infidelity represents a threatened loss of self. Also, since there is a certain degree of merged identity, when a wife has sexual relations with another man, that man symbolically has had sexual access to her husband as well. This may elicit feelings in the husband of having been raped, or arouse panic over homosexual themes. It is not uncommon for men to violently assault their wives under such circumstances. The fact that men are most likely to perpetrate such acts of violence suggests that the autonomy and individuation to which men aspire is often surrendered in their intimate relationships with women. One may also speculate that some instances of wife battering are based on a pathological fear of abandonment and the subsequent need to completely control or dominate the woman.

The actual incidence of such violence is supported by a number of social conditions and should not be analyzed strictly in terms of intrapsychic events. Paramour laws indicate a certain social tolerance for homicidal rages predicated on intimate relationships. Thus, in the past the wronged party could seek violent retribution with impugnity. Initially, paramour laws applied only to men (theoretically enraged over a violation of their property). When such laws were made sex fair, many of them were repealed.

Psychic dependency does not always lead to diagnostic pathology or homicide. Everyone retains a certain amount of psychic dependency. The process of acquiring a sense of self, independent from the views and expectations of others, is an ongoing existential task. The sense of self continually undergoes reevaluation and discovery. Periodic diffusion of boundaries between self and other may ultimately promote personal growth. The question is how diffuse the boundaries become and how much permanent psychic dependency results. Often blurring of boundaries simply represents a means of experiencing vicarious pleasures. For example, the father who recounts his son's athletic accomplishments while using plural pronouns probably is exhibiting some psychic dependency.

Contemporary feminist theorists have developed new perspectives on dependency, where dependency does not reflect lack of individuation but instead reflects a desire to be in relationship to others. For convenience, this will be termed *relational identity*. Ideally, it is based on the ability to be empathic without being engulfed. Relational identity involves the desire to be in relation to others, connected to others, and to attend to relationships.

This more recent approach recognizes that dependency was defined historically as negative because it was identified with women and that which is female (Stiver, 1984). However, affirmative views of feminine style recognize that a sense of self is often developed and maintained through relational experiences (Miller, 1976; Gilligan, 1982; Surrey, 1983, 1984a). In fact, women are more likely to view interpersonal events as opportunities for growth, competence, and achievement than are men (Stein & Bailey, 1973; Travis, Burnett-Doering, & Reid, 1982).

Although relationships are often less than perfect and sometimes involve inequities and disappointments, the desire to pursue sound, healthy relationships should be viewed as a strength and not a weakness. The capacity to genuinely take pleasure in being in relationship to others, to feel enhanced by relationships, and to freely support others in relationships is a worthy developmental goal.

Women, more than men, seem to be consciously aware of their need to be in relation to others and to purposefully invest their energy in attending to and maintaining these relationships. Social expectations allow women to invest their energy in relationships (although they are somewhat ridiculed for doing so). The continued choice of homemaker roles as career options among women is probably partly the result of women's desire to pursue life-styles where relationships are the principle arenas of endeavor and exchange.

In contrast, men are not given social permission to attend to relationships and may fear that needs to be in relation to others are indicative of weakness. Because society is more accepting of female relational dependency, men more often evidence their relational dependency in disguised form. Sexual gratification, presented as a need for physical release, is one area where men frequently also seek gratification of their needs for closeness and connection (Stiver, 1984). Women, on the other hand, are likely to consciously experience sexuality as an aspect of being in relationship.[1] The psychological significance of sexual intercourse for men is often revealed in rage reactions to infidelity by their partners. The infidelity represents not only a confrontation with the separateness of the other but also contains threats to the satisfaction of dependency needs.

These different patterns of women and men contribute to much conflict, the typical pattern being that women want more emotional expressiveness and relational investment from men. This is in some ways ironic because it is probable that women already know a good deal more about men's emotional needs and states than men know about those of women.

The feminist movement has acknowledged the value of being in relationship to others, and communal, as opposed to agentic, styles are encouraged. However, healthy relational work cannot be pursued effectively unless all parties have a firm sense of self as unique and independent from others. Consequently, feminists have also encouraged women to develop a sense of identity separate from the roles they hold in relation to parents, spouses, and children.

Unfortunately, balancing the search for independent identity with relational investment is not easy. Many women have responded negatively to rhetoric focused only on pursuit of an autonomous self. The real threat of this message, and a possible explanation for why women's liberation initially found so little grass roots support, was the implication that women should restructure their sense of self and give up the significance of being connected to others.

As women have struggled with these issues, new insights have emerged. Contemporary feminist views suggest that empathy and the ability to be in relationship to others represents a far more complex and developmentally advanced process than implied in traditional developmental theory and perhaps than implied in early feminist rhetoric (Jordan, 1983; Surrey, 1983; Kaplan, 1983). These theorists argue that for women, competence and initiative are developed in the context of important relationships. The desire to understand and to be understood play an important role in self-acceptance for women (Jordan, 1983). The importance of this empathic

---

[1]This description should not be taken as a universal pattern, nor a dichotomous one. The degree to which sexuality is a recreational act, an expression of dominance, or affirmative and mutual acceptance (and so on) varies on a continuum for both sexes.

state may be appreciated when one realizes that the development of empathy is one of the first steps in psychotherapy and precedes transference, insight, or growth (Kaplan, 1983a).

Being-in-relation, and the associated empathy, has implications for dominance relations. In a dyadic relationship, the less "needy" partner is in a more powerful position because that person can always exert influence by a threat of withdrawal or indifference. To the extent that women, more than men, are aware of their own needs to be related, women are the ones who are most likely to make compromises to retain a relationship. That is, women are more likely to perceive a threat to the relational commitment at an early stage of conflict. Men frequently do not realize the extent of their own need for relationship until they have lost it. For example, it is routinely the case that in couples therapy, it is the woman who has initiated therapeutic contact, while her partner protests that nothing is wrong.

Anger

Common assumptions are that men readily express their anger and that women do not. However, both women and men have difficulty in managing anger and expressing it effectively. Both sexes disguise and redirect their feelings in these areas. For example, it has been suggested that women often say they are hurt when in fact they are really angry (Lerner, 1980). In contrast, men may say they are angry, when in fact they are hurt (Miller, 1983). Both women and men may somaticize their anger, high blood pressure being a frequent consequence. Depression may be another outcome of difficulty in the management and expression of anger. Social sanctions, affiliative needs, and cognitive belief systems all operate to shape the expression of anger, and each has implications for dominance relations.

Social sanctions are differentially applied to women and men regarding the expression of anger. Compared to men, women risk paying a higher social cost when they express anger. A good deal of social pressure is exerted by labeling aggressive women as "man-haters," "castrating bitches," and various other perjoratives. Such labeling excludes women from acceptable social company, not only of men but often of other women as well.

It has been suggested that this social pressure partially draws its impact from a deep psychic fear that women have the potential for omnipotent destructiveness (Lederer, 1968; Lerner, 1980). Individuals who carefully monitor and control their emotions often do so because they feel that particular emotion is so strong it might become overwhelmingly destructive, of the self as well as others. However, the suggestion here is that society in general perceives female anger as being especially violent and disruptive. From a societal perspective, angry men are apparently not as threatening as angry women. If a lot of men are angry, there is a strike or a coup. If a lot of women are angry, the breakdown of society is imminent.

Affiliative needs and the desire to be in relation to others may also contribute to diffiulties women have in expressing their anger. Anger carries a threat to relationships and thereby elicits separation anxiety (Lerner, 1980). Anger implies a distinctiveness and separation from others. Women often deal with such threats by denying they are angry or exhibiting tears and weeping in conjunction with the expression of anger. This is often accompanied by statements of hurt feelings. Even while experiencing anger, women may feel a compulsion to reassure the other that an emotional commitment still exists. Further, there may be considerable pull from the other to reaffirm commitment. The essence of conflict over affiliation, separation and anger is captured in the following quote.

> The expression of legitimate anger and protest is more than a statement of dignity and self-respect. It is also a statement that one will risk standing alone, even in the face of disapproval or the potential loss of love from others (Lerner, 1980, p. 145).

Separation anxiety is, however, based on more than the threat of lost love. Many women, especially those with young children, are financially dependent on support from a man, even when the woman herself is employed. Thus, anger or even strong criticism might potentially jeopardize not only her well-being but that of her children as well.

Conditions that seem to inhibit the expression of anger in women also seem to give power to men. Separation anxiety may greatly restrict the ability of women to assume a firm negotiating position in interpersonal relationships. It may often be the case that women are more likely than men to abandon an argument or ignore an area of conflict than jeopardize the relationship (Gilligan, 1982). The fact that men more easily express their anger, and that it may take violent forms, further tips the scale of influence in favor of men.

Additionally, men may gain in negotiating strength because the expression of anger is frequently viewed as an indication of the legitimacy of one's position. This is based on the belief that only virtuous people can be indignant. Getting angry can also be adopted as a strategy to forestall future criticisms or conflict. Thus, one party can make conflict so emotionally traumatic that the costs of resolving sensitive problems are made to far outweigh potential gains.

Cognitive factors also contribute to the experience of anger and dominance relations. Miller (1983) has suggested that subordinates, of either sex, hold belief systems that complicate anger. The most common beliefs are (1) I am weak, (2) I am unworthy, and (3) I have no right to be angry. These belief systems are fostered and supported to some degree by important others and certainly those who stand to gain in dominance exchange.

The self-estimate of weakness is a relational assessment, crediting the power of overwhelming retaliation to those at whom the anger is directed. Retaliation may take the form of physical abuse, temper tantrums, harangues, love withdrawal, pouting, and so on. This belief is also often accompanied by a fundamental attribution error that the perceived weakness is a permanent personality trait not subject to change.

A shakey self-esteem contributes to the feeling that one cannot reasonably expect better treatment, that is, the belief one is not worthy. This belief also rests partly on the fact that in dominance relations the legitimacy of subordinates' experiences is often denied or trivialized. Thus, feelings of anger may be judged inappropriate or signs of a flawed personality.

Finally, subordinates often come to believe that the division of goods and resources is equitable, and they have no right to be angry. Equity theory suggests that people generally expect to be rewarded according to their investment or costs and that others should be similarly rewarded (Walster, Berscheid, & Walster, 1973; Berkowitz & Walster, 1976; Walster, Walster, & Berscheid, 1978). A variety of conditions and factors appear to influence whether principles of equity or equality are followed by subjects in experimental settings (Kahn & Gaeddert, 1985).

If women believe equity has been established in their relationships, then they have no right to be angry. An implicit *just world hypothesis* (Lerner, Miller, & Holmes, 1976) often operates to convince subordinates that equity does exist. The belief that individuals get their just desserts is commonly supported in American society. It is, to some extent, a comforting thought that if one works hard, success will follow. It is a belief that contributes to a sense of control and predictability. Of course, the obverse also holds; if one does not work hard, failure ensues. By extension and causal inference, if one has fewer rewards than others, one has not worked hard enough. Thus, the belief in a just world lends itself to the acceptance of individualism and the unequal distribution of goods as equitable and fair.

The apparent acceptance of inequities and lack of anger among women may well be traced to the belief that the distribution of rewards is just. That is, women may contribute substantially to the financial security of the family, manage the physical comforts of home and hearth, and provide emotional support and nurturance for their male partners who maintain a single role, that of the "good provider". It would seem that in many cases, fulfillment of that single role completes the male part of a relational contract. Research on dual career couples indicates that seldom do men in these relationships contribute equally to household tasks or child care (Weingarten, 1978). Further, it is generally agreed that men do not nurture their wives to the extent that women nurture their husbands. For example, forgotten anniversaries and birthdays are so common among men as to provide standard source material for cartoonists and comedians.

These conflicts and difficulties are not unique to women. If men could experience and express their anger effectively, they would commit far fewer violent acts. The primitive reaction of physical acting out is probably indicative of feelings of ineptitude and an inability to produce alternative, more favorable outcomes. Men have limited repertoires in managing their anger. Therefore, instead of assertive insistence on fair treatment or change, they resort to table pounding and posturing. The supposition that women are more emotional than men is substantially weakened if data on violence are examined.

Power

Common conceptions of power tend to identify it with domination and ruthlessness. Power is generally assumed to exist in a zero-sum framework; that is, power is limited and to the extent that if individual "A" has more power, "B" must have less power. Clearly this sets power as a scarce commodity, acquired primarily by conflict and exploitation (Miller, 1976).

Social psychologists have offered somewhat more complex views of power bases (French & Raven, 1959). They suggest five sources of power: legitimate, expert, reward, coercive, and referent power. Legitimate power is that source of influence accorded to individuals who occupy formal positions of leadership or control. Expert power refers to influence that may be wielded due to special knowledge or skills that are perceived as important or necessary for the accomplishment of group goals. Referent power is based on personal charisma and the attractiveness of the individual to others who wish to emulate those same positive traits. Reward and coercive power simply refer to the control of resources and sanctions.

The conceptualization of power translates readily to issues involved in dominance relations; it is probably partly due to this ready translation that women have experienced so much conflict over power. As subordinates, women should want to gain control of their lives, to insure more responsive attention to their own needs, and to establish new social structures. However, women consistently deny that they want power or often that they even need it.

The desire of women to be in relation to others affects their use of power. To the extent that power is perceived to be usurpation of limited resources or exploitation of others, women tend to avoid expressions of power or influence. This is partly because women tend to see such agentic actions as selfish. Themes of giving and concern over selfishness routinely emerge when women discuss their conflicts involving power (Miller, 1982). Pursuing personal preferences is often perceived as selfish, irresponsible, and sometimes immoral (Gilligan, 1982). Additionally, women often fear evoking the displeasure of others, especially a man. There is an unacknowledged expectation that the man will simply leave; thus fears of abandonment also produce inhibitions in the use of power.

Further experience with power may reveal options beyond those of cultural stereotypes. For example, in some circumstances, power does not have to exist in a zero-sum framework (Kimmel, 1985). Jointly assuming power as a communal act may result in an increased sense of competence, enthusiasm, and feelings of accomplishment for all involved. This sort of experience is termed *empowerment*. To become empowered with respect to one's own strengths and capabilities does not imply conflict with others and is a major goal of feminist therapy (Imes & Clance, 1984). Additionally, power may be developed in a communal framework whereby a coalition is formed to implement change. This feminist view of power assumes that power can have growthful consequences for others and can be a product of cooperative relationships. One contribution of feminist analyses of power will be the development of new conceptions in the acquisition and expression of power, not only for women but for men as well.

SUMMARY

There are no fixed schools of feminist alternatives in theory and therapy; considerable overlap exists and developments have been guided by relatively general principles. These principles focus on the fact that women must be viewed as possessing basically healthy and powerful sources of personal growth and expression. Women's experiences are viewed as important in their own right. Furthermore, these principles advocate a balance between person and context or figure and ground, acknowledging the intimate interplay of self and social frameworks. Additionally, feminist analyses focus more directly on sexism and its effects. Symptoms of dysfunction may be produced by characteristics of traditional feminine roles, role overload, or role conflict and may also be seen as survival tactics among individuals with limited power.

The experience of limited power may be played out in numerous subtle dominance relations, whereby women have limited access to resources and therefore limited opportunities to constructively effect change. The fact that these experiences are often ignored or rejected as invalid have a number of consequences for dependency and anger.

As women acquire a sense of their own authenticity, their expressions of power should be less conflicted. For example, when women feel their needs are as legitimate as those of their families, spouses, children, colleagues, and so on, it will be easier to press others to attend to those needs. Accepting one's own comprehension of the world as a valid basis for responding to it enhances the sense that one is entitled to the judgments, emotions, and actions based on that comprehension.

References

Abernethy, D. R., Greenblatt, D. J., Divall, M., Arendt, R., Ochs, H. R., & Shader, S. (1982). Impairment of diazepam metabolism by low-dose estrogen-containing oral-contraceptive steroids. *Medical Intelligence, 306* (13), 791–792.

Abramson, L. Y., Seligman, M. E., & Teasdale, J. D. (1978). Learned helplessness in humans: Critique and reformulation. *Journal of Abnormal Psychology, 87,* 49–57.

Adelstein, A., & White, G. (1977). Alcoholism and mortality, *Population Trends, 6,* 7–13.

Agras, S., & Werne, J. (1977). Behavior modification in anorexia nervosa: Research foundations. In R. A. Vigersky (Ed.), *Anorexia nervosa* (pp. 291–303). New York: Raven Press.

Al-Issa, I. (1980). *The psychopathology of women.* Englewood Cliffs, NJ: Prentice Hall.

Allan, C. A., & Cooke, D. J. (1985). Stressful life events and alcohol misuse in women: A critical review. *Journal of Studies on Alcohol, 46,* 147–152.

Allen, R. P., Wagman, A., Tallaici, L. A., & McIntosh, M. (1971). Electroencephalographic (EEG) sleep recovery following prolonged alcohol intoxication in alcoholism. *Journal of Nervous and Mental Disease, 153,* 425–433.

Allgeier, E. (1979, August). The relationship of androgyny to several indices of psychological functioning. Paper presented at the American Psychological Association meetings, New York.

Anderson, S. C. (1980). Patterns of sex-role identification in alcoholic women. *Sex Roles, 6,* 231–243.

Angrist, S., Dinitz, S., Lefton, M., & Pasamanick (1961). Rehospitalization of female mental patients. *Archives of American Psychiatry, 4,* 363.

Angrist, S., Dinitz, S., Lefton, M., & Pasamanick, B. (1968). *Women after treatment.* New York: Appleton-Century Crofts.

Ardrey, R. (1966). *The territorial imperative.* New York: Atheneum.

Ashley, M. J., Olin, J. S., Le-Riche, W. H., Kornaczewski, A., Schmidt, W., & Rankin, J. G. (1977). Morbidity in alcoholics: Evidence for accelerated development of physical disease in women. *Archives of Internal Medicine, 137,* 883–887.

Asma, E. E., Eggert, R. L., & Hilker, R. R. (1971). Long-term experience with rehabilitation of alcoholic employees. *Journal of Occupational Medicine, 13,* 581–585.

Bailey, M. B., Haberman, P. W., & Alksne, H. (1965). The epidemiology of alcoholism in an urban residential area. *Quarterly Journal of Studies on Alcohol, 26,* 19–40.

Bakan, D. (1966). *The duality of human existence.* Chicago: Rand McNally.

Baker, M. A., Berheide, C. W., Greckel, F. R., Gugin, L. C., Lipetz, M. J., & Segal, M. T. (1980). *Women today.* Monterey, CA: Brooks/Cole Publishing Co.

Bandura, A. (1977). Self-efficacy: Toward a unifying theory of behavioral change. *Psychological Review, 84,* 191–215.

Barr, H. L., & Cohen, A. (1979). The problem-drinking drug addict. National Institute on Drug Abuse Services Research Report. DHEW Publication No. (ADW) 79-893, U.S. Government Printing Office.

Barrett, C. J., Berg, P. I., Eaton, E. M., & Pomeroy, E. L. (1974). *Psychotherapy: Theory, Research & Practice, 11*(1), 11–15.

Bart, P. (1971). Depression in middle-aged women. In V. Gornick & B. Moran (Eds.), *Women in Sexist Society.* New York: Basic Books.

Beck, A. T. (1967). *Depression: Clinical and theoretical aspects.* New York: Harper & Row.

Beck, A. T., & Greenberg, R. L. (1974). Cognitive therapy with depressed women. In V. Frank & V. Burtle, (Eds.), *Women in therapy.* New York: Brunner/Mazel.

Beck, A. T., Rush, A. J., Shaw, B. F., & Emery, G. (1979). *Cognitive therapy of depression.* New York: Guilford Press.

Beck, J. C., & Worthen, K. (1972). Precipitating stress, crisis theory and hospitalization in schizophrenia and depression. *Archives of General Psychiatry, 26,* 123–129.

Beckman, L. J. (1975). Women alcoholics: A review of the social psychological studies. *Journal of Studies on Alcohol, 36,* 797–824.

Beckman, L. J. (1976). Alcoholism problems and women: An overview. In: M. Greenblatt & M. A. Schucket (Eds.), *Alcoholism Problems in Women* (pp. 367–380). New York: Grune & Stratton.

Beckman, L. J. (1977). Psychosocial aspects of alcoholism in women. *Alcoholism—Clinic and Experimental Research, 1,* 177.

Beckman, L. J. (1978). Sex role conflict in alcoholic women: Myth or reality. *Journal of Abnormal Psychology, 87,* 408–417.

Beckman, L. J. (1979). Reported effects of alcohol on the sexual feelings and behavior of women alcoholics and nonalcoholics. *Journal of Studies on Alcohol, 40,* 272–282.

Beckman, L. J., & Amaro, H. (1984). Patterns of women's use of alcohol treatment agencies. In: S. Wilsnack & L. Beckman (Eds.), *Alcohol problems in women* (pp. 319–348). New York & London: Guilford Press.

Beckman, L. J., & Amaro, H. (1986). Personal and social difficulties faced by women and men entering alcoholism treatment. *Journal of Studies in Alcoholism, 47*, 135–145.

Belfer, M. L., & Shader, R. I. (1976). Premenstrual factors as determinants of alcoholism in women. In: M. Greenblatt & M. A. Schuckit (Eds.), *Alcoholism Problems in Women* (pp. 97–102). New York: Grune & Stratton.

Belfer, M. L., Shader, R. I., Carroll, M., & Hermatz, J. S. (1971). Alcoholism in women. *Archives of General Psychiatry, 25*, 540–544.

Bell, H., & Nordhagen, R. (1980). HLA antigens in alcoholics with special reference to alcoholic cirrhosis. *Scandinavian Journal of Gastroenterology, 15*, 453–456.

Belle, D. (1980). Who uses mental health facilities? In M. Guttentag, S. Salasin, & D. Belle (Eds.), *The mental health of women*. New York: Academic Press.

Belle, D., & Goldman, N. (1980). Patterns of diagnoses received by men and women. In M. Guttentag, S. Salasin, & D. Belle (Eds.), *The mental Health of women*. New York: Academic Press.

Belsky, J., & Rovine, M. (1984, May). Social-network contact, family support, and the transition to parenthood. *Journal of Marriage and the Family*, pp. 455–462.

Bem, S. L. (1974). The measurement of psychological androgyny. *Journal of Consulting and Clinical Psychology, 42*, 155–162.

Bem, S. L. (1975a). Probing the promise of androgyny. Address presented at the APA-NIMH Conference on the Research Needs of Women, Madison, Wisconsin.

Bem, S. L. (1975b). Sex role adaptability: One consequence of psychological androgyny. *Journal of Personality and Social Psychology, 31*, 634–643.

Bem, S. L. (1981). Gender schema theory: A cognitive account of sex-typing. *Psychological Review, 88*, 354–364.

Bem, S. L., & Lenney, E. (1976). Sex typing and the avoidance of cross-sex behavior. *Journal of Personality and Social Psychology, 33*, 48–54.

Bemis, K. M. (1978). Current approaches to the etiology and treatment of anorexia nervosa. *Psychological Bulletin, 85*(3), 593–617.

Benjamin, J. (1984). The convergence of psychoanalysis and feminism: Gender identity and autonomy. In C. M. Brody (Ed.), *Women therapists working with women*. New York: Springer Publishing Co.

Benjaminsen, S. (1981). Stressful life events preceding the onset of neurotic depression. *Psychological Medicine, 11*, 369–378.

Bennett, W., & Gurin, J. (1982). *The dieter's dilemma*. New York: Basic Books.

Benston, M. (1971). The political economy of women's liberation. In J. Sochen (Ed.), *The new feminism in twentieth-century America*. Lexington, MA: D.C. Health & Company, 192–202.

Bergin, A. E., & Lambert, M. J. (1971). The evaluation of therapeutic outcomes. In A. E. Bergin & S. L. Garfield (Eds.), *Handbook of psychotherapy and behavior change*. New York: Wiley.

Bergman, H., Borg, S., Hindmarsh, T., Idestrom, C. M., & Mutzell, S. (1980). Computed tomography of the brain and neuropsychological assessment of male alcoholic patients and a random sample from the general male population. *Acta Psychiatrica Scandinavia, 62* (Suppl. 286), 47–56.

Berkman, L. F. (1984). Assessing the physical health effects of social networks and social support. *Annual Review of Public Health, 5,* 413–432.

Berkman, L. F., & Syme, L. (1979). Social networks, host resistance, and mortality: A nine-year follow-up study of Alameda County residents. *American Journal of Epidemiology, 109*(2), 186–204.

Berkowitz, L., & Walster, E. (1976). *Equity theory: Toward a general theory of social interaction. Advances in experimental social psychology* (Vol. 9). New York: Academic Press.

Biddle, B. J., Bank, B. J., & Martin, M. M. (1980). Social determinants of adolescent drinking. What they think, what they do and what I think and do. *Journal of Studies on Alcohol, 41,* 215–241.

Billings, A. G., & Moos, R. H. (1982). Social support and functioning among community and clinical groups: A panel model. *Journal of Behavioral Medicine, 5*(3), 295–311.

Bird, C. (1968). *Born female.* New York: David McKay Co., Inc.

Blatt, S. J., Wein, S. J., Chevron, E., & Quinlan, D. M. (1979). Parental representations and depression in normal young adults. *Journal of Abnormal Psychology, 88*(4), 388–397.

Blazer, D. (1980). Life events, mental health functioning and the use of health care services by the elderly. *American Journal of Public Health, 70*(11), 1174–1179.

Blechman, E. A. (1980). Behavior therapies. In A. M. Brodsky & R. T. Hare-Mustin (Eds.), *Women and psychotherapy.* New York: The Guilford Press.

Block, J. H. (1984). *Sex role identity and ego development.* San Francisco: Jossey-Bass Publishers.

Bohman, M., Sigvardsson, S., & Cloninger, R. (1981). Maternal inheritance of alcohol abuse. Cross fostering analyses of adopted women. *Archives of General Psychology, 38,* 965–969.

Bootzin, R. R., & Max, D. (1980). Learning and behavioral theories. In I. L. Kutash & L. B. Schlesinger (Eds.), *Handbook on stress and anxiety.* San Francisco: Jossey-Bass Publishers.

Bordin, E. S. (1974). *Research strategies in psychotherapy.* New York: John Wiley & Sons.

Boskind-Lodahl, M. (1976). Cinderella's stepsisters: A feminist perspective on anorexia nervosa and bulimia. *Signs: Journal of Women in Culture and Society, 2*(2), 342–356.

Boskind-Lodahl, M., & White, W. C. (1978). The definition and treatment of bulimarexia nervosa and bulimia. *Signs, 2,* 342–356.

Boss, G. R., & Seegmiller, J. E. (1979). Hyperuricemia and gout: Classification, complications and management. *New England Journal of Medicine, 300,* 1459–1468.

Bowen, M. (1978). *Family therapy in clinical practice.* New York: Aronson.

Boyar, R. M., Hellman, L. D., & Roffwarg, H. (1977). Cortisol secretion and metabolism in anorexia nervosa. *New England Journal of Medicine, 296,* 190–193.

Braatoy, T. (1937). Is it probable that the sociological situation is a factor in schizophrenia? *Acta Psychiatrica Scandinavica, 12*, 109–138.

Braiker, H. (1984). Therapeutic issues in the treatment of alcoholic women. In: S. Wilsnack & L. Beckman (Eds.), *Alcohol problems in women* (pp. 349–368). New York & London: Guilford Press.

Brenner, M. H., & Mooney, A. (1983). Unemployment and health in the context of economic change. *Social Science and Medicine, 17*, 1125–1138.

Brewer, C., & Perrett, L. (1971). Brain damage due to alcohol consumption: An air-encephalographic, psychometric and electroencephalographic study. *British Journal of Addiction, 66*, 170–112.

Brodsky, A. M., & Hare-Mustin, R. T. (1980). *Women and psychotherapy: An assessment of research and practice.* New York: Guilford Press.

Brody, C. (1984). *Women therapists working with women.* New York: Springer.

Brook, G. K. (1977). Acute gastric dilatation in anorexia nervosa. *British Medical Journal, 20*, 499–500.

Brooks, J., Ruble, D., & Clark, A. (1977). College women's attitudes and expectancies concerning menstrual-related changes. *Psychosomatic Medicine, 39*, 288–298.

Brotman, A. W., Rigotti, N., & Herzog, D. B. (1985). Medical complications of eating disorders: Outpatient evaluation and management. *Comprehensive Psychiatry, 26*, 258–272.

Brotman, A. W., & Stern, T. A. (1983). Case report of cardiovascular abnormalities in anorexia nervosa. *American Journal of Psychiatry, 140*, 1227–1228.

Broverman, I. K., Broverman, D. M., Clarkson, F. E., Rosenkrantz, P. S., & Vogel, S. R. (1970). Sex-role stereotypes and clinical judgments of mental health. *Journal of Consulting and Clinical Psychology, 34*(1), 1–7.

Brown, G. M. (1983). Endocrine alterations in anorexia nervosa. In P. L. Darby, P. E. Garfinkel, D. M. Garner, & D. V. Coscina (Eds.), *Anorexia nervosa: Recent developments in research* (pp. 231–247). New York: Alan R. Liss, Inc.

Brown, G. W., & Harris, T. (1978). *Social origins of depression: A study of psychiatric disorder in women.* New York: Free Press.

Brown, G. W., & Harris, T. (1982). Fall-off in the reporting of life events. *Social Psychiatry, 17*, 23–28.

Brown, G. W., Harris, T., & Peto, J. (1973). Life events and psychiatric disorders. II: Nature of causal link. *Psychological Medicine, 3*, 159–176.

Brown, J. (1971). Editorial. In J. Agel (Ed.), *The radical therapist.* New York: Ballantine.

Brownell, A., & Shumaker, S. A. (1984). Social support: An introduction to a complex phenomenon. *Journal of Social Issues, 40*(4), 1–9.

Browning, C., & Miller, S. (1968). Anorexia nervosa: A study in prognosis and management. *American Journal of Psychiatry, 124*(8), 1128–1132.

Bruch, H. (1973). *Eating disorders: Obesity, anorexia nervosa, and the person within.* New York: Basic Books, Inc.

Bruch, H. (1977). Psychological antecedents of anorexia nervosa. In R. A. Vigersky (Ed.), *Anorexia nervosa* (pp. 1–10). New York: Raven Press.

Bruch, H. (1978). *The golden cage: The enigma of anorexia nervosa.* Cambridge, MA: Harvard University Press.

Bruch, H. (1985). Four decades of eating disorders. In D. M. Garner & P. E. Garfinkel (Eds.), *Handbook of psychotherapy for anorexia nervosa and bulimia.* New York: The Guilford Press.

Bunney, W. E. Jr., & Davis, J. M. (1965). Norepinephrine in depressive reactions. *Archives of General Psychiatry, 13,* 483–494.

Burchardt, C. J., & Serbin, L. A. (1982). Psychological androgyny and personality adjustment in college and psychiatric populations. *Sex Roles, 8,* 835–851.

Byrne, D. G. (1981). Sex differences in the reporting of symptoms of depression in the general population. *British Journal of Clinical Psychology, 20,* 83–92.

Cadoret, R. J., Winokur, G., Dorzab, J., & Baker, M. (1972). Depressive disease: life events and onset of illness. *Archives of General Psychiatry, 26,* 133–136.

Calahan, D., Cisin, I., & Crossley, H. (1969). American drinking practices. Rutgers Center of Alcohol Studies Monograph. No. 6. New Brunswick, NJ.

Cannon, W. B. (1929). *Bodily changes in pain, hunger, fear, and rage: An account of recent researches into the function of emotional excitement.* New York: Appleton-Century Crofts.

Caranosos, G. J., Stewart, R. B., Cluff, L. E. (1974). Drug-induced illness leading to hospitalization. *Journal of American Medical Association, 228*(6), 713–717.

Casper, R. C. (1983). Some provisional ideas concerning the psychologic structure in anorexia nervosa and bulimia. In P. L. Darby, P. E. Garfinkel, D. M. Garner, & D. V. Coscina (Eds.), *Anorexia nervosa: Recent developments in research.* New York: Alan R. Liss.

Casper, R., & Davis, J. M. (1977). On the course of anorexia nervosa. *American Journal of Psychiatry, 134*(9), 974–978.

Casper, R. C., Eckert, E. D., Halmi, K. A., Goldberg, S. C., & Davis, J. M. (1980). Bulimia: Its incidence and clinical importance in patients with anorexia nervosa. *Archives of General Psychiatry, 37,* 1030–1035.

Cassel, J. (1976). The contribution of the social environment to host resistance. *American Journal of Epidemiology, 104*(2), 107–123.

Chambers, C. D., Inciardi, J. A., & Siegal, H. A. (1975). *Chemical coping: A report on legal drug use in the United States.* New York: Spectrum Publications.

Chasnoff, I. J. (1985). Fetal alcohol syndromes in twin pregnancy. *Acta Genetical Medical et Gemelloligiae, 34,* 229–232.

Chesler, P. (1972). *Women and madness.* New York: Doubleday & Co.

Chevron, E. S., Quinlan, D. M., & Blatt, S. J. (1978). Sex roles and gender differences in the experience of depression. *Journal of Abnormal Behavior, 87*(6), 680–683.

Chodorow, N. (1978). *The reproduction of mothering.* Berkeley: University of California Press.

Christoffel, K. K., & Salafsky, I. (1975). Fetal alcohol syndrome in dizygotic twins. *Journal of Pediatrics, 87,* 963–967.

Clancy, K., & Gove, W. (1974). Sex differences in mental illness: An analysis of response bias in self-reports. *American Journal of Sociology, 80,* 205–216.

Clark, W. B., Midankik, L., & Knupfer, G. (1981). Alcohol use and alcohol problems among U.S. Adults: Results of the 1979 survey (working draft). Berkeley, CA: Social Research Group, School of Public Health, University of California at Berkeley.

Cobb, S. (1976). Social support as a moderator of life stress. *Psychosomatic Medicine*, *38*, 300–314.

Coffman, D. A. (1984). A clinically derived treatment model for the binge-purge syndrome. In R. C. Hawkins, W. J. Frenouw, P. F. Clement (Eds.), *The Binge-Purge Syndrome* (pp. 211–226). New York: Springer Publishing Co.

Cohen, J., & Halpern, A. (1978). A practice counsellor. *Journal of the Royal College of General Practitioners*, *28*, 481–484.

Cohen, S., & McKay, G. (1984). Social support, stress, and the buffering hypothesis: A theoretical analysis. In A. Baum, J. E. Singer, & S. E. Taylor (Eds.), *Handbook of psychology and health*, (Vol. 4). Hillsdale, NJ: Lawrence Erlbaum Associates.

Cohen, S., & Syme, S. L. (1985). Issues in the study and application of social support. In S. Cohen & Syme, S. L. (Eds.), *Social support and health*. Orlando: Academic Press.

Connor, B., & Babcock, M. (1980). The impact of feminist psychotherapy on the treatment of women alcoholics. Focus on women. *Journal of Addictions and Health*, *2*, 77–92.

Consentino, F., & Heilbrun, A. B. (1964). Anxiety correlates of sex-role identity in college students. *Psychological Reports*, *14*, 729–730.

Constantinople, A. (1973). Masculinity-femininity: An exception to a famous dictum? *Psychological Bulletin*, *80*(5), 389–407.

Cook, E. P. (1985). *Psychological androgyny*. New York: Pergamon.

Cooke, D. J., & Allan, C. A. (1984). Stressful life events and alcohol abuse in women: A general population study. *British Journal of Addiction*, *79*, 425–430.

Cooper, H. M. (1979). Statistically combining independent studies: A meta-analysis of sex differences in conformity research. *Journal Personality & Social Psychology*, *37*, 131–146.

Cooperstock, R. (1971). Sex differences in the use of mood-modifying drugs: An explanatory model. *Journal of Health and Social Behavior*, *12*, 238–244.

Cooperstock, R. (1978). Sex differences in psychotropic drug use. *Social Science & Medicine 12B:* 179–186.

Cooperstock, R. (1980). Special problems of psychotropic drug use among women. *Canada's Mental Health* 28 (2): 3–5.

Corrigan, E. M. (1980). *Alcoholic women in treatment*. New York: Oxford University Press.

Costrich, N., Feinstein, J., Kidder, L., Marecek, J., & Pascale, L. (1975). When stereotypes hurt: Three studies of penalities for sex-role reversals. *Journal Experimental Social Psychology*, *11*, 520–530.

Crisp, A. H. (1965). Some aspects of the evolution, presentation and follow-up of anorexia nervosa. *Proceedings Royal Society of Medicine*, *58*, 814–820.

Crisp, A. H. (1977). Some psychobiological aspects of adolescent growth and their relevance for the fat/thin syndrome (anorexia nervosa). *International Journal of Obesity*, *1*, 231–238.

Crisp, A. H. (1981-82). Anorexia nervosa at normal body weight! The abnormal normal weight control syndrome. *International Journal of Psychiatry in Medicine*, *11*(3), 203–233.

Crisp, A. H. (1983a). Anorexia nervosa. *British Medical Journal*, *287*, 855–858.

Crisp, A. H. (1983b). Some aspects of the psychopathology of anorexia nervosa. In P. L. Darby, P. E. Garfinkel, D. M. Garner, & D. V. Coscina (Eds.), *Anorexia nervosa: Recent developments in research* (pp. 15–28). New York: Alan R. Liss, Inc.

Crisp, A. H., & Bhat, A. V. (1982). "Personality" and anorexia nervosa—the phobic avoidance stance. *Psychotherapy and Psychosomatics, 38*, 178–200.

Crisp, A. H., & Kalucy, R. S. (1974). Aspects of the perceptual disorder in anorexia nervosa. *British Journal of Medical Psychology, 47*, 349–361.

Crisp, A. H., Kalucy, R. S., Lacey, J. H., & Harding, B. (1977). The long-term prognosis in anorexia nervosa: Some factors predictive of outcome. In R. A. Vigersky (Ed.), *Anorexia Nervosa* (pp. 55–65). New York: Raven Press.

Crisp, A. H., Palmer, R. L., & Kalucy, R. S. (1976). How common is anorexia nervosa? A prevalence study. *British Journal of Psychiatry, 128*, 549–554.

Crisp, A. H., & Toms, D. A. (1972). Primary anorexia nervosa or weight phobia in the male. Report on 13 cases. *British Medical Journal, 1*, 334–338.

Crisp, A. H., Hsu, L. K. G., Harding, B., & Hartshorn, J. (1980). Clinical features of anorexia nervosa. *Journal of Psychosomatic Research, 24*, 179–191.

Curlee, J. (1970). A comparison of male and female patients at an alcohol treatment center. *Journal of Psychology, 74*, 239–247.

Dahlgren, L., & Idestrom, C-M. (1979). Female alcoholics. V. Morbidity. *Acta Psychiatrica Scandinavica, 60*, 199–213.

Dahlgren, L., & Myrhed, M. (1977). Female Alcoholics II. Causes of death with reference to sex differences. *Acta Psychiatrica Scandinavica, 56*, 81–97.

Daly, M. (1978). *Gyn/ecology*. Boston, MA: Beacon Press.

Dare, C. (1983). Family therapy for families containing an anorectic youngster. In *Understanding Anorexia and Bulimia*, Report of the Fourth Ross Conference on Medical Research (pp. 28–37). Columbus, Ohio: Ross Laboratories.

Davidson, C. V., & Abramowitz, S. I. (1980). Sex bias in clinical judgment: Later empirical returns. *Psychology of Women Quarterly, 4*(3), 377–395.

Davis, V. E., & Walsh, M. J. (1970a). Alcohol amines and alkaloids: A possible biochemical basis for alcohol addiction. *Science, 167*, 1005–1007.

Davis, V. E., & Walsh, M. J. (1970b). Alcohol addiction and tetrahydropapaveroline. *Science, 169*, 171–174.

DeCrow, K. (1974). *Sexist justice*. New York: Random House.

Depner, C. E., Wethington, E., & Ingersoll-Dayton, B. (1984). Social support: Methodological issues in design and measurement. *Journal of Social Issues, 40*(4), 37–54.

Der-Karabetian, A., & Smith, A. J. (1977). Sex-role stereotyping in the United States: Is it changing? *Sex Roles, 3*(2), 193–198.

Deykin, E. Y., Jacobson, S., Klerman, G., & Solomon, M. (1966). The empty nest: Psychosocial aspects of conflict between depressed women and their grown children. *American Journal of Psychiatry, 122*, 1422–1426.

Dinnerstein, D. (1976). *The mermaid and the minotaur*. New York: Harper & Row.

Doherty, W. J., Schrott, H. G., Metcalf, L., & Lasiello-Vailas, L. (1983). Effect of spouse support and health beliefs on medication adherence. *The Journal of Family Practice, 17*(5), 837–841.

Dohrenwend, B. P., & Dohrenwend, B. S. (1969). *Social status and psychological disorder: A causal inquiry*. New York: John Wiley & Sons.

Dohrenwend, B. S., & Dohrenwend, B. P. (1967). Field studies of social factors in relation to three types of psychological disorder. *Journal of Abnormal Psychology, 72*, 369–378.

Dohrenwend, B. P., & Dohrenwend, B. S. (1976). Sex differences and psychiatric disorders. *American Journal of Sociology, 81*(6), 1447–1454.

Dorgan, M., Goebel, B. L., & House, A. E. (1983). Generalizing about sex role and self-esteem: Results or effects? *Sex Roles, 9*(6), 719–724.

Dowie, M., & Johnston, T. (1977). A case of corporate malpractice and the Dalkon Shield. In C. Dreifus (Ed.), *Seizing our bodies*. New York: Vintage Books.

Driscoll, G. Z., & Barr, H. L. (1972). Comparative study of drug dependent and alcoholic women. Procedings of the 23rd Annual Meeting of the Alcohol and Drug Problems Association of North America. Atlanta, Georgia.

Drossman, D. A. (1983). Anorexia nervosa: A comprehensive approach. In G. H. Stollerman (Ed.), *Advances in internal medicine* (Vol. 28). Chicago: Yearbook Medical Publishers, Inc.

Dunbar, R. (1971). Female liberation as the basis for social revolution. In J. Sochen (Ed.), *The new feminism in twentieth-century America* (179–191). Lexington, MA: D. C. Health & Company.

Dunnell, K., & Cartwright, A. (1972). Medicine takers, prescribers, and hoorders. London: Routledge & Kegan Paul.

Eagly, A. H. (1983). Gender and social influences—A social psychological analysis. *American Psychologist, 38*(9), 971–981.

Eagly, A. H., & Carli, L. L. (1981). Sex of researchers and sex-typed communications as determinants of sex differences in influenceability: A meta-analysis of social influence studies. *Psychological Bulletin, 90*, 1–20.

Eagly, A. H., & Wood, W. (1982). Inferred sex differences in status as a determinant of gender stereotypes about social influence. *Journal of Personality & Social Psychology, 43*, 384–394.

Eaton, W. W., Holzer, C. E., Korff, M. V., Anthony, J. C., Helzer, J. E., George, L., Burnam, M. A., Boyed, J. H., Kessler, L. G., & Locke, B. Z. (1984). The design of epidemiological catchment area surveys. *Archives of General Psychiatry, 41*, 942–948.

Eckert, E. D. (1983). Behavior modification in anorexia nervosa: A comparison of two reinforcement schedules. In P. L. Darby, P. E. Garfinkel, D. M. Garner, & D. V. Coscina (Eds.), *Anorexia Nervosa: Recent Developments in Research* (pp. 377–385). New York: Alan R. Liss, Inc.

Ehrenreich, B., & Ehrenreich, J. (1974). Health care and social control. *Social Policy, 5*, 26–40.

Eichenbaum, L., & Orbach, S. (1984). Feminist psychoanalysis: Theory and practice. In C. M. Brody (Ed.), *Women therapists working with women*. New York: Springer Publishing Co.

Eisenstein, Z. R., (Ed.) (1979). *Capitalist patriarchy and the case for socialist feminism*. New York: Monthly Review Press.

Ellis, A. (1974). The treatment of sex and love problems in women. In V. Franks & V. Burtle (Eds.), *Women in therapy*. New York: Brunner/Mazel Publishers.

Enright, A. B., Butterfield, P., & Berkowitz, B. (1985). Self-help and support groups in the management of eating disorders. In D. M. Garner & P. E. Garfinkel (Eds.), *Handbook of psychotherapy for anorexia nervosa and bulimia*. New York: The Guilford Press.

Erickson, B. E. (1980). Emotional, cognitive and physical variations during the menstrual cycle. II. Differences among women. From an unpublished doctoral dissertation, Department of Psychology, Duke University, Durham, N.C., 27710.

Erikson, E. (1950). Childhood and society. New York: Norton.

Etzion, D. (1984). Moderating effect of social support on stress-burnout relationship. *Journal of Applied Psychology, 69*(4), 615–622.

Eysenck, H. J. (1952). The effects of psychotherapy: An evaluation. *Journal Consulting Psychology, 16*, 319–324.

Fabian, M. S., Jenkins, R. L., & Parsons, O. A. (1981). Gender, alcoholism and neuropsychological functioning. *Journal of Consulting and Clinical Psychology, 49*, 139–141.

Fairbairn, W. R. D. (1952). *An object-relations theory of personality*. New York: Basic Books.

Fairburn, C. G. (1980). Self-induced vomiting. *Journal of Psychosomatic Research, 24*, 193–197.

Fairburn, C. G. (1983). The place of a cognitive behavioral approach in the management of bulimia. In P. L. Darby, P. E. Garfinkel, D. M. Garner, & D. V. Coscina (Eds.), *Anorexia nervosa: Recent developments in research*. New York: Alan R. Liss.

Fairburn, C. G. (1985). Cognitive-behavioral treatment for bulimia. In D. M. Garner & P. E. Garfinkel (Eds.), *Handbook of psychotherapy for anorexia nervosa and bulimia*. New York: Guilford Press.

Fairburn, C. G., & Cooper, P. J. (1982). Self-induced vomiting and bulimia nervosa: An undetected problem. *British Medical Journal, 284*, 1152–1155.

Fee, E. (Ed.) (1975). *Women and health: The politics of sex in medicine*. Farmingdale, N.Y.: Baywood Publishing Co., Inc.

Felkner, M. (1982). The political economy of sexism in industrial health. *Social Science & Medicine, 16*, 3–13.

Fidell, L. S. (1981). Sex differences in psychotropic drug use. *Professional Psychiatry, 12*(1), 156–162.

Fillmore, K. M. (1984). "When angels fall" Women's drinking as cultural preoccupation and as reality. In: S. C. Wilsnack & L. J. Beckman, (Eds.). *Alcohol Problems in Women* (pp. 7–36). New York & London: Guilford Press.

Finkelhor, D., Gelles, R. J., Hotaling, G. T., & Straus, M. A. (1983). *The dark side of families*. Beverly Hills, CA: Sage.

Firestone, S. (1970). *The dialectic of sex*. New York: William Morrow & Co., Inc.

Fisher, E. (1979). *Women's creation*. New York: Doubleday & Co.

Fiske, S. T., & Taylor, S. E. (1983). *Social Cognition*, Reading, MA: Addison-Wesley.

Fitzgerald, L. E. (1973). Women's changing expectations . . . New insights, new demands. *Counseling Psychologist, 4*, 90–95.

Fliegel, Z. O. (1982). Half a century later: Current status of Freud's controversial views on women. *Psychoanalytic Review, 69*(1), 7–28.

Foch, T. T., & McClearn, G. E. (1980). Genetics, body weight, and obesity. In A. J. Stunkard (Ed.), *Obesity*, Philadelphia: W. B. Saunders Co.

Forrest, A. D., Fraser, R. H., & Priest, R. G. (1965). Environmental factors in depressive illness. *British Journal of Psychiatry, 111*, 243–253.

Forslund, M. A., & Guftason, T. J. (1970). Influences of peers and parents and sex differences in drinking by high school students. *Quarterly Journal of Studies on Alcohol 31*, 868–875.

Foushee, H. C., Helmreich, R. L., & Spence, J. T. (1979). Implicit theories of masculinity and femininity: Dualistic or bipolar? *Psychology of Women Quarterly, 3*(3), 259–269.

Fox, H. (1945). Neurotic resentment and dependence overseas. *Psychiatry, 8*(2), 131–138.

Frank, J. D. (1961). *Persuasion and healing*. Baltimore: The Johns Hopkins Press.

Frankel, B. G., & Nuttall, S. (1984). Illness behaviour: An exploration of determinants. *Social Science and Medicine, 19*(2), 147–155.

Frankel, R. S., & Jenkens, J. S. (1975). Hypothalamic-pituitary function in anorexia nervosa. *Acta Endocrinology, 78*, 209–21.

Frankfort, E. (1972). Vaginal politics. New York: Quadrangle/The New York Times Book Co.

French, J. R. P., Jr., & Raven, B. (1959). The bases of social power. In D. Cartwright (Ed.), *Studies in social power*. Ann Arbor: University of Michigan Press.

Freud, S. (1933). New introductory lectures on psychoanalysis. In *Collected papers* (Vol. 22). London: Hogarth Press.

Freud, S. (1905). Three essays in the theory of sexuality. In J. Strachey (Ed.), *Standard edition of the complete psychological works*, London: Hogarth Press.

Freud, S. (1917). Mourning and melancholia, in *Collected papers* (Vol. 4). London: Hogarth Press, 1956.

Freud, S. (1925). Some psychological consequences of the anatomical distinction between the sexes, in *Collected papers* (Vol. 5). London: Hogarth Press, 1956.

Freud, S. (1931). Female sexuality. in *Collected papers*, Vol. 5, London: Hogarth Press, 1956.

Frey, K. S. (1979). Differential teaching methods used with girls and boys of moderate and high achievement levels. Paper presented at the annual meeting of the Society for Research in Child Development, San Francisco.

Fried, M. (1963). Grieving for a lost home. In L. J. Duhl (Ed.), *The urban condition*. New York: Basic Books.

Friedan, B. (1963). *The feminine mystique*. New York: Norton.

Friedman, M., & Rosenman, R. H. (1974). *Type A behavior and your heart*. New York: Knopf.

Fries, H. (1977). Studies on a secondary amenorrhea, amectic behavior, and body-image perception: Importance for the early recognition of anorexia nervosa. In R. A. Vigersky (Ed.), *Anorexia nervosa* (pp. 163–176). New York: Raven Press.

Fries, H., & Nillius, S. J. (1973). Dieting, anorexia nervosa and amenorrhea after oral contraceptive treatment. *Acta Psychiatry Scandinavia, 49*, 669–679.

Frisch, R. E. (1975). Demographic implications of the biological determinants of female fecundity. *Social Biology, 22*, 17–22.

Frisch, R. E. (1977). Food intake, fatness and reproductive ability. In R. A. Vigersky (Ed.), *Anorexia nervosa* (pp. 149–161). New York: Raven Press.

Frisch, R. E. (1983). Fatness and reproduction: Delayed menarche and amenorrhea of ballet dancers and college athletes. In P. L. Darby, P. E. Garfinkel, D. M. Garner, & D. V. Coscina (Eds.), *Anorexia nervosa: Recent developments in research* (pp. 343–363). New York: Alan R. Liss, Inc.

Frisch, R. E., & Revelle, R. (1971). Height and weight at menarche and a hypothesis of menarche. *Archives of Diseases Child, 46*, 695–701.

Gall, M. D. (1969). The relationship between masculinity-femininity and manifest anxiety. *Journal of Clinical Psychology, 25*, 294–295.

Garfield, S., & Bergin, A. (Eds.) (1978). *Handbook of psychotherapy and behavior change*. New York: Wiley.

Garfinkel, P. E., & Garner, D. M. (1982). *Anorexia nervosa: A multidimensional perspective*. New York: Brunner/Mazel Publishers.

Garfinkel, P. E., & Garner, D. M. (1983). The multidetermined nature of anorexia nervosa. In P. L. Darby, P. E. Garfinkel, D. M. Garner, & D. V. Coscina (Eds.), *Anorexia nervosa: Recent developments in research* (pp. 3–14). New York: Alan R. Liss, Inc.

Garfinkel, P. E., Moldofsky, H., & Garner, D. M. (1977). Prognosis in anorexia nervosa as influenced by clinical features, treatment, and self-perception. *Canadian Medical Association Journal, 117*, 1041–1045.

Garfinkel, P. E., Moldofsky, H., & Garner, D. M. (1980). The heterogeneity of anorexia nervosa: Bulimia as a distinct subgroup. *Archives of General Psychiatry, 37*, 1036–1040.

Garfinkel, P. E., Moldofsky, H., Garner, D. M., Stancer, H. C., & Coscina, D. V. (1978). Body awareness in anorexia nervosa: Disturbances in "body image" and "satiety." *Psychosomatic Medicine, 40*(6), 487–498.

Garner, D. M., & Bemis, K. M. (1985). Cognitive therapy for anorexia nervosa. In D. M. Garner & P. E. Garfinkel (Eds.), *Handbook of psychotherapy for anorexia nervosa and bulimia*. New York: The Guilford Press.

Garner, D. M., & Garfinkel, P. E. (1979). The eating attitudes test: An index of the symptoms of anorexia nervosa. *Psychological Medicine, 9*, 273–279.

Garner, D. M., & Garfinkel, P. E. (1981-82). Body image in anorexia nervosa: Measurement, theory and clinical implications. *International Journal of Psychiatry in Medicine, 11*(3), 263–284.

Garner, D. M., Garfinkel, P. E., & Olmsted, M. P. (1983). An overview of sociocultural factors in the development of anorexia nervosa. In P. L. Darby, P. E. Garfinkel, D. M. Garner, & D. V. Coscina (Eds.), *Anorexia nervosa: Recent developments in research* (pp. 65–82). New York: Alan R. Liss, Inc.

Garner, D. M., Garfinkel, P. E., Schwartz, D., & Thompson, M. (1980). Cultural expectations of thinness in women. *Psychological Reports, 47*, 483–491.

Garner, D. M., Olmsted, M. P., & Polivy, J. (1983). The eating disorder inventory: A measure of cognitive-behavioral dimensions of anorexia nervosa and bulimia. In P. L. Darby, P. E. Garfinkel, D. M. Garner, & D. V. Coscina (Eds.), *Anorexia nervosa: Recent developments in research*. New York: Alan R. Liss, Inc.

Garrett, G. R., & Bahr, M. (1973). Women on skid row. *Quarterly Journal of Studies on Alcohol, 34*, 1228–1243.

Gatchel, R. J., & Baum, A. (1983). *An introduction to health psychology*. Reading, MA: Addison-Wesley.

Gelles, R. J. (1979). *Family violence*. Beverly Hills, CA: Sage.

Gilbert, L. C. (1980). Feminist therapy. In A. M. Brodsky & R. T. Hare-Mustin (Eds.), *Women and psychotherapy*. New York: The Guilford Press.

Gilbert, L. A. (1981). Toward mental health: The benefits of psychological androgyny. *Professional Psychology, 12*(1), 29–38.

Gilligan, C. (1982). *In a different voice*. Cambridge, MA: Harvard University Press.

Glass, D. C. (1977). Stress, behavior patterns, and coronary disease. *American Scientist, 65*, 177–187.

Glenn, M. & Kunnes, R. (1973). *Repression or revolution? Therapy in the United States today*. NY: Harper & Row.

Glenn, N. D., & Zody, R. E. (1970). Cohort analysis with national survey data. *The Gerontologist, 10*, 233–240.

Goddard, H. H. (1921). *The Kallikah Family: A study in the heredity of feeblemindedness*. New York: McMillian.

Goble, F. C. (1975). Sex as a factor in metabolism, toxicity and efficacy of pharmacodynamic and chemotherapentic agents. *Advances in Pharmacolology and Chemothery, 13*, 173–252.

Gold, M. S., Pottash, A. C., Martin, D., Extein, I., & Howard, E. (1981-82). The 24 hour LH test in the diagnosis and assessment of response to treatment of patients with anorexia nervosa. *International Journal of Psychiatry in Medicine, 11*(3), 245–250.

Golden, N., & Sacker, I. M. (1984). An overview of the etiology, diagnosis, and management of anorexia nervosa. *Clinical Pediatrics, 23*(4), 209–214.

Goldman, N., & Ravid, R. (1980). Community surveys: Sex differences in mental illness. In M. Guttentag, S. Salasin, & D. Belle (Eds.), *The mental health of women*. New York: Academic Press.

Golub, S. (1976). The magnitude of premenstrual anxiety and depression. *Psychosomatic Medicine, 38*, 4–12.

Gomberg, E. S. (1976). Alcoholism in women. In: B. Kissen & H. Begleiter (Eds.), *The Biology of Alcoholism, 4, Social Aspects of Alcoholism* (pp. 117–166). New York & London: Plenum.

Gomberg, E. S. (1980). *Drinking and problem drinking among the elderly*. Ann Arbor: Institute of Gerontology, University of Michigan.

Goodsitt, A. (1985). Self psychology and the treatment of anorexia nervosa. In D. M. Garner & P. E. Garfinkel (Eds.), *Handbook of psychotherapy for anorexia nervosa and bulimia*. New York: The Guilford Press.

Goodwin, D. W. (1985). Alcoholism and genetics. *Archives of General Psychiatry, 34*, 751–755.

Goodwin, D. W., Schulsinger, F., Knop, J., Mednick, S., & Guze, S. B. (1977a). Alcoholism and depression in adopted-out daughters of alcoholics. *Archives of General Psychiatry, 34*, 751–755.

Goodwin, D. W., Schulsinger, F., Knop, J., Mednick, S., & Guze, S. B. (1977b). Psychopathology in adopted and nonadopted daughters of alcoholics. *Archives of General Psychiatry, 34*, 1005–1009.

Gordon, D. S., Clance, P. R., & Simerly, D. E. (1985). The feminist therapy model: Evolution and definition. manuscript.

Gore, S. (1985). Social support and styles of coping with stress. In S. Cohen & S. L. Syme (Eds.), *Social support and health*. Orlando: Academic Press.

Gormally, J. (1984). The obese binge eater: Diagnosis, etiology, and clinical issues. In R. C. Hawkins, W. J. Femouw, & P. F. Clement (Eds.), *The binge-purge syndrome: Diagnosis, treatment, and research*. New York: Springer Publishing Co.

Gottdiener, J. S., Gross, H. A., Henry, W. L., Borer, J. S., & Ebert, M. H. (1978). Effects of self-induced starvation on cardiac size and function in anorexia nervosa. *Circulation, 58*, 425–433.

Gove, W. R. (1972). The relationship between sex roles, marital status, and mental illness. *Social Forces, 51*, 34–44.

Gove, W. R. (1978). Sex differences in mental illness among adult men and women: An evaluation of four questions raised regarding the evidence on the higher rates of women. *Social Science and Medicine, 12B*, 187–198.

Gove, W. R., & Geerken, M. R. (1976). Response bias in surveys of mental health: An empirical investigation. *American Journal of Sociology, 82*(6), 1289–1317.

Gove, W. R., & Geerken, M. R. (1977). The effect of children and employment on the mental health of married men and women. *Social Forces, 56*(1), 66–76.

Gove, W. R., & Hughes, M. (1979). Possible causes of the apparent sex differences in physical health: An empirical investigation. *American Sociological Review, 44*, 126–146.

Gove, W. R., Hughes, M., & Style, C. B. (1983). Does marriage have positive effects on the psychological well-being of the individual? *Journal of Health and Social Behavior, 24*, 122–131.

Gove, W. R., & Tudor, J. F. (1973). Adult sex roles and mental illness. *American Journal of Sociology, 78*(4), 812–835.

Greenblatt, D. J., & Miller, R. R. (1977). Rational use of psychotropic drugs. I. Hypnatics. In Russell R. Miller & David J. Greenblatt (Eds.), *Drug therapy reviews* (Vol. 1) (pp. 37–48). New York: Masson Publishing.

Greenblatt, D. J., & Shader, R. I. (1977a). Rational use of psychotropic drugs. II. Antianxiety agents. In Russell R. Miller & David J. Greenblatt (Eds.), *Drug therapy reviews* (Vol. 1) (pp. 49–58). New York: Masson Publishing.

Greenblatt, D. J., & Shader, R. I. (1977b). Rational use of psychotropic drugs. III. Major tranquilizers. In Russell R. Miller & David J. Greenblatt (Eds.), *Drug therapy reviews* (Vol. 1) (pp. 59–72). New York: Masson Publishing.

Greenblatt, D. J., & Shader, R. I. (1977c). Rational use of psychotropic drugs. IV. Antidepressants. In Russell R. Miller & David J. Greenblatt (Eds.), *Drug Therapy Reviews* (Vol. 1) (pp. 73–84). New York: Masson Publishing.

Greenwood, M. R. C., & Turkenkopf, I. J. (1983). Genetic and metabolic aspects. In M. R. C. Greenwood (Ed.), *Obesity*, New York: Churchill Livingstone, Inc.

Grunberger, B. (1964). Outline for the study of narcissism in female sexuality. In J. Chassequet-Smirgel (Ed.), *Female sexuality*. Ann Arbor: University of Michigan Press.

Gull, W. W. (1868). The address in medicine delivered before the annual meeting of the BMA at Oxford. *Lancet, 2*, 171.

Gurman, A. S. (1977). The patient's perception of the therapeutic relationship. In A. S. Gurman & A. M. Razin, (Eds.), *Effective psychotherapy: A handbook of research*. New York: Pergamon Press.

Hagen, R. L., & Kahn, A. (1975). Discrimination against competent women. *J. Applied Social Psychology, 5*, 362–376.

Hall, A. (1985). Group psychotherapy for anorexia nervosa. In D. M. Garner & P. E. Garfinkel (Eds.), *Handbook of psychotherapy for anorexia nervosa and bulimia*. New York: The Guilford Press.

Halmi, K. A. (1974). Anorexia nervosa: Demographic and clinical features in 94 cases. *Psychosomatic Medicine, 36*(1), 18–26.

Halmi, K. A. (1981-82). Catacholamine metabolism in anorexia nervosa. *International Journal of Psychiatry in Medicine, 11*(3), 251–254.

Halmi, K. A., & Falk, J. T. (1983). Behavioral and dietary discrimination of menstrual function in anorexia nervosa. In P. L. Darby, P. E. Garfinkel, D. M. Garner, & D. V. Coscina (Eds.), *Anorexia nervosa: Recent developments in research* (pp. 323–329). New York: Alan R. Liss, Inc.

Halmi, K. A., Falk, J. R., & Schwartz, E. (1981). Binge eating and vomiting: A survey of a college population. *Psychological Medicine, 11*, 697–706.

Halmi, K. A., Goldberg, S. C., Casper, R. C., Eckert, E. D., & Davis, J. M. (1979). Pretreatment predictors of outcome in anorexia nervosa. *British Journal of Psychiatry, 134*, 71–78.

Halmi, K. A., Goldberg, S. C., Eckert, E., Casper, R., & Davis, J. M. (1977). Pretreatment evaluation in anorexia nervosa. In R. A. Vigersky (Ed.), *Anorexia nervosa* (pp. 43–54). New York: Raven Press.

Hamilton, R. (1978). *The liberation of women*. Boston: George Allen University.

Hammer, M., Gutwirth, L., & Phillips, S. L. (1982). Parenthood and social networks. *Social Science & Medicine, 16*, 2091–2100.

Hanisch, C. (1971). The personal is political. In J. Agel (Ed.), *The radical therapist*. New York: Ballantine.

Hannum, R. D., Rosellini, R. A., & Seligman, M. (1978). Learned helplessness and the rat: Retention and immunization. *Developmental Psychology, 12*, 449–454.

Harder, D. W., Strauss, J. S., Kokes, R. F., Ritzler, B. A., & Gift, T. E. (1980). Life events and psychopathologicy severity among first psychiatric admissions. *Journal of Abnormal Psychology, 89*(2), 165–180.

Hare-Mustin, R. T. (1983). An appraisal of the relationship between women and psychotherapy: 80 years after the case of Dora. *American Psychologist, 38*, 593–601.

Harlap, J., & Shiono, D. H. (1980). Alcohol, smoking, and incidence of spontaneous abortions in the first and second trimester, *Lancet, 2*, 173–176.

Hatcher, E. M., Jones, M. K., & Jones, B. M. (1977). Cognitive deficits in alcoholic women. *Alcoholism: Clinical and experimental research, 1*, 371–377.

Haw, M. A. (1982). Women, work and stress: A review and agenda for the future. *Journal of Health and Social Behavior, 23*(2), 132–144.

Hawkins, R. C., & Clements, P. F. (1980). Development and construct validation of a self-report measure of binge eating tendencies, *Addictive Behaviors, 5*, 219–226.

Hay, W., Nathan, P., Hurmans, H., & Frankenstein, W. (1984). Menstrual cycle tolerance and blood alcohol levels discrimination ability. *Addictive Behaviors, 9*, 67–77.

Heilbrun, A. B., & Schwartz, H. L. (1982). Sex-gender differences in level of androgyny. *Sex Roles, 8*(2), 201–214.

Heller, K., & Mansbach, W. E. (1984). The multifaceted nature of social support in a community sample of elderly women. *Journal of Social Issues, 40*(4), 99–112.

Herman, C. P., Olmsted, M. P., & Polivy, J. (1983). Obesity, externality, and susceptibility to social influence: An integrated analysis. *Journal of Personality & Social Psychology, 45*, 926–934.

Herz, A., & Emrich, H. M. (1983). Opioid systems and the regulation of Mood: Possible significance in depression? In J. Angst (Ed.), *The origins of depression: Current concepts and approaches.* New York: Springer-Verlag.

Herzog, D. B. (1982). Bulimia: The secretive syndrome. *Psychosomatics, 23*, 481–483.

Hicks, R., Okonek, A., & Davis, J. M. (1980). The psychopharmacological approach. In I. L. Kutash & L. B. Schlesinger (Eds.), *Handbook on stress and anxiety.* San Francisco: Jossey-Bass Inc.

Hill, S. Y. (1984). Vulnerability to the biomedical consequences of alcoholism and alcohol-related problems in women. In S. C. Wilsnack & L. J. Beckman (Eds.), *Alcohol problems in women* (pp. 121–154). New York & London: Guilford Press.

Hirsch, B. J. (1980). Natural support systems and coping with major life changes. *American Journal of Community Psychology, 8*(2), 159–172.

Hoffman, H., & Wefring, L. R. (1972). Sex and age differences in psychiatric symptoms of alcoholics. *Psychology Reports, 30*, 887–889.

Hollister, L. E. (1978a). I. Tricyclic antidepressants. *New England Journal of Medicine, 299*(20), 1106–1109.

Hollister, L. E. (1978b). II. Tricyclic antidepressants. *New England Journal of Medicine, 299*(21), 1168–1172.

Hollister, L. E. (1982a). Drugs for treating affective disorders. In W. Modell (Ed.), Drugs of choice 1982–1983. St. Louis: C. V. Mosby.

Hollister, L. E. (1982b). Drugs for treating anxiety. In W. Modell (Ed.), Drugs of choice 1982–1983. St. Louis: C. V. Mosby Company.

Holmes, T. H., & Rahe, R. H. (1967). The social readjustment scale. *Journal of Psychosomatic Research, 11*, 213–218.

Holroyd, J. C., & Brodsky, A. M. (1977). Psychologists' attitudes and practices regarding erotic and nonerotic physical contact with patients. *American Psychologist, 32*(10), 843–849.

Homiller, J. (1977). Women and alcohol: A guide for state and local decision makers. Washington, DC: Alcohol and Drug Problems Association of North America.

Horowitz, M. J. (1980). Psychoanalytic therapy. In I. L. Kutash, & L. B. Schlesinger (Eds.), *Handbook on stress and anxiety*. San Francisco: Jossey-Bass Publishers.

Horwitz, A. V. (1982). Sex-role expectations, power, and psychological distress. *Sex Roles, 8*(6), 607–623.

Howard, K. I., Orlinsky, D. E., & Hill, J. A. (1977). The therapist's feelings in the psychotherapeutic process: Type of problem, age of client, and sex of counselor. *Journal of Counseling Psychology, 24*, 60–65.

Howard, K. I., & Orlinsky, D. E. (1979, August). What effect does therapist gender have on outcome for women in psychotherapy? Presentation at the conference of the American Psychological Association, New York.

Hsu, L. K. G. (1980). Outcome of anorexia nervosa. *Archives of General Psychiatry, 37*, 1041–1046.

Hubbard, R., Henifin, M. S., & Fried, B. (Eds.) (1979). *Women look at biology looking at women*. Boston, MA: Schenkman Publishing Co.

Hubbard, R., & Lowe, M. (Eds.) (1979). *Genes and gender: II Pitfalls in research on sex and gender*. New York: Gordion Press.

Hudgens, R. W., Morrison, J. R., & Barchha, R. (1967). Life events and onset of primary affective disorders. A study of 40 hospitalized patients and 40 controls. *Archives of General Psychiatry, 16*, 134–145.

Humphrey, L. L. (1983). A sequential analysis of family processes in anorexia and bulimia. In *Understanding anorexia nervosa and bulimia*, Report of the Fourth Ross Conference on Medical Research. Columbus, OH: Ross Laboratories.

Hyde, J. S. (1985). *Half the human experience* (3rd ed.). Lexington, MA: D. C. Heath & Co.

Hyde, J. S., & Linn, M. C. (1986). *The psychology of gender*. Baltimore: Johns Hopkins Press.

Imes, S., & Clance, P. R. (1984). Treatment of the imposter phenomenon in high achieving women. In C. Brody (Ed.), *Women working with women*. New York: Springer Publishing.

Imlah, N. (1970). Drugs in modern society. London: Geoffrey Chapman.

Ivey, M. E., & Bardwick, M. J. (1968). Patterns of affective fluctuation in the menstrual cycle. *Psychosomatic Medicine, 30*, 336–345.

Jackson, G., Korts, D., Hanbury, R., Sturiano, V., Wolpert, L., Cohen, M., & Stimmel, B. (1982). Alcohol consumption in persons on methadone maintenance therapy. *American Journal of Drug and Alcohol Abuse, 9*, 69–76.

Jackson, L. A. (1983). The perception of androgyny and physical attractiveness: Two is better than one. *Personality and Social Psychology Bulletin, 9*(3), 405–413.

Jacobsen, E. (1964). The theoretical basis for the chemotherapy of depression. In E. B. Davies (Ed.), *Depression: Proceedings of the symposium held at Cambridge, 1959*. Cambridge: Cambridge University Press.

Jacobson, S., Deykin, E., Prusoff, B. (1977). Process and outcome of therapy with depressed women. *American Journal of Orthopsychiatry, 47*(1), 140–148.

Jagger, A. M., & Struhl, P. R. (1978). *Feminist frameworks*. New York: McGraw-Hill.

Janis, I. L. (1951). *Air war and emotional stress.* New York: McGraw Hill.

Janis, I. L. (1983). The role of social support in adherence to stressful decisions. *American Psychologist, 38,* 143–160.

Jellison, J. M., & Green, J. A. (1981). A self-presentation approach to the fundamental attribution error: The norm of internality. *Journal of Personality and Social Psychology, 40,* 643–469.

Jenkins, C. D. (1979). Psychosocial modifiers of response to stress. In J. E. Barrett (Ed.), *Stress and mental disorder.* Manchester: Manchester University Press.

Jesser, R., & Jesser, S. L. (1977). *Problem behavior and psychological development: A longitudinal study of youth.* New York: Academic Press.

Johnson, C. L., Lewis, C., Love, S., Stuckey, M., & Lewis, L. (1983). A descriptive survey of dieting and bulimic behavior in a female high school population. In *Understanding anorexia nervosa and bulimia,* Report of the Fourth Ross Conference on Medical Research, (pp. 14–18). Columbus, OH: Ross Laboratories.

Johnson, P. (1974, April). Social power and sex role stereotypes. Paper presented at the meeting of the Western Psychological Association, San Francisco.

Johnson, P. B. (1982). Sex differences, women's roles and alcohol use: Preliminary national data. *Journal of Social Issues, 38,* 93–116.

Johnson, P., Armour, D. J., Plidi, S., & Stambul, H. (1977). U.S. adult drinking practices: Time trends, social correlates and sex roles, prepared for the National Institute on Alcohol Abuse and Alcoholism, Santa Monica, CA.

Johnston, L. D., Backman, J. G., & O'Malley, P. M. (1984). Drugs and American high school students: 1975–1983. U.S. Department of Health and Human Services Publications. Washington, DC: U.S. Government Printing Office.

Jones, B. (1970). The dynamics of marriage and motherhood. In R. Morgan (Ed.), *Sisterhood is powerful.* New York: Random House.

Jones, B. M. (1975). Alcohol and women: Intoxication levels and memory impairment as related to the menstrual cycle. *Alcohol Technical Reports, Oklahoma State Dept. of Mental Health Division on Alcoholism, 4,* 1–11.

Jones, B. M., & Jones, M. K. (1976a). Alcohol effects in women during the menstrual cycle. *Annuals of the New York Academy of Science, 273,* 567–587.

Jones, B. M., & Jones, M. K. (1976b). Women and alcohol: Intoxication, metabolism and the menstrual cycle. In: M. Greenblatt & M. A. Schuckit (Eds.), *Alcoholism Problems in Women and Children* (pp. 103–136). New York: Grune & Stratton.

Jones, B. M., & Jones, M. K. (1977). Interaction of alcohol, oral contraceptives and the menstrual cycle with stimulus-response compatability. In: F. A. Seixas (Ed.), *Currents in Alcoholism* (pp. 457–477). New York: Grune & Stratton.

Jones, C., & Aronson, E. (1973). Attribution of fault to a rape victim as a function of respectability of the victim. *Journal of Personality and Social Psychology, 26,* 415–420.

Jones, K. L., Smith, D. W., Clelland, C. N., & Streissguth, A. P. (1973). Pattern of malformation in offspring of chronic alcoholic mothers. *Lancet, 1,* 1267–1271.

Jones, M. L. (1971). Personality antecedants and correlates of drinking patterns of women. *Journal of Consultative Clinical Psychology, 36,* 61–69.

Jones, W. H., Chernovetz, M. E., & Hanson, R. O. (1978). The enigma of androgyny: Differential implications for males and females? *Journal of Consulting and Clinical Psychology, 46,* 298–313.

Jordan, J. V. (1983). Empathy and the mother-daughter relationship. *Work in Progress,* No. 82-02. Wellesley: Stone Center.

Jung, C. G. (1953). Anima and Animus. In two essays on analytical psychology: *Collected Works of C. G. Jung,* vol. 7 (pp. 186–209). New York: Bollinger Foundation.

Kahn, A. S., & Gaeddert, W. P. (1985). From theories of equity to theories of justice: The liberating consequences of studying women. In V. E. O'Leary, R. K. Unger, & B. S. Wallston (Eds.), *Women, gender, and social psychology.* Hillsdale, NJ: Lawrence Erlbaum Associates.

Kallman, F. J. (1946). The genetic theory of schizophrenia: An analyses of 691 schizophrenic index families. *American Journal of Psychology, 103,* 309–322.

Kalucy, R. S., Crisp, A. H., & Harding, B. (1977). A study of 56 families with anorexia nervosa. *British Journal of Medical Psychology, 50,* 381–395.

Kalucy, R. S., Gilchrist, P. N., McFarlane, C. M., & McFarlane, A. C. (1985). The evolution of a multitherapy orientation. In D. M. Garner & P. E. Garfinkel (Eds.), *Handbook of psychotherapy for anorexia nervosa and bulimia.* New York: The Guilford Press.

Kaplan, A. G. (1976). Androgyny as a model of mental health for women: From theory to therapy. In A. G. Kaplan & J. P. Bean (Eds.), *Beyond sex-role stereotypes: Reading toward a psychology of androgyny.* Boston: Little, Brown and Co.

Kaplan, A. G. (1979). Clarifying the concept of androgyny: Implications for therapy. *Psychology of Women Quarterly, 3*(3), 223–230.

Kaplan, A. G. (1983). Empathic communication in the psychotherapy relationship. *Work in Progress,* No. 82-02. Wellesley: Stone Center.

Kaplan, A. G. (1984). Female or male psychotherapists for women: New Formulations. *Work in Progress,* No. 82-02. Wellesley: Stone Center.

Kaplan, A. G., Fibel, B., Grief, A. C., McComb, A., Sedney, M. A., & Shapiro, E. (1983). The process of sex-role integration in psychotherapy: Contributions from a training experience. *Psychotherapy: Theory, Research, and Practice, 20*(4), 476–485.

Kaplan, A. G., & Sedney, M. A. (1980). *Psychology and sex roles: An androgynous perspective.* Boston: Little Brown.

Kaplan, A. G., & Yasinski, L. (1980). Psychodynamic perspectives. In A. M. Brodsky & R. T. Hare-Mustin (Eds.), *Women and psychotherapy.* New York: The Guilford Press.

Kaplan, B. H., Cassel, J. C., & Gore, S. (1977). Social support and health. *Medical Care, 15*(5) (Suppl.), 47–58.

Kaplan, M. (1983a). A woman's view of DSM-III. *American Psychologist, 38*(7), 786–792.

Kaplan, M. (1983b). The issue of sex bias in DSM-III. *American Psychologist, 38*(7), 802–803.

Kazdin, A. E. (1982). Methodology of psychotherapy outcome research: Recent developments. In J. H. Harvey & M. M. Parks (Eds.), *Psychotherapy research and behavior change.* Washington, D.C.: American Psychological Association.

Keesey, R. E. (1980). A set-point analysis of the regulation of body weight. In A. J. Stunkard (Ed.), *Obesity*. Philadelphia: W. B. Saunders Co.

Kellet, J., Trimble, M., & Thorley, A. (1976). Anorexia nervosa after menopause. *British Journal of Psychiatry, 128*, 555–558.

Kelly, J. A., & Worell, J. (1977). New formulations of sex roles and androgyny: A critical review. *Journal of Consulting and Clinical Psychology, 45*, 1574–1586.

Kent, T. A., Campbell, J. L., Pazdernik, T. L., Hunter, R., Gunn, W. H., & Goodwin, D. W. (1985). Blood platelet uptake of serotonin in men alcoholics. *Journal of Studies on Alcohol, 46*, 357–359.

Kent, T. A., Pazdernik, T. L., Gunn, W. H., Penick, E. L., Marples, B. W., Jones, M. P., & Goodwin, D. H. (1983). Platelet uptake of serotnin in ethanol intoxication: A preliminary study. *Biological Pschiatry, 18*, 929–933.

Kenworthy, J. A. (1979). Androgyny in psychotherapy: But will it sell in Peoria? *Psychology of Women Quarterly, 3*(3), 231–240.

Khantzian, J. (1978). Drug-Alcohol problems in women: A clinical perspective. *Psychiatric Opinion*, pp. 18–20.

Kimmel, E. (1985, May). Women and Power. Invited address presented at the University of Tennessee, Knoxville.

King, E. (1980). Sex bias in psychoactive drug advertisements. *Psychiatry, 43*, 129–137.

Kinney, E. L., Trautmann, J., Gold, J. A., Vesell, E. S., & Zelis, R. (1981). Underrepresentation of women in new drug trials. *Annals of Internal Medicine, 95*(4), 495–499.

Kinsey, B. A. (1966). *The female alcoholic: A social psychological study*, Springfield, IL: C. C. Thomas.

Kirsh, B. (1974). Consciousness-raising groups as therapy for women. In V. Franks & V. Burtle (Eds.), *Women in Therapy*, New York: Brunner/Mazel publishers.

Kirstein, L. (1981-82). Diagnostic issues in primary anorexia nervosa. *International Journal of Psychiatry in Medicine, 11*(3), 235–244.

Klein, R. B., & Snyder, D. K. (1985). Replicated MMPI Subtypes for alcoholic men and women: Relationship to self-reported drinking behaviors, *Journal of Consulting and Clinical Psychology, 53*, 70–79.

Kline, J., Shrout, P., Stein, Z., Susser, M., & Warburton, D. (1980). Drinking during pregnancy and spontaneous abortion. *Lancet, 2*, 176–180.

Knupfer, G. (1967). The epidemiology of problem drinking. *American Journal of Public Health, 57*, 973–986.

Koedt, A., Levine, D., & Rapone, A. (1973). *Radical feminism*. New York: Quadrangle Books.

Kohut, H. (1971). *The analysis of the self*. New York: International Universities Press.

Kohut, H. (1977). *The restoration of the self*. New York: International Universities Press.

Kohut, H., & Wolf, E. (1978). The disorders of the self and their treatment: An outline. *International Journal of Psychoanalysis, 59*, 413–424.

Koumjian, K. (1981). The use of valium as a form of social control. *Social Science Medicine, 15E*, 245–249.

Krasner, N., Davis, M., Portmann, B., & Williams, R. (1977). Changing pattern of alcoholic liver disease in Great Britain: Relation to sex and signs of autoimmunity. *British Medical Journal, 1,* 1497–1550.

Kravetz, D. (1978). Consciousness-raising groups in the 1970's. *Psychology of Women Quarterly, 3,* 168–186.

Kravetz, D. (1980). Consciousness-raising and self-help. In A. M. Brodsky & R. T. Hare-Mustin (Eds.), *Women and psychotherapy.* New York: The Guilford Press.

Kupfer, D. J., & Reynolds, C. F. (1983). Neurophysiologic studies of depression: State of the art. In J. Angst (Ed.), *The origins of depression: Current concepts and approaches.* New York: Springer-Verlag.

Lacey, J. H. (1985). Time-limited individual and group treatment for bulimia. In D. M. Garner & P. E. Garfinkel (Eds.), *Handbook of psychotherapy for anorexia nervosa and bulimia.* New York: The Guilford Press.

Lagos, J. M. (1981-82). Family therapy in the treatment of anorexia nervosa: Theory and technique. *International Journal of Psychiatry in Medicine, 11*(3), 291–302.

Lakoff, R. (1973). Language and woman's place. *Language and Society, 2,* 45–79.

Langer, T. S., & Michael, S. T. (1963). *Life stress and mental health.* New York: Free Press of Glencoe.

Launer, M. A. (1978). Anorexia nervosa in late life. *British Journal of Medical Psychology, 51,* 375–377.

Laws, J. L. (1978). Work motivation and work behavior of women: New perspectives. In J. Sherman & F. Denmark (Eds.), *Psychology of women: Future directions and research.* New York: Psychological Dimensions.

Laws, J. L. (1979). *The second x.* New York: Elsevier.

Lazarus, A. (1968). Learning theory in the treatment of depression. *Behavioral Research Therapy, 6,* 28–40.

Lederer, W. (1968). *The fear of women.* New York: Grune & Stratton.

Lee, A. G. (1982). Psychological androgyny and social desirability. *Journal of Personality Assessment, 46*(2), 147–152.

Lee, A. G., & Scheurer, V. L. (1983). Psychological androgyny and aspects of self-image in women and men. *Sex Roles, 9*(3), 289–306.

Lee, K., Moller, L., Hardt, F., Hauber, A., & Jensen, E. (1979). Alcohol induced brain damage in young males. *Lancet, 2,* 759–761.

Lennard, H. L., Epstein, L. T., Bernstein, A., & Kansom, D. C. (1970). Hazards implicit in prescribing psychoactive drugs. *Science, 169,* 438–441.

Leopold, R. L., & Dillon, H. (1963). Psychoanatomy of a disaster: A long term study of post-traumatic neurosis in survivors of a marine explosion. *American Journal of Psychiatry, 119,* 913–921.

Lerner, H. E. (1980). Internal prohibitions against female anger. *The American Journal of Psychoanalysis, 40*(2), 137–148.

Lerner, H. E. (1983). Female dependency in context: Some theoretical and technical considerations. *American Journal of Orthopsychiatry, 53*(4), 697–705.

Lerman, H. (1985, August). From Freud to feminist personality theory: Getting here from there. Presidential Address for Division 35 presented at the American Psychological Association meetings, Los Angeles.

Lerner, M. J., Miller, D. T., & Holmes, J. G. (1976). Deserving the emergence of forms of justice. In L. Berkowitz (Ed.), *Advances in experimental social psychology* (Vol. 9). New York: Academic Press.

Lerner, M. J. (1970). The desire for justice and reactions to victims. In J. Mc-Cauley & L. Berkowitz (Eds.), *Altruism and helping behavior*. New York: Academic Press.

Lerner, M. J. (1980). *The belief in a just world: A fundamental delusion*. New York: Plenum Books.

Lerner, M. J., & Simmons, C. H. (1966). Observer's reaction to the innocent victim: Compassion or rejection. *Journal of Personality and Social Psychology, 4,* 203–210.

Levine, H. G. (1980). Temperance and women in 19th-Century United States. In O. J. Kalant (Ed.), *Alcohol and drug related problems in women* (pp. 25–67). Research Advances in Alcohol and Drug Problems, New York & London: Plenum Press.

Levy, R. L. (1983). Social support and compliance: A selective review and critique of treatment integrity and outcome measurement. *Social Science and Medicine, 17*(18), 1329–1338.

Lewinsohn, P. M. (1975). The behavioral study and treatment of depression. In M. Hersen (Ed.), *Progress in behavioral modification*. New York: Academic Press.

Lisansky, E. S. (1957). Alcoholism in women: Social and psychological concomitants. *Quarterly Journal of Studies on Alcohol, 18,* 588–623.

Little, R. E. (1976). Alcohol consumption during pregnancy as reported to the obstetrician and to an independent interviewer. *Annuals of the New York Academy of Sciences, 273,* 588–592.

Little, R. E., & Ervin, C. H. (1984). Alcohol use and reproduction. In: S. C. Wilsnak & L. J. Beckman (Eds.), *Alcohol problems in women: Antecedents, consequences and intervention* (pp. 155–188). New York & London: Guilford Press.

Little, R. E., Mandell, W., & Schultz, F. A. (1977). Consequences of retrospective measurment of alcohol consumption. *Journal of Studies on Alcohol, 38,* 1777–1780.

Little, R. E., Moore, D. E., Guzinski, G. M., & Perez, A. (1980). Absence of effect of exogenous estradiol on alcohol consumption in women. *Substance and Alcohol Actions/Misuse, 1,* 551–556.

Little, R. E., Schultz, F. A., & Mandell, W. A. (1976). Drinking during pregnancy. *Journal of Studies on Alcohol, 37,* 375–379.

Little, R. E., & Streissguth, A. D. (1978). Drinking during pregnancy in alcoholic women. *Alcoholism: Clinical and Experimental Research, 2,* 179–183.

Locksley, A., & Colten, M. E. (1979). Psychological androgyny: A case of mistaken identity? *Journal of Personality and Social Psychology, 37*(6), 1017–1031.

Logue, P. E., Gentry, D., Linnoila, M., & Ervin, C. (1978). The effect of alcohol consumption on state anxiety changes in male and female nonalcoholics. *American Journal of Psychiatry, 135,* 1079–1081.

Lokander, S. (1962). Sick absence in a Swedish company: A sociometric study. *Acta Medica Scandinavia, 171,* (Suppl. 377), 8–169.

Long, C. G., & Cordle, C. J. (1982). Psychological treatment of binge eating and self-induced vomiting. *British Journal of Medical Psychology, 55,* 139–145.

Loro, A. D. (1984). Binge-eating: A cognitive behavioral treatment approach. In R. C. Hawkins, W. J. Frenouw, & R. F. Clement (Eds.), *The Binge-Purge Syndrome* (pp. 183–210). New York: Springer Publishing Co.

Lott, B. (1981). A feminist critique of androgyny: Toward the elimination of gender attributions for learned behavior. In C. Mayo & N. Henley (Eds.), *Gender and nonverbal behavior.* New York: Springer-Verlag.

Luborsky, L., Singer, B., & Luborsky, L. (1975). Comparative studies of psychotherapies: Is it true that "Everybody has won and all must have prizes?" *Archives of General Psychiatry, 32,* 995.

Maas, J. W., Fawcett, J. A., & Dekirmenjian, H. (1972). Catecholamine metabolism, depressive illness and drug response. *Archives of General Psychiatry, 26,* 252–262.

Maccoby, E. E., & Jacklin, C. N. (1974). *The psychology of sex differences.* Stanford, CA: Stanford University Press.

Maffeo, P. A. (1979). Thoughts on Stricker's "Implications of research for psychotherapeutic treatment of women." *American Psychologist, 34*(8), 690–695.

Maffeo, P. A. (1982). Gender as a model for mental health. In I. Al-Issa (Ed.), *Gender and psychopathology.* New York: Academic Press.

Maier, S. F., & Seligman, M. (1976). Learned helplessness: Theory and evidence. *Journal of Experimental Psychology, 105,* 3–46.

Major, B. (1980). Information acquisition and attribution processes. *Journal of Personality and Social Psychology, 39,* 1010–1023.

Maloney, M. J., & Farrell, M. K. (1980). Treatment of severe weight loss in anorexia nervosa with hyperalimentation and psychotherapy. *American Journal of Psychiatry, 137*(3), 310–314.

Mandel, L., & North, S. (1982). Sex roles, sexuality and recovering alcoholics: Program issues. *Journal of Psychoactive Drugs, 14,* 163–166.

Marecek, J. (1979). Social change, positive mental health, and psychological androgyny. *Psychology of Women Quarterly, 3*(3), 241–247.

Marecek, J., & Johnson, M. (1980). Gender and the process of therapy. In A. M. Brodsky & R. T. Hare-Mustin (Eds.), *Women and psychotherapy.* New York: The Guilford Press.

Marecek, J., & Kravetz, D. (1977). Women and mental health: A review of feminist change efforts. *Psychiatry, 40,* 323–330.

Maracek, J., Kravetz, D., & Finn, S. E. (1979, August). Women's life stresses and psychiatric symptoms formation. Paper presented at the meetings of the American Psychological Association.

Margulies, R. Z., Kessler, R. C., & Kandel, D. B. (1977). A longitudinal study of onset of drinking among high-school students. *Journal of Studies in Alcohol, 38,* 897–912.

Marieskind, H. (1980). *Women in the health system.* St. Louis, MI: C. V. Mosby Company.

Marsh, G. N., & Barr, J. (1975). Marriage guidance counselling in a group practic. *Journal of the Royal College of General Practitioners, 25,* 73–75.

Martin, F. (1983). Subgroups in anorexia nervosa: A family systems study. In P. L. Darby, P. E. Garfinkel, D. M. Garner, & D. V. Cooscina (Eds.), *Anorexia nervosa: Recent developments in research*. New York: A. R. Liss.

Martin, W. T. (1976). Status integration, social stress, and mental illness: Accounting for marital status variations in mental hospitalization rates. *Journal of Health and Social Behavior, 17,* 280–294.

Masters, W., & Johnson, V. (1966). *Human sexual response.* Boston: Little Brown.

Matazarro, J. D. (1965). Psychotherapeutic processes. In P. R. Farnsworth & Q. McNemar (Eds.), *Annual Review of Psychology* (pp. 181–224) (Vol. 16). Palo Alto: Annual Reviews.

Matazarro, J. D. (1967). Some psychotherapists make patients worse! *International Journal of Psychiatry, 3*(3), 156–157.

Matarazzo, J. D. (1971). The practice of psychotherapy is art and not science. In A. R. Mahrer & L. Pearson (Eds.), *Creative Developments in Psychotherapy* (Vol. I). Cleveland: Press of Case Western Reserve University.

McClelland, D., Davis, W., Kalin, R., & Wanner, E. (1972). *The Drinking Man.* New York: Free Press.

McCord, W., & McCord, J. (1960). *Origins of Alcoholism.* Stanford, CA: Stanford University Press.

McPherson, K. S., & Spetrino, S. K. (1983). Androgyny and sex-typing: Differences in beliefs regarding gender polarity in ratings of ideal men and women. *Sex Roles, 9*(4), 441–451.

McRee, C., Corder, B. F., & Haizlip, T. (1974). Responses to sexual bias advertising. *American Journal of Psychiatry, 131*(11), 1273–1275.

Medhus, A. (1974). Morbidity among female alcoholics. *Scandinavian Journal of Social Medicine, 2,* 5–11.

Medhus, A., Edwards, G., & Kyle, E. (1975). Alcoholics admitted to four hospitals in England. *Quarterly Journal of Studies on Alcohol, 35,* 841–855.

Megargee, E. I. (1969). Influence of sex roles on the manifestation of leadership. *Applied Psychology, 53,* 377–382.

Meile, R. L., Johnson, D. R., & Peter, L. S. (1976). Marital role, and mental disorder among women: Test of an interaction hypothesis. *Journal of Health and Social Behavior, 17,* 295–301.

Mellinger, G. D., Balter, M. B., & Manherner, D. I. (1971). Patterns of psychotropic drug use among adults in San Francisco. *Archives of General Psychiatry, 25,* 385–394.

Mello, N. K., & Mendelson, J. H. (1972). Drinking patterns during work contingent and non-contingent alcohol acquisition. *Psychosomatic Medicine, 34,* 139–164.

Mello, N. K., & Mendelson, J. H. (1978). Alcohol and human behavior. In L. L. Iverson, S. D. Iverson, & S. H. Snyder (Eds.), *Handbook of Psychopharmacology, Vol. 12, Drugs of Abuse,* New York & London: Plenum. 235–317,

Meltzoff, J., & Kornreich, M. (1970). *Research in Psychotherapy.* New York: Atherton.

Melville, A. (1980). Reducing whose anxiety? A study of the relationship between repeat prescribing of minor tranquillisers and doctors' attitudes. In R. E. Mapes (Ed.), *Prescribing practice and drug usage.* London: Croom Helm.

Mestrovic, S., & Glassner, B. (1983). A Durkheimian hypothesis on stress. *Social Science & Medicine, 17*(18), 1315–1327.

Metzner, H. L. (1980). Role and role conflict in women's drinking practices: Report of the pilot study. Ann Arbor: School of Public Health, University of Michigan.

Miller, D., & Jang, M. (1977). Children of Alcoholics: A 20 year longitudinal study. *Social Work Research and Abstracts, 13,* 23–29.

Miller, J. B. (1983). The constuction of anger in women and men. *Work in progress*, No. 83-01. Wellesley: Stone Center.

Miller, J. B. (1976). *Toward a new psychology of women.* Boston: Beacon Press.

Miller, J. B. (1982). Women and power. *Work in Progress*, No. 82-01, Wellesley: Stone Center.

Miller, J. B., & Mothner, I. (1971). Psychological consequences of sexual inequality. *American Journal of Orthopsychiatry, 41*(5), 767–775.

Miller, J. B. (1984). The development of women's sense of self. *Work in Progress*, No. 84-01. Wellesley: Stone Center Working Paper Series.

Miller, R. R. (1977). Clinically important drug interactions. Pp. 85–99 In Russell R. Miller & David J. Greenblatt (Eds.) *Drug Therapy Reviews*, (Vol. 1) (pp. 85–99). New York: Mason Publishing.

Miller, W. R., Rosellini, R. A., & Seligman, M. E. P. (1977). Learned helplessness and depression. In J. D. Maser & M. E. P. Seligman (Eds.), *Psychopathology: Experimental models.* San Francisco: Freeman.

Millet, K. (1970). *Sexual politics.* Garden City, N.Y.: Doubleday & Company, Inc.

Millon, T. (1983). The DSM-III: An insider's perspective. *American Psychologist, 38*(7), 804–814.

Minuchin, S. (1974). *Families and family therapy.* Cambridge: Harvard University Press.

Minuchin, S., Rosman, B. L., & Baker, L. (1978). *Psychosomatic families.* Cambridge: Harvard University Press.

Mitchell, J. (1974). *Psychoanalysis and feminism.* New York: Pantion Books.

Mitchell, J. E., Hatsukami, D., Goff, G., Pyule, R. L., Eckert, E. D., & Davis, L. E. (1985). Intensive outpatient group treatment for bulimia. In D. M. Garner & P. E. Garfinkel (Eds.), *Handbook of psychotherapy for anorexia nervosa and bulimia.* New York: The Guilford Press.

Mogar, R. E., Wilson, W. M., & Helm, S. T. (1970). Personality subtypes of male and female alcoholic patients. *International Journal of Addictions, 5,* 99–113.

Montague, A. (1952). *The natural superiority of women.* New York: Collier Macmillian Publishers.

Moore, D. C. (1977). Amitriptyline therapy in anorexia nervosa. *American Journal of Psychiatry, 134*(11), 1303–1304.

Moos, R. H. (1969). Typology of menstrual cycle symptoms. *American Journal of Obstetrics and Gynecology, 103,* 390–401.

Morgan, E. (1972). *The descent of women.* New York: Stein & Day Publishers.

Morgan, H. G., & Russell, G. F. M. (1975). Value of family background and clinical features as predictors of long-term outcome in anorexia nervosa: Four-year follow-up study of 41 patients. *Psychological Medicine, 5,* 355–371.

Morgan, M. Y., & Sherlock, S. (1977). Sex-related differences among 100 patients with alcoholic liver disease. *British Medical Journal, 1,* 939–941.

Morgan, R. (1970). *Sisterhood is powerful.* New York: Random House.

Morris, D. (1967). *The naked ape.* London: Johnathan Cape.

Morton, R. (1689). *Phthisiological: Or a treatise of consumptions.* London: San Smith and Benjamin Walford.

Mulford, H. A. (1977). Women and men problem drinkers. *Journal of Studies on Alcoholism, 38,* 1624–1639.

Myers, J. K., Weissman, M. M., Tischler, G. L., Holzer, C. E., Leaf, P. J., Orvaschel, H., Anthony, J. C., Boyed, J. H., Burke, J. D., Kramer, M., & Stoltzman, R. (1984). Six-month prevalence of psychiatric disorders in three communities. *Archives of General Psychiatry, 41,* 959–967.

Nagera, H. (1975). *Female sexuality and the oedipus complex.* New York: Jason Aronson.

Nanji, A. A., & French, S. W. (1986). Correlations between deviations from expected cirrohsis mortality and serum uric acid and dietary protein intake. *Journal of Studies on Alcohol, 47,* 253–255.

Nassi, A. J., & Abramowitz, S. I. (1978). Raising consciousness about womens groups: Process and outcome research. *Psychology of Women Quarterly, 3*(2), 139–156.

National Center for Health Statistics. (1982a). B. K. Cypress: Drug utilization in office visits to primary care physicians: National Ambulatory Medical Care Survey 1980. Advance data from vital and health statistics, No. 86. DHHS Pub. No. (PHS) 82-1250. Public Health Service, Hyattsville, MD. October 8, 1982.

National Center for Health Statistics. (1982b). H. Koch: Drug utilization in office practice by age and sex of the patient: National ambulatory medical care survey, 1980. Advance data from vital and health statistics, No. 81 DHHS Pub. No. (PHS) 82-1250. Public health service, Hyattsville, MD. July 26, 1982.

National Center for Health Statistics. (1983). H. Koch: Utilization of psychotropic drugs in office-based ambulatory care, National ambulatory Medical care survey 1980 and 1981. Advance Data from Vital and Health Statistics, No. 90. DHHS Pub. No. (PHS) 83-1250. Public health service, Hyattsville, MD. June 15, 1983.

National Institute of Alcohol Abuse and Alcoholism. (1981). Fourth Special Report to U.S. Congress in Alcohol and Health. (DHHS) Publication Number ADM82-1080. Washington, DC: U.S. Government Printing Office.

National Institute in Alcohol Abuse and Alcoholism. (1983a). Alcohol Health and Research World, 7, (DDHS) Publication Number ADM83-151. Washington, DC: U.S. Government Printing Office.

National Institute in Alcohol Abuse and Alcoholism. (1983b). Advances in Alcoholism Treatment Service for Women. (DDHS) Publication No. ADM82-1217, Washington, DC: U.S. Government Printing Office.

Navarro, V. (1975). Women in health care. *New England Journal of Medicine, 292,* 398–402.

Needleman, H. L., & Waber, D. (1977). The use of amitriptyline in anorexia nervosa. In R. A. Vigersky (Ed.), *Anorexia nervosa.* New York: Raven Press.

Nicholls, P., Edwards, G., & Kyle, E. (1974). Alcoholics admitted to four hospitals in England. *Quarterly Journal of Studies on Alcohol, 35*, 841–855.

Nillius, S. J. (1983). Weight and the menstrual cycle. In *Understanding anorexia nervosa and bulimia*, Report of the Fourth Ross Conference on Medical Research (pp. 77–80). Columbus, OH: Ross Laboratories.

Novack, D. H. (1981). Psychosocial aspects of illness. *Southern Medical Journal, 74*(11), 1376–1381.

Nuckolls, K. B., Cassel, J., & Kaplan, B. H. (1972). Pychosocial assets, life crisis, and the prognosis of pregnancy. *American Journal of Epidemiology, 95*, 431–441.

Nylander, I. (1971). The feeling of being fat and dieting in a school population. *Acta Socio-Medica Scandinavica, 3*, 17–26.

O'Connell, S. (1983). The placebo effect and psychotherapy. *Psychotherapy: Theory, Research, & Practice, 20*(3), 337–345.

Orbach, S. (1978). *Fat is a feminist issue.* New York: Berkley Books.

Orbach, S. (1985). Accepting the symptom: A feminist psychoanalytic treatment of anorexia nervosa. In D. M. Garner & P. E. Garfinkel (Eds.), *Handbook of psychotherapy for anorexia nervosa and bulimia.* New York: The Guilford Press.

O'Leary, V. E., Unger, R. K., & Wallston, B. S. (1985). *Women, gender, and social psychology.* Hillsdale, N.J.: Lawrence Erlbaum.

Orleans, C. T., & Barnett, L. R. (1984). Bulimarexia: Guidelines for behavioral assessment. In R. C. Hawkins, W. J. Fremouw, & P. F. Clement (Eds.), *The binge-purge syndrome: Diagnosis, treatment, and research.* New York: Springer Publishing Co.

Orlinsky, D. E., & Howard, K. I. (1978). The relation of process to outcome in psychotherapy. In S. L. Garfield & A. E. Bergin (Eds.), *Handbook of psychotherapy and behavior change: An empirical analysis* (2nd ed.). New York: Wiley.

Orlinsky, D. E., & Howard, K. I. (1980). Gender and psychotherapeutic outcome. In A. M. Brodsky & R. T. Hare-Mustin (Eds.), *Women and psychotherapy.* New York: The Guilford Press.

Orloff, K. (1978). The trap of androgyny. *Regionalism and the Female Imagination, 4*(ii), 61–80.

Orlofsky, J. L., & Windle, M. T. (1978). Sex role orientation, behavioral adaptability and personal adjustment. *Sex Roles, 4*, 801–811.

Osofsky, J. D., & O'Connell, E. J. (1972). Parent-child interaction: Daughters' effects on mothers' and fathers' behavior. *Developmental Psychology, 7*, 157–168.

Ostrum, A. (1975). Childbirth in America. In S. Hammer (Ed.), *Women body and culture.* New York: Perennial Library.

Pagelow, M. D. (1981). *Woman-battering.* Beverly Hills, CA: Sage.

Palmer, R. L. (1979). The dietary chaos syndrome: A useful new term. *British Journal of Medical Psychology, 52*, 187–190.

Parker, F. B. (1972). Sex role adjustment in women alcoholics. *Quarterly Journal in Studies of Alcohol, 33*, 647–657.

Parker, F. B. (1975). Sex role adjustment and drinking disposition of women college students. *Quarterly Journal on Studies of Alcohol, 36*, 1570–1573.

Parlee, M. B. (1973). The premenstrual syndrome, *Psychiatric Bulletin, 80*, 454–465.

Parlee, M. B. (1974). Sterotypic beliefs about menstruation: A methodological note on the Moos Menstrual Distress Questionnaire and some new data. *Psychosomatic Medicine, 36*, 225–240.

Parloff, M. B. (1979). Can psychotherapy research guide the policymaker? A little knowledge may be a dangerous thing. *American Psychologist, 34*, 296.

Parry, H. J. (1968). Use of psychotropic drugs by U.S. Adults. *Public Health Reports, 83*(10), 799–810.

Parry, H. J., Bodler, M. B., Mellinger, G. D., Cisin, I. H., & Manheiner, D. I. (1973). National patterns of psychotherapeutic drug use. *Archives of General Psychiatry, 28*, 769–783.

Parsons, O. A. (1977). Neuropsychological deficits in alcoholics: Facts and fancies. *Alcoholism, 1*, 51–56.

Parsons, T., & Bales, R. F. (1955). *Family, socialization and interaction process.* Glencoe, IL: Free Press.

Pasamanick, B., Knobloch, H., & Lilienfeld, A. (1956). Socio-economic status and some precursors of neuropsychiatric disorder. *American Journal of Orthopsychiatry, 26*, 183–191.

Paykel, E. S. (1980). Recall and reporting of life events. *Archives of General Psychiatry, 37*, 485.

Pearlin, L. I. (1985). Social structure and process of social support. In S. Cohen & S. L. Syme (Eds.), *Social support and health.* Orlando: Academic Press.

Pedhazur, E. J., & Tetenbaum, T. J. (1979). Bem Sex Role Inventory: A theoretical and methodological critique. *Journal of Personality and Social Psychology, 37*(6), 996–1016.

Pernanen, K. (1974). Validity of survey data on alcohol use. In R. J. Gibbins, Y. Israel, H. Kalant, R. E. Popham, W. Schmidt, & R. B. Smart (Eds.), *Research Advances in Alcohol and Drug Problems, 1* (pp. 355–374). New York: Wiley.

Perrucci, C. C., Potter, H. R., & Rhoads, D. L. (1978). Determinants of male-female role performance. *Psychology of Women Quarterly, 3*(1), 53–66.

Pertschuk, M. J. (1977). Behavior therapy: Extended follow-up, In R. A. Vigersky (Ed.), *Anorexia nervosa.* New York: Raven Press.

Peterson, D. S., & Barkmeier, W. W. (1983). Oral signs of frequent vomiting in anorexia. *American Family Physician, 27*, 199–200.

Petursson, H., & Lader, M. H. (1981). Benzodiazepine dependence. *Brit Journal of Addiction, 76*, 133–145.

Phillips, D., & Segal, B. (1969). Sexual status and psychiatric symptoms. *American Sociological Review, 34*, 58–72.

Pihl, R. O., Marinier, R., Lapp, J., & Drake, H. (1982). Psychotropic drug use by women: Characteristics of high consumers. *International Journal of Addiction, 17*(2), 259–269.

Pillay, M., & Crisp, A. H. (1977). Some psychological characteristics of patients with anorexia nervosa whose weight has been newly restored. *British Journal of Medical Psychology, 50*, 375–380.

Plant, M. (1980). Women with drinking problems. *British Journal of Psychology, 137*, 289–290.

Polivy, J., & Herman, C. P. (1985). Dieting and binging: A causal analysis. *American Psychologist, 40*(2), 193–201.

Polivy, J., Herman, C. P., & Garner, D. M. (in press). Cognitive assessment of eating disorders. In G. A. Marlatt & D. H. Donovan (Eds.), *Assessment of addictive behaviors*. New York: Guilford Press.

Polivy, J., & Thomsen, L. (in press). Behavioral medicine for women: Eating disorders.

Pope, H. G., Jr., & Hudson, J. I. (1984). *New hope for binge eaters*. New York: Harper & Row.

Pope, H. G., Hudson, J. I., & Yurgelun-Todd, D. (1984). Anorexia nervosa and bulimia among 300 suburban women shappers. *American Journal of Psychiatry, 141*(2), 292–294.

Popour, J. (1983). Planning women's alcohol and drug services in Michigan. Office of Substance Abuse Services. Michigan Department of Public Health.

Porsolt, R. D. (1983). Pharmacological models of depression. In J. Angst (Ed.), *The origins of depression: Current concepts and approaches*. New York: Springer-Verlag.

Prather, J., & Fidell, S. (1975). Sex differences in the content and style of medical advertisements. *Social Science and Medicine, 9*, 23–26.

President's Commission on Mental Health (1978a). Summary subpanel report of the special populations subpanel on mental health of women. Washington, DC: Government Printing Office.

President's Commission on Mental Health (1978b). *Task panel report on community support systems*. Washington, DC: Government Printing Office.

Rachal, J. V., Griess, L. L., Hubbard, R. L., Maisto, S. A., Cavanaugh, E. R., Waddell, R., & Benrud, C. H. (1980). The 1974 and 1978 national sample studies (report prepared for the National Institute on Alcohol Abuse and Alcoholism). (NTIS #PB81-199267). Research Triangle Park, NC: Research Triangle Institute.

Rachal, J. V., Williams, J. R., Brehm, M. L., Cavanaugh, B., Moore, R. D., & Eckerman, W. C. (1975). Adolescent drinking behavior, attitudes and correlates: A national study. (Final report, Research Triangle Institute, RTI Project #236-891). Research Triangle Park, NC: Research Triangle Institute.

Rachman, S. (1973). The effects of psychological treatment. In H. Eysenck (Ed.), *Handbook of abnormal psychology*. New York: Basic Books.

Radelet, L. (1981). Health Beliefs, Social networks, and tranquilizer use. *Journal Health and Social Behavior, 22*, 165–173.

Radloff, (1975). Sex differences in depression: The effects of occupation and marital status. *Sex Roles, 1*(3), 249–265.

Rakoff, V. (1983). Multiple determinants of family dynamics in anorexia nervosa. In P. L. Darby, P. E. Garfinkel, D. M. Garner, & D. V. Coscina (Eds.), *Anorexia nervosa: Recent developments in research* (pp. 29–40). New York: Alan R. Liss, Inc.

Rau, J. H., & Green, R. S. (1984). Neurological factors affecting binge eating: Body over mind. In R. C. Hawkins, W. J. Fremouw, P. F. Clement (Eds.), *The binge-purge syndrome* (pp. 123–143). New York: Springer Publishing Co.

Raven, B. H. (1974, April). Power relations in home and school. Paper presented at the meeting of the Western Psychological Association, San Francisco.

Redstockings. (1970). Redstockings manifesto. In R. Morgan (Ed.), *Sisterhood is powerful: An anthology of writings from the women's liberation movement*. New York: Random House.

Redstockings. (1979). *Radical feminism*, New York: Random House.

Regier, D. A., Myers, J. K., Kramer, M., Robins, L. N., Glazer, D. G., Hough, R. L., Eaton, W. W., & Locke, B. Z. (1984). The NIMH epidemiologic catchment area program. *Archives of General Psychiatry, 41*, 934–941.

Reich, W. (1942). *The function of the orgasm*. New York: Orgone Institute Press.

Reich, W. (1973). *The function of the orgasm*. New York: Farrar, Straus & Giroux (originally published, 1942).

Rich, A. (1976). *Of woman born*. New York: Bantam.

Rigotti, N. A., Nussbaum, S. R., Herzog, D. B., & Neer, R. M. (1984). Osteoporosis in women with anorexia nervosa. *New England Journal of Medicine, 311*, 1601–1606.

Rist, F., & Watzl, H. (1983). Self assessment of relapse risk and assertiveness in relation to treatment outcome of female alcoholics, *Addictive Behavior, 8*, 121–127.

Robins, L. N., Helzer, J. E., Weissman, M. M., Orvaschel, H., Gruenberg, E., Burke, J. D., & Regier, D. A. (1984). Lifetime prevalence of specific psychiatric disorders in three sites. *Archives General Psychiatry, 41*, 949–958.

Robinson, L. S. (1978). *Sex, class, and culture*. Bloomington: Indiana University Press.

Rockwell, J. K., Ellinwood, Jr., E. H., Dougherty, G. G., & Brodie, K. H. (1982). Anorexia nervosa: Review of current treatment practices. *Southern Medical Journal, 75*(9), 1101–1107.

Rodin, J. (1976). The role of perception of internal and external signals on regulation of feeing in overweight and nonobese individuals. In T. Silverstone (Ed.), *Appetite and food intake*. New York: Pergamon Press.

Rodin, J., & Slochower, J. (1976). Externality in the nonobese: The effects of environmental responsiveness on weight. *Journal of Personality & Social Psychology, 29*, 557–565.

Rosenfield, S. (1982). Sex roles and societal reactions in mental illness: The labeling of deviant deviance. *Journal of Health and Social Behavior, 23*, 18–24.

Rosenkrantz, P. S., Vogel, S. R., Bee, H., Broverman, I. K., & Broverman, D. M. (1968). Sex-role stereotypes and self-concepts in college students. *Journal of Consulting and Clinical Psychology, 32*, 287–295.

Rosenman, R. H., Brand, R. J., Sholtz, R. I., & Friedman, M. (1976). Multivariate prediction of coronary heart disease during 8.5 year follow-up in the Western Collaborative Group Study. *American Journal of Cardiology, 37*, 903–910.

Rosenthal, N. B. (1984). Consciousness raising: From revolution to reevaluation. *Psychology of Women Quarterly, 8*(4), 309–326.

Rosman, B. L., Minuchin, S., Baker, L., & Liebman, R. (1977). A family approach to anorexia nervosa: Study, treatment, and outcome. In R. A. Vigersky (Ed.), *Anorexia Nervosa* (pp. 341–348). New York: Raven Press.

Rosman, B., Minuchin, S., & Liebman, R. (1975). Family lunch session. An introduction to family therapy in anorexia nervosa. *American Journal of Orthopsychiatry, 45*(5), 846–853.

Ross, L. D., Amabile, T. M., & Steinmetz, J. L. (1977). Social roles, social control, and biases in social-perception process. *Journal of Personality & Social Psychology, 35*, 485–494.

Rossi, A. (1964). Equality between the sexes: An immodest proposal. *Daedalus, 93.*

Rossi, A. (1976). Sex equality: The beginnings of ideology. In A. G. Kaplan & J. P. Bean (Eds.), *Beyond sex role stereotypes*, Boston: Little Brown & Co. 80-88.

Rotter, N. G., & O'Connell, A. N. (1982). The relationships among sex-role orientation, congitive complexity, and tolerance for ambiguity. *Sex Roles, 8*(12), 1209–1220.

Royce, J. E. (1981). *Alcohol Problems and Alcoholism: A comprehensive survey.* New York: The Free Press. 140–158.

Rubin, R. T., & Poland, R. E. (1983). Neuroendocrine function and depression. In J. Angst (Ed.), *The origins of depression: Current concepts and approaches.* New York: Springer-Verlag.

Ruble, D. (1977). Premenstrual symptoms: A reinterpretation. *Science, 197,* 291–292.

Russell, D. E. H. (1984). *Sexual exploitation.* Beverly Hills, CA: Sage.

Russell, G. (1979). Bulimia nervosa: An ominous variant of anorexia nervosa. *Psychological Medicine, 9,* 429–448.

Russell, G. F. M. (1983). Delayed puberty due to anorexia nervosa of early onset. In P. L. Darby, P. E. Garfinkel, D. M. Garner, & D. V. Coscina (Eds.), *Anorexia nervosa: Recent developments in research* (pp. 331–342). New York: Alan R. Liss, Inc.

Russell, M., & Bigler, L. (1979). Screening for alcohol-related problems in an outpatient obstetric-gynecologic clinic. *American Journal of Obstetrics and Gynecology, 134,* 4–12.

Ryan, W. (1971). *Blaming the victim.* New York: Vintage Books.

Rychlak, J. F., & Legerski, A. T. (1967). A sociocultural theory of appropriate sexual role identification and level of personal adjustment. *Journal of Personality, 35,* 31–49.

Safilios-Rothschild, C. (1974). *Women & social policy.* Englewood Cliffs, NJ: Prentice-Hall, Inc.

Sanders, G. S. (1982). Social comparison and perceptions of health and illness. In G. S. Sanders & J. Suls (Eds.), *Social psychology of health and illness.* Hillsdale, NJ: Lawrence Erlbaum Associates.

Sandmaier, M. (1980). *The invisible alcoholics: Women and alcohol abuse in America.* New York: McGraw Hill.

Sandmaier, M. (1982). *Helping women with alcohol problems: A guide to community caregivers.* Philadelphia, PA: Women's Health Communications.

Sarason, I. G., & Sarason, B. R. (1984). Life changes, moderators of stress and health. In A. Baum, S. E. Taylor, & J. E. Singer (Eds.), *Handbook of pschology and health* (Vol. 4). Hillsdale, NJ: Lawrence Erlbaum.

Saxe, L., Yates, B. T., Newman, F. (1980). Background paper #3: The efficacy and cost effectivness of psychotherapy. *The implications of cost-effectiveness analysis of medical technology.* Office of Technology Assessment, Washington, DC: U.S. Government Printing Office.

Sayers, J. (1982). *Biological politics*. New York: Tavistock Publications.

Schacht, T. E. (1985). DSM-III and the politics of truth. *American Psychologist, 40*(5), 513–522.

Schachter, S., & Gross, L. (1968). Manipulated time and eating behavior. *Journal of Personality & Social Psychology, 10*, 98–106.

Schachter, S., & Singer, J. (1962). Cognitive, social, and physiological determinants of emotional state. *Psychological Review, 69*, 379–399.

Schildkraut, J. J. (1965). Catecholamine hypothesis of affective disorders: A review of supporting evidence. *American Journal of Psychiatry, 122*, 509–522.

Schlegel, R. P., & Sanborn, M. D. (1979). Religious affiliation and adolescent drinking. *Journal of Studies on Alcohol, 40*, 693–703.

Schlesier-Stropp, B. (1984). Bulimia: A Review of the literature. *Psychological Bulletin, 95*(2), 247–257.

Schlossberg, N. K., & Pietrofesa, J. J. (1973). Perspectives on counseling bias: Implications for counselor education. *Counseling Psychologist, 4*, 44–54.

Schmidt, W., & de Lint, J. (1972). Causes of death of alcoholics. *Quarterly Journal of Studies on Alcohol, 33*, 171–185.

Schuckit, M. (1972). The alcoholic woman: A literature review. *Psychiatric Medicine, 3*, 37–43.

Schuckit, M. A., & Morrissey, E. R. (1976). Alcoholism in women: Some clinical and social perspectives with an emphasis on possible subtypes. In M. Greenblatt & M. A. Schuckit (Eds.). *Alcoholism problems in women and children* (pp. 5–36). New York: Grune & Stratton.

Schuckit, M. A., Pitts, F. N., Jr., Reich, T., King, L. J., & Winokur, G. (1969). Alcoholism I. Two types of alcoholism in women. *Archives of General Psychiatry, 20*, 301–306.

Schulder, D. B. (1970). Does the law oppress women. In R. Morgan (Ed.), *Sisterhood is powerful* (139–160). New York: Random House.

Schulz, M. R. (1975). The semantic derogation of women. In B. Thorne & N. Henley (Eds.), *Language and sex: Differences and dominance*. Rowley, MA: Newbury House.

Schwab-Bakman, N., Appelt, H., & Rist, F. (1981). Identification in women alcoholics and depressives, *Journal of Studies on Alcohol, 42*, 654–660.

Schwartz, D. M., Thompson, M. G., & Johnson, C. L. (1983). Eating disorders and culture. In P. L. Darby, P. E. Garfinkel, D. M. Garner, & D. V. Coscina (Eds.), *Anorexia Nervosa: Recent Developments in Research* (pp. 83–94). New York: Alan R. Liss, Inc.

Sclare, A. B. (1970). The female alcoholic. *British Journal of Addiction, 65*, 99–107.

Scott, H. (1974). *Does socialism liberate women*. Boston: Beacon Press.

Seaman, B. (1977). The dangers of oral contraception. In C. Dreifus (Ed.), *Seizing our bodies*. New York: Vintage Books.

Sedlak, A. J. (1984, August). Understanding vilence between intimate partners: The effects of personal experience and victim reactions on labelling it "battering" and allocating blame. Paper presented at the annual meeting of the American Psychological Association, Toronto, Canada.

Seiden, A. M. (1976). Overview: Research of the psychology of women II. Women in families, work, and psychotherapy. *American Journal of Psychiatry, 133,* 1111–1123.

Seidenberg, R. (1971). Drug advertising and perception of mental illness. *Mental Hygiene, 55*(1), 21–31.

Seligman, M. (1975). *Helplessness.* San Francisco: W. H. Freeman.

Seligman, M., & Weiss, J. M. (1980). Coping behavior: Learned helplessness, physiological change and learned inactivity. *Behavioral Research Therapy, 18,* 459–512.

Selvini-Palazzoli, M. P. (1978). *Self-starvation: From individual to family therapy.* New York: Jason Aronson.

Selye, H. (1946). The general adaptation syndrome and the diseases of adaptation. *Journal of Clinical Endocrinology, 6,* 117–230.

Serbin, L. A. (1973). A comparison of teacher response to the preacademic and problem behavior of boys and girls. *Child Development, 44,* 796–804.

Shainess, N. (1970). Is there a separate feminine psychology? *New York State Journal of Medicine, 70*(24), 3007–3009.

Shapiro, S., Skinner, E. A., Kessler, L. G., Korff, M. V., German, P. S., Tischler, G. L., Leaf, P. J., Benham, L., Cottler, L., & Regier, D. A. (1984). Utilization of health and mental health services. *Archives of General Psychiatry, 41,* 971–978.

Sheatsley, P. B., & Feldman, J. (1964). The assassination of President Kennedy: Public reaction. *Public Opinion Quarterly, 28,* 189–215.

Sherman, B. M., & Halmi, K. A. (1977). Effect of nutritional rehabilitation on hypothalamic-pituitary function in anorexia nervosa. In R. A. Vigersky (Ed.). *Anorexia nervosa,* New York: Raven Press.

Sherman, J. A. (1980). Therapist attitudes and sex-role stereotyping. In A. M. Brodsky & R. Hare-Mustin (Eds.), *Women and psychotherapy.* New York: The Guilford Press.

Shinn, M., Lehmann, S., & Wong, N. W. (1984). Social interaction and social support. *Journal of Social Issues, 40*(4), 55–76.

Shumaker, S. A., & Brownell, A. (1984). Toward a theory of social support: Closing conceptual gaps. *Journal of Social Issues, 40*(4), 11–36.

Siegel, S. (1986). Alcohol and opiate dependence: Reevaluation of the Victorian Perspective, In H. Cappell, Y. Israel, H. Kalant, W. Schmidt, E. M. Seibers, R. G. Smart (Eds.), *Research advances in alcohol and drug problems, Vol. 9,* New York: Plenum.

Silbergeld, S., Brast, N., & Noble, E. P. (1971). The menstrual cycle: A double-blind study of symptoms, mood and behavior, and biochemical variables using Enovid and placebo, *Psychosomatic Medicine, 33,* 411–428.

Silberstein, J. A., & Parson, O. A. (1979). Neuropsychological impairment in female alcoholics. In M. Galanter (Ed.), *Currents in Alcoholism, 7,* (pp. 481–495). New York: Grune & Stratton.

Silverman, M., & Lee, P. R. (1974). *Pills, profits and politics.* London: University of California Press.

Singer, J. E., & Lord, D. (1984). The role of social support in coping with chronic or life-threatening illness. In A. Baum, S. E. Taylor, & J. E. Singer (Eds.),

Handbook of pschology and health, (Vol. IV). Hillsdale, NJ: Lawrence Erlbaum Associates.

Skegg, K., Skegg, D. C. G., & Richards, S. M. (1983). Incidence of self poisoning in patients prescribed psychotropic drugs. *British Medical Journal (Clinical Research) 286*, 841–843.

Smilkstein, F., Helsper-Lucas, A., Ashworth, C., Montano, D., & Pagel, M. (1984). Prediction of pregnancy complications: An application of the biopsychosocial model. *Social Science and Medicine, 18*(4), 315–321.

Smith, D. W. (1979). The fetal alcohol syndrome. *Hospital Practice, 14*, 121–128.

Smith, M. C. (1977). Appeals used in adventisements for psychotropic drugs. *American Journal of Public Health, 67*(2), 171–173.

Smith, S. L. (1975). Mood and the menstrual cycle. In E. G. Sacker (Ed.), *Topics in Psychoneuroendocrinology* (pp. 19–58). New York: Grune & Stratton.

Smith, M. L., & Glass, G. V. (1977). Meta-analysis of psychotherapy outcome studies. *American Psychologist, 32*, 752–760.

Smith, M. L., Glass, G. V., & Miller (1981). *The benefits of psychotherapy*. Baltimore: Johns Hopkins University Press.

Sokol, R. J., Miller, S. I., & Reed, G. (1980). Alcohol abuse during pregnancy: An epidemiologic study. *Alcoholism: Clinical and Experimental Research, 4*, 135–145.

Solomon, Z., & Bromet, E. (1982). The role of social factors in affective disorder: An assessment of the vulnerability model of Brown and his colleagues. *Psychology Medicine, 12*, 123–130.

Sours, J. A. (1969a). The anorexia nervosa syndrome: Phenomenologic and psychodynamic components. *Psychiatry Quarterly, 43*(2), 240–256.

Sours, J. A. (1969b). Anorexia nervosa: Nosology, diagnosis, developmental patterns and power-control dynamics. In G. Caplan & S. Lebovici (Eds.), *Adolescence: Psychological perspectives*. New York: Basic Books.

Sours, J. A. (1980). *Starving to death in a sea of objects: The anorexia nervosa syndrome.* New York: Jason Aronson.

Spence, J. T., & Helmreich, R. L. (1978). *Masculinity and femininity*. Austin: University of Texas Press.

Spence, J. T., Helmreich, R., & Stapp, J. (1974). The personal attributes questionnaire: A measure of sex role stereotypes and masculinity-femininity. *Catalog of Selected Documents in Psychology, 4*, ms. no. 617.

Spence, J. T., Helmreich, R., & Stapp, J. (1975). Ratings of self and peers on sex role attributes and their relation to self-esteem and conceptions of masculinity and femininity. *Journal of Personality and Social Psychology, 32*(1), 29–39.

Spitzer, R. L., & Williams, J. B. W. (1983). An empirical study of the issue of sex bias in the diagnostic criteria of DSM-III axis II personality disorders. *American Psychologist, 38*(7), 802–803.

Stacey, J. (1979). When partriarchy kowtows: The significance of the Chinese family revolution for feminist theory. In Z. R. Eisenstein (Ed.), *Capitalist patriarchy and the case for socialist feminism* (299–354). New York: Monthly Review Press.

Stein, A. H., & Bailey, M. (1973). The socialization of achievement orientation in females. *Psychological Bulletin, 80*, 343–366.

Steiner, M., & Carroll, B. J. (1977). The psychobiology of pre-menstrual dysphoria: Review of theories and treatments. *Psychoneuroendocrinology, 2*, 321–335.

Stimmel, B., Hambury, R., Sturiano, V., Korts, D., Jackson, G., & Cohen, M. (1982). Alcoholism as a risk factor in methadone maintenance. *The American Journal of Medicine, 73*, 631–636.

Stimson, G. V. (1975). The message of psychotropic drug ads. *Journal of Communication, 25*(3), 153–160.

Stiver, I. P. (1984). The meanings of dependency in female-male relationships. *Work in Progress*, No. 83-07. Wellesley: Stone Center.

Stangler, R. S., & Printz, A. M. (1980). DSM-III: Psychiatric diagnosis in a university population. *American Journal of Psychiatry, 137*, 937–940.

Streissguth, A. D., Barr, H. M., Martin, D. C., & Herman, C. S. (1980). Effects of maternal alcohol, nicotine and caffeine use during pregnancy on infant mental and motor development at 8 months. *Alcoholism: Clinical and Experimental Research, 4*, 152–154.

Stricker, G. (1977). Implications of research for psychotherapeutic treatment of women. *American Psychologist, 32*(1), 14–22.

Strickland, B. R. (1984). Sex-related differences and women's health, paper presented at the Southeastern Psychological Association meeting.

Strickland, B., Hall, J. H., Chamberlain, J., Kahn, R., Kobayashi, J., Parron, D., & Schneider, S. (1985). *Developing a national agenda to address women's mental health needs: A conference report.* Washington, DC: American Psychological Association.

Strober, M. (1981). The relation of personality characteristics to body image disturbances in juvenile anorexia nervosa: A multivariate analysis. *Psychosomatic Medicine, 43*(4), 232–330.

Strober, M. (1983). Subclassification of anorexia nervosa: Psychologic and biologic correlates. In, Report of the Fourth Ross Conference on Medical Research, *Understanding anorexia nervosa and bulimia.* Columbus, Ohio: Ross Laboratories.

Strupp, H. H. (1982). The outcome problem in psychotherapy: Contemporary perspectives. In J. H. Harvey & M. M. Parks (Eds.), *Psychotherapy research and behavior change.* Washington, DC: American Psychological Association.

Strupp, H. H., Fox, R. E., & Lessler, K. (1969). *Patients view their psychotherapy.* Baltimore: Johns Hopkins University Press.

Strupp, H. H., Wallach, M. S., & Wogan, M. (1964). Psychotherapy experience in retrospect: Questionnaire survey of former patients and their therapists. *Psychological Monographs, 78*(11), 588.

Stunkard, A. J. (1976). *The pain of obesity,* Palo Alto, CA: Bull Publishing Co.

Stunkard, A. J. (1980). Psychoanalysis and psychotherapy. In A. J. Stunkard (Ed.), *Obesity,* Philadelphia: W. B. Saunders Co.

Stunkard, A. J., & Koch, C. (1964). The interpetation of gastric motility. I. Apparent bias in the reports of hunger by obese persons. *Archives of General Psychiatry, 11*, 74–82.

Sturdivant, S. (1980). *Therapy with women: A feminist philosophy of treatment.* New York: Springer Publishing.

Suematsu, H., Ishikawa, H., Kuboki, T., & Ito, T. (1985). Statistical studies on anorexia nervosa in Japan: Detailed clinical data on 1,011 patients. *Psychotherapy and Psychosomatics, 43,* 96–103.

Suematsu, H., Kuboki, T., & Ito, T. (1985). Statistical studies on the prognosis of anorexia nervosa. *Psychotherapy and Psychosomatics, 43,* 104–112.

Suls, J. (1982). Social support, interpersonal relations, and health: benefits and liabilities. In G. S. Sanders & J. Suls (Eds.), *Social psychology of health and illness.* Hillsdale, NJ: Lawrence Erlbaum Associates.

Surrey, J. (1983). The relational self in women: Clinical implications. *Work in Progress,* No. 82-02. Wellesley: Stone Center.

Surrey, J. (1984a). Self-in-relation: A theory of women's development. Presented at the Stone Center Colloquium Series, Wellesley College.

Surrey, J. L. (1984b). Eating patterns as a reflection of women's development. Stone Center for Developmental Services and Studies, *Work in Progress.* No. 83-06, Wellesley: Stone Center.

Sutker, P., Libet, J., Albert, A., & Randall, C. (1983). Alcohol use, negative mood states and menstrual cycle phases. *Alcoholism Clinical and Experimental Research, 7,* 327–334.

Sweeney, D. R., Gold, M. S., Pottash, A. L. C., & Davies, R. K. (1980). Neurobiological theories. In I. L. Kutash, L. B. Schlesinger (Eds.), *Handbook on stress and anxiety.* San Francisco: Jossey-Bass.

Swinson, R. P. (1980). Sex differences in the inheritance of alcoholism. In O. J. Kalant (Ed.), *Alcohol and Drug Problems in Women* (pp. 233–262). 5, New York & London: Plenum Press.

Syrotuik, J., & D'Arcy, C. (1984). Social support and mental health: Direct, protective and compensatory effects. *Social Science and Medicine, 18*(3), 229–236.

Szasz, T. (1961). *The myth of mental illness: Foundations of a theory of personal conduct.* New York: Hoeber-Harger.

Szasz, T. (1973). *The second sin.* Garden City, New York: Anchor Books.

Szasz, T. (1976). *Heresies.* Garden City, New York: Anchor Books.

Szmukler, G. I. (1983a). Weight and food preoccupation in a population of English schoolgirls. In *Understanding Anorexia Nervosa and Bulimia,* Report of the Fourth Ross Conference on Medical Research (pp. 21–28). Columbus, OH: Ross Laboratories.

Szmukler, G. I. (1983b). A study of family therapy in anorexia nervosa: Some methodological issues. In P. L. Darby, P. E. Garfinkel, D. M. Garner, & D. V. Coscina (Eds.), *Anorexia nervosa: Recent developments in research.* New York: Alan R. Liss, Inc.

Tamerin, J. S., Tolor, A., & Harrington, B. (1976). Sex differences in alcoholics: A comparison of male and female alcoholics' self and spouse perceptions. *American Journal of Drug and Alcohol Abuse, 3,* 457–472.

Tarter, R. E., & Edwards, K. L. (1986). Multifactorial etiology of neuro-psychological impairment in alcoholics. *Alcoholism: Clinical and Experimental Research, 10,* 128–135.

Task Force on Clinical Training and Practice (1984). Final report to the executive committee Division of the Psychology of Women, American Psychological Association. Task Force Chairs B. L. Claster, J. Marecek.

Task Force on Sex Bias and Sex-Role Stereotyping in Psychotherapeutic Practice. (1975). *American Psychologist, 30*, 1169–1172.

Task Force on Sex Bias and Sex Role Stereotyping in Psychotherapeutic Practice. (1978). Guidelines for therapy with women. *American Psychologist, 41*, 1122–1123.

Tavris, C. (1977). Masculinity. *Psychology Today, 19*(8), 34.

Temerlin, M. K. (1968). Suggestion effects in psychiatric diagnosis. *Journal of Nervous and Mental Disease, 47*, 349–353.

Tennov, D. (1975). *Psychotherapy: The hazardous cure.* New York: Abelard-Schuman.

Teri, L. (1982). Effects of sex and sex-role style on clinical judgment. *Sex Roles, 8*(6), 639–649.

Terrance, R. G. (1980). Sex differences in the prevalence of problem drinking. In O. J. Kalant (Ed.), *Alcohol and Drug Problems in Women* (pp. 69–124). New York & London: Plenum Press.

Theander, S. (1983). Long-term prognosis of anorexia nervosa: A preliminary report. In P. L. Darby, P. E. Garfinkel, D. M. Garner, & D. V. Coscina (Eds.), *Anorexia nervosa: Recent developments in research.* New York: Alan R. Liss, Inc.

Thompson, K. M., & Wilsnack, R. W. (1984). Drinking and drinking problems among female adolescents: Patterns and influences. In S. C. Wilsnack, & L. J. Beckman, (Eds.). *Alcohol Problems in Women* (pp. 37–65). New York, London: Guilford Press.

Tietze, C., Lemkau, P. V., & Cooper, M. (1941). Schizophrenia, manic-depressive psychosis, and social-economic status. *American Journal of Sociology, 47*, 167–175.

Tiger, L., & Fox, R. (1971). *The imperial animal.* New York: Holt, Rinehardt and Winston.

Tobach, E., & Rosoff, B. (Eds.). (1978). *Genes & gender I.* New York: Gordian Press.

Travis, C. B. (1976). Women's liberation among two groups of women. *Psychology of Women Quarterly, 1*, 189–199.

Travis, C. B., Burnett-Doering, J., & Reid, P. T. (1982). The impact of sex, achievement domain, and conceptual orientation on causal attributions. *Sex Roles, 8*, 443–454.

Travis, C. B., & Seipp, P. H. (1978). An examination of secondary reinforcement, operant conditioning, and status envy hypotheses in relation to sex-role ideology. *Sex Roles, 4*(4), 525–538.

Unger, R. K. (1979). *Female and male.* New York: Harper and Row.

Vandereycken, W., & Pierloot, R. (1983). Combining drugs and behavior therapy in anorexia nervosa: A double-blind placebo/pimozide study. In P. L. Darbey, P. E. Garfinkel, D. M. Garner, & D. V. Coscina (Eds.), *Anorexia nervosa: Recent developments in research.* New York: Alan R. Liss.

Verbrugge, L. M. (1979). Female illness rates & illness behavior: Testing hypotheses about sex differences in health. *Women and Health, 4*(1), 61–75.

Verbrugge, L. M. (1980). Sex differences in complaints and diagnoses. *Journal of Behavioral Medicine, 3*(4), 327–355.

Verbrugge, L. M. (1982). Sex differences in legal drug use. *Journal of Social Issues, 38*(2): 59–76.

Verbrugge, L. M. (1983, March). Multiple roles and physical health of women and men. *Journal of Health and Social Behavior, 24,* 16–30.

Vetter, L. (1973). Career counseling for women. *Counseling Psychologist, 4,* 55–66.

Videla, L. A., & Valenzuela, A. (1982). Alcohol ingestion, liver glutathione lipoperoxidation: Metabolic interrelations and pathological implications. *Life Science, 31,* 2395–2407.

Vigersky, R. A., & Loriaux, D. L. (1977a). The effect of cyproheptadine in anorexia nervosa: A double-blind trial. In R. A. Vigersky (Ed.), *Anorexia nervosa.* New York: Raven Press.

Vigersky, R. A., & Loriaux, D. L. (1977b). Anorexia nervosa as a model of hypothalic dysfunction. In R. A. Vigersky (Ed.), *Anorexia nervosa.* New York: Raven Press.

Von Knorring, A., Cloninger, C. R., Bohman, M., & Sigvardsson, S. (1983). An adoption study of depressive disorders and substance abuse. *Archives of General Psychiatry, 40,* 943–950.

Waites, E. A. (1982). Female self-representation and the unconscious: A reply to Amy Galen. *Psychoanalytic Review, 69*(1), 29–41.

Wakeling, A., & DeSouza, V. F. A. (1983). Differential endocrine and menstrual response to weight change in anorexia nervosa. In P. L. Darby, P. E. Garfinkel, D. M. Garner, & D. V. Coscina (Eds.), *Anorexia nervosa: Recent developments in research* (pp. 271–277). New York: Alan R. Liss, Inc.

Waller, J. V., Kaufman, M. R., & Deutsch, F. (1940). Anorexia nervosa: A psychosomatic entity. *Psychosomatic Medicine, 2,* 3–16.

Wallston, B. S. (1985). Social psychology of women and gender. *Journal of Applied Social Psychology,* in press.

Wallston, B. S., Alagna, S. W., DeVellis, B. M., & DeVellis, R. F. (1983). Social support and physical health. *Health Psychology, 2,* 367–391.

Walsh, B. T. (1982). Endocrine disturbances in anorexia nervosa and depression. *Psychosomatic Medicine, 44*(1), 85–91.

Walster, E., Berscheid, E., & Walster, G. W. (1973). New directions in equity research. *Journal of Personality and Social Psychology, 25,* 151–176.

Walster, E., Walster, G. W., & Berscheid, E. (1978). *Equity theory & research.* Boston: Allyn & Bacon.

Warren, S. E., & Steinberg, S. M. (1979). Acid-base and electrolyte disturbances in anorexia nervosa. *American Journal of Psychiatry, 136,* 415–418.

Weingarten, K. (1978). The employment pattern of professional couples and their distribution of involvements in the family. *Psychology of Women Quarterly, 3*(1), 43–52.

Weiss, K. (1977). What medical students learn about women. In C. Dreifus (Ed.), *Seizing Our Bodies.* New York: Vintage Books, Random House.

Weiss, K. (Ed.) (1984). *Women's health care: A guide to alternatives.* Reston, Virginia: Reston Publishing Co., Prentice-Hall.

Weissman, M. M., & Klerman, G. L. (1977). Sex differences and the epidemiology of depression. *Archives of General Psychiatry, 34,* 98–111.

Weissman, M. M., & Paykel, E. S. (1974). *The depressed woman*. Chicago: University of Chicago Press.

Westbrook, M. T., & Mitchel, R. A. (1979). Changes in sex-role stereotypes from health to illness. *Social Science and Medicine, 13a*, 297–302.

Wetzel, J. W. (1984). *Clinical handbook of depression*. New York: Gardner Press.

White, M. (1983). Anorexia nervosa: A transgenerational system perspective. *Family Process, 22*(3), 255–273.

White, W. C., & Boskind-White, M. (1984). An experimental-behavioral treatment program for bulimarexic women. In R. C. Hawkins, W. J. Fremouw, R. F. Clement (Eds.), *The Binge-Purge Syndrome* (pp. 77–103). New York: Springer Publishing Co.

Whitehead, W. E., Blackwell, B., DeSilva, H., & Robinson, A. (1977). Anxiety and anger in hypertension. *Journal of Psychosomatic Research, 21*, 383–389.

Widseth, J. C., & Mayer, J. (1971). Drinking behavior and attitudes toward alcohol in delinquent girls. *International Journal of the Addictions, 6*, 453–461.

Wilcoxson, L. A., Schrader, S. L., & Shery, C. W. (1976). Daily self-report on activities, life events, moods and somatic changes during the menstrual cycle. *Psychosomatic Medicine, 38*, 399–417.

Wilkinson, P., Santamaria, J. N., & Rankin, J. B. (1969). Epidemiology of alcoholic cirrhosis. *Australian Annals of Medicine, 18*, 222.

Williams, C. N., & Klerman, L. V. (1984). Female alcohol abuse: Its effects on the family. In: S. C. Wilsnack & L. J. Beckman (Eds.), *Alcohol problems in women: Antecedents, consequences and interventions* (pp. 280–312). New York & London: Guilford Press.

Williams, J. H. (1973). Sexual role identification and personality functioning in girls: A theory revisited. *Journal of Personality and Social Psychology, 41*(1), 1–8.

Williams, R. R., & Horn, J. W. (1977). Association of cancer sites with tobacco and alcohol consumption and socioeconomic status of patients: Interview study from the third National Cancer Survey. *Journal of the National Cancer Institute, 58*, 525–547.

Wilsnack, S. C. (1973). Sex role identity in female alcoholism. *Journal of Abnormal Psychology, 82*, 253–261.

Wilsnack, S. C. (1974). The effects of social drinking on women's fantasy. *Journal of Personality, 42*, 43–61.

Wilsnack, S. C. (1976). The impact of sex roles on women's alcohol use and abuse. In M. Greenblatt & M. A. Schuckit (Eds.), *Alcoholism Problems in Women and Children* (pp. 37–64). New York: Grune & Stratton.

Wilsnack, S. C. (1984). Drinking, sexuality and sexual dysfunction in women. In S. C. Wilsnack & L. J. Beckman (Eds.), *Alcohol Problems in Women: Antecedents, consequences and interventions* (pp. 189–227). New York & London: Guilford Press.

Wilsnack, R. W., Wilsnack, S. C., & Klassen, A. D. (1984). Women's drinking and drinking problems: Patterns from a 1981 national survey. *American Journal of Public Health, 74*, 1231–1238.

Wilson, G. T. (1984). Toward the understanding and treatment of binge eating. In R. C. Hawkins, W. J. Fremouw, P. F. Clement (Eds.), *The Binge-Purge Syndrome* (pp. 264–289). New York: Springer Publishing Co.

Wooley, S., & Wooley, O. (1979). Obesity and women. I. A closer look at the facts. *Women's Studies International Quarterly, 2,* 669–679.

Wooley, S. C., & Wooley, O. W. (1985). Intensive outpatient and residential treatment for bulimia. In D. M. Garner & P. E. Garfinkel (Eds.), *Handbook of psychotherapy for anorexia nervosa and bulimia.* New York: The Guilford Press.

Wortman, C. B., & Conway, T. L. (1985). The role of social support in adaptation and recovery from physical illness. In S. Cohen & Syme, S. L. (Eds.), *Social support and health.* Orlando: Academic Press.

Wright, C. T., Meadow, A., Abramowitz, S. I., & Davidson, C. V. (1980). Psychiatric diagnosis as a function of assessor profession and sex. *Psychology of Women Quarterly, 5*(2), 240–242.

Yager, J. (1982). Family issues in the pathogenesis of anorexia nervosa. *Psychosomatic Medicine, 44*(1), 43–60.

Yudkovitz, E. (1983). Bulimia: Growing awareness of an eating disorder. *Social Work, 28,* 472–478.

Yudkovitz, E. (1984). Power, authority and femininity integrated: Resolution of the binge-purge cycle. Workshop presented at the conference: The Psychology of Women and the Psychotherapy of Eating Disorders, Center for the Study of Anorexia and Bulimia, New York.

Zaix, M., Gardner, E. A., & Hart, W. (1967). A survey of the prevalance of alcoholism in Monroe County, New York. *Quarterly Journal of Studies on Alcoholism, 28,* 316–327.

Zelen, S. L. (1985). Sexualization of therapeutic relationships: The dual vulnerability of patient and therapist. *Psychotherapy: Theory, Research, Practice, Training, 22*(2), 178–185.

Zucker, R. A., & Devoe, C. I. (1975). Life history characteristics associated with problem drinking and antisocial behavior in adolescent girls: A comparison with male findings. In: R. D. Wirt, G. Winokur, & M. Roff (Eds.), *Life history research in psychopathology, 4,* Minneapolis: University of Minnesota Press.

Zweig, M. (1971). Is women's liberation a therapy group? In J. Agel (Ed.), *The radical therapist.* New York: Ballantine.

Author Index

Subject Index

271